THE THEOLOGY OF THE BOOKS OF HAGGAI AND ZECHARIAH

Tucked away at the end of the Minor Prophets, the Books of Haggai and Zechariah offer messages of challenge and hope to residents of the small district of Yehud in the Persian Empire in the generations after the return from Babylonian exile. In this volume, Robert Foster focuses on the distinct theological message of each book. The Book of Haggai uses Israel's foundational event – God's salvation of Israel from Egypt – to exhort the people to finish building the Second Temple. The Book of Zechariah argues that the hopes the people had in the prophet Zechariah's days did not come true because the people failed to keep God's long-standing demand for justice, though hope still lies in the future because of God's character. Each chapter in this book closes with a substantive reflection on the ethics of the major sections of the Books of Haggai and Zechariah and their implications for contemporary readers.

Robert L. Foster is Lecturer in Religion and New Testament at the University of Georgia. He is the author of *We Have Heard, O Lord: An Introduction to the Theology of the Psalter* (2018) and is a member of the editorial board of *Horizons in Biblical Theology*.

OLD TESTAMENT THEOLOGY

GENERAL EDITORS

Brent A. Strawn

Professor of Old Testament and Professor of Law

Duke University

Stephen B. Chapman

Associate Professor of Old Testament

Duke University

Patrick D. Miller[†]

Charles T. Haley Professor of Old Testament Theology, Emeritus

Princeton Theological Seminary

This series aims to remedy the deficiency of available published material on the theological concerns of the Old Testament books. Here, specialists explore the theological richness of a given book at greater length than is usually possible in the introductions to commentaries or as part of other Old Testament theologies. They are also able to investigate the theological themes and issues of their chosen books without being tied to a commentary format or to a thematic structure provided from elsewhere. When complete, the series will cover all the Old Testament writings and will thus provide an attractive, and timely, range of short texts around which courses can be developed.

PUBLISHED VOLUMES

The Theology of the Book of Kings, Keith Bodner
The Theology of the Book of Amos, John Barton
The Theology of the Book of Genesis, R. W. L. Moberly
The Theology of the Book of Jeremiah, Walter Brueggemann

THE THEOLOGY OF THE BOOKS OF HAGGAI AND ZECHARIAH

ROBERT L. FOSTER

University of Georgia

CAMBRIDGE
UNIVERSITY PRESS

University Printing House, Cambridge CB2 8BS, United Kingdom

One Liberty Plaza, 20th Floor, New York, NY 10006, USA

477 Williamstown Road, Port Melbourne, VIC 3207, Australia

314–321, 3rd Floor, Plot 3, Splendor Forum, Jasola District Centre, New Delhi – 110025, India

79 Anson Road, #06-04/06, Singapore 079906

Cambridge University Press is part of the University of Cambridge.

It furthers the University's mission by disseminating knowledge in the pursuit of education, learning, and research at the highest international levels of excellence.

www.cambridge.org
Information on this title: www.cambridge.org/9781108475501
DOI: 10.1017/9781108688321

© Cambridge University Press 2021

This publication is in copyright. Subject to statutory exception and to the provisions of relevant collective licensing agreements, no reproduction of any part may take place without the written permission of Cambridge University Press.

First published 2021

Printed in the United Kingdom by TJ Books Limited, Padstow Cornwall

A catalogue record for this publication is available from the British Library.

Library of Congress Cataloging-in-Publication Data
NAMES: Foster, Robert L., 1970– author.
TITLE: The theology of the Books of Haggai and Zechariah / Robert L. Foster.
DESCRIPTION: 1. | New York : Cambridge University Press, 2020. | Series: Old testament theology | Includes bibliographical references and index.
IDENTIFIERS: LCCN 2020021929 (print) | LCCN 2020021930 (ebook) | ISBN 9781108475501 (hardback) | ISBN 9781108468589 (paperback) | ISBN 9781108688321 (ebook)
SUBJECTS: LCSH: Bible. Haggai–Criticism, interpretation, etc. | Bible. Zechariah–Criticism, interpretation, etc.
CLASSIFICATION: LCC BS1655.52 .F67 2020 (print) | LCC BS1655.52 (ebook) | DDC 224/.9706–dc23
LC record available at https://lccn.loc.gov/2020021929
LC ebook record available at https://lccn.loc.gov/2020021930

ISBN 978-1-108-47550-1 Hardback
ISBN 978-1-108-46858-9 Paperback

Cambridge University Press has no responsibility for the persistence or accuracy of URLs for external or third-party internet websites referred to in this publication and does not guarantee that any content on such websites is, or will remain, accurate or appropriate.

In memoriam, Roy F. Melugin, 1937–2008

Contents

General Editors' Preface	page xiii
Preface	xvii
List of Abbreviations	xx

1	PROPHETS TO A REMNANT.	1
	Prophets and People in the "Middle Territory"	2
	Social Divisions in the Yehud Community	11
	Personal Perspectives in Performing Biblical Theology	15
2	I AM WITH YOU: THE BOOK OF HAGGAI	19
	YHWH of Hosts: A Troubling Presence	20
	I Will Fill This House with Glory	31
	From This Day, Blessing	38
	YHWH's Engraving	44
	Biblical Theology and Theological Ethics	48
3	RETURN TO YHWH: THE INTRODUCTION TO THE BOOK OF ZECHARIAH.	53
	Biblical Theology and Theological Ethics	58

4	YHWH HAS RETURNED TO YOU: ZECHARIAH'S VISION	61
	YHWH, God of Comfort and Motherly Compassion	62
	A Wall of Fire, an Indwelling Presence	66
	Guilt Removed	73
	Finishing the House of YHWH	80
	The Return of YHWH: A Curse upon Thieves and Liars	85
	Removing Wickedness from the Land	87
	YHWH's Anger Fully Pacified	89
	A Final, Dramatic Action: The Priest, the Branch, and Peace	91
	Biblical Theology and Theological Ethics	95
5	LOVE TRUTH AND PEACE	100
	YHWH Called but They Would Not Listen	101
	Nothing Is Impossible for God	104
	Nations Will Seek the Favor of YHWH	112
	Biblical Theology and Theological Ethics	115
6	VICTORY FOR THE HOUSE OF JUDAH, SALVATION FOR THE HOUSE OF JOSEPH	121
	Rejoice Greatly, Daughter of Zion	124
	Ask YHWH	136
	Wail, Cypress and Oaks of Bashan	145
	Biblical Theology and Theological Ethics	148
7	WOE TO THE WORTHLESS SHEPHERD	154
	Merchants of Humanity	155
	A Broken Covenant with the Nations	159
	The Broken Family Bond	163

	A Woeful End	166
	Biblical Theology and Theological Ethics	169
8	ON THAT DAY....................	172
	YHWH Creates	173
	Salvation and Purifications	176
	YHWH Sabaoth, Great King over All the Earth	187
	Biblical Theology and Theological Ethics	194
9	THE THEOLOGY OF THE BOOKS OF HAGGAI AND ZECHARIAH WITHIN THE OLD TESTAMENT	199
	The Theology of the Books of Haggai and Zechariah	199
	The Theology of the Books of Haggai, Zechariah, and Malachi	202
	Haggai and Zechariah and the Book of the Twelve	205
	Haggai and Zechariah and the Books of Isaiah, Jeremiah, and Ezekiel	209
	Haggai and Zechariah and the Books of Daniel and Esther	212
	Haggai and Zechariah and the Books of Ezra and Nehemiah	215
	Haggai and Zechariah and the Book of the Psalms	217
	Haggai and Zechariah and the Books of the Torah	219
	Biblical Theology and Theological Ethics	222
Further Reading		235
Author Index		240
Scripture Index		242
Subject Index		250

General Editors' Preface

Some years ago, Cambridge University Press, under the editorship of James D. G. Dunn, initiated a series entitled New Testament Theology. The first volumes appeared in 1991, and the series was brought to completion in 2003. For whatever reason, a companion series that would focus on the Old Testament/Hebrew Bible was never planned or executed. The present series, Old Testament Theology, is intended to rectify this need.

The reasons for publishing Old Testament Theology are not, however, confined solely to a desire to match New Testament Theology. Instead, the reasons delineated by Dunn that justified the publication of New Testament Theology continue to hold true for Old Testament Theology. These include, among other things, the facts that (1) given faculty and curricular structures in many schools, the theological study of individual Old Testament writings is often spotty at best; (2) most exegetical approaches (and commentaries) proceed verse by verse such that theological interests are in competition with, if not completely eclipsed by, other important issues, whether historical, grammatical, or literary; and (3) commentaries often confine their discussion of a book's theology to just a few pages in the introduction. The dearth of materials focused exclusively on a particular book's theology may be seen as a result of factors like these; or, perhaps, it is the cause of such factors. Regardless, as Dunn concluded, without adequate theological resources, there is little incentive for teachers or students to engage the theology of specific books; they must be content with what are mostly general overviews. Perhaps the most serious problem resulting from all this is that students are at a disadvantage, even incapacitated, when it comes to the matter of integrating their study of the Bible with other courses in religion and theology. There is, therefore, an urgent need for a series to bridge the gap between the too-slim theological précis and the too-full commentary where theological concerns are lost among many others.

All of these factors commend the publication of Old Testament Theology now, just as they did for New Testament Theology more than two decades ago. Like its sister series, Old Testament Theology is a place where Old Testament scholars can write at greater length on the theology of individual biblical books and may do so without being tied to the linear, verse-by-verse format of the commentary genre or a thematic structure of some sort imposed on the text from outside. Each volume in the series seeks to describe the biblical book's theology as well as to engage the book theologically – that is, each volume intends to *do* theology through and with the biblical book under discussion, as well as delineate the theology contained within it. Among other things, theological engagement with the composition includes paying attention to its contribution to the canon and appraising its influence on and reception by later communities of faith. In these ways, Old Testament Theology seeks to emulate its New Testament counterpart.

In the intervening years since New Testament Theology was first conceived, however, developments have taken place in the field that provide still further reasons for the existence of Old

Testament Theology; these have impact on how the series is envisioned and implemented and also serve to distinguish it, however slightly, from its companion series. Three developments in particular are noteworthy:

1. *The present hermeneutical climate*, often identified (rightly or wrongly) as "postmodern," is rife with possibility and potential for new ways of theologizing about Scripture and its constituent parts. Theologizing in this new climate will of necessity look (and be) different from how it has ever looked (or been) before.
2. *The ethos change in the study of religion, broadly, and in biblical studies in particular.* No longer are the leading scholars in the field only Christian clergy, whether Catholic priests or mainline Protestant ministers. Jewish scholars and scholars of other Christian traditions are every bit as prominent, as are scholars of non- or even anti-confessional stripes. In short, now is a time when "Old Testament Theology" must be conducted without the benefits of many of the old consensuses and certainties, even the most basic ones relating to epistemological frameworks and agreed-upon interpretative communities along with their respective traditions.
3. Finally, recent years have witnessed *a long-overdue rapprochement among biblical scholars, ethicists, and systematic theologians.* Interdisciplinary studies between these groups are now regularly published, thus furthering and facilitating the need for books that make the theology of Scripture widely available for diverse publics.

In brief, the time is ripe for a series of books that will engage the theology of specific books of the Old Testament in a new climate for a new day. The result will not be programmatic, settled, or altogether certain. Despite that – or, in some ways, *because* of that – it is hoped that Old Testament Theology will contain highly useful volumes that are ideally poised to make significant contributions on a number of fronts, including (1) the ongoing discussion of biblical theology in confessional and nonconfessional modes as well as in postmodern and canonical contexts, (2) the theological exchange between Old Testament scholars and those working in cognate and disparate disciplines, and (3) the always-pressing task of introducing students to the theology of the discrete canonical unit: the biblical books themselves.

Brent A. Strawn
Professor of Old Testament and Professor of Law, Duke University

Stephen B. Chapman
Associate Professor of Old Testament, Duke University

Patrick D. Miller[†]
Princeton Theological Seminary, Emeritus

Preface

The Books of Haggai and Zechariah, tucked as they are in the back of the Book of the Twelve, are two of the most neglected books in the Old Testament. The Book of Haggai barely registers with its two chapters, and though the Book of Zechariah is more substantive, for some reason it fails to capture the attention not only of many Christian or Jewish lay readers, it often fails to attract the attention of Old Testament scholars, though the past decades have seen a more robust production of scholarship on the book. For me, over the decades I have pondered what I consider to be the genius of these prophets and the scribes who treasured and expanded upon their traditions, whose theological interpretations of the experiences of the people living in Yehud during the Persian Period eventually garnered their books a place in the canon.

In fact, my interest in these two books dates back to a rather mediocre paper I wrote on these two books in a course on Old Testament theology taught by John T. Willis at Abilene Christian University. Eventually, one of the more enigmatic passages in the Old Testament, Zechariah 11:4–17, became the subject of my master's thesis and later an article published in the *Journal of*

Biblical Literature.¹ Several years later, I authored another article on the theology of the Book of Zechariah that followed the rhetorical development of the whole book, an article that serves as the foundation for a (now further developed) large portion of this book.² And I have continued to teach it in public settings, most often in churches, which always generates a good deal of interest in the gems that arise from these much neglected books.

The production of this book mainly occurred during the past six years at the University of Georgia (UGA). I have some formidable colleagues in biblical studies who, each in their own way, have encouraged my work: Wayne Coppins, Dick Friedman, and Baruch Halpern. Tyler Kelley, an outstanding PhD candidate at UGA, read the first edition of this manuscript in its entirety and offered excellent criticism, for which I offer my thanks. I am grateful to have experienced "the full Strawn" effect in the careful editing by Brent Strawn. His words pushed me to greatly improve the final manuscript, but the reader already knows that any problems that remain are all my own.

I dedicate this book to the memory of Roy Melugin, who, in his later careers was Research Professor of Hebrew Bible at Brite Divinity School in Ft. Worth, Texas, and whom I met originally while in my MA program at Abilene Christian University as I drove over to attend the Southwest Biblical Studies Colloquy that he spearheaded. First in my time at Abilene and later while working on my PhD at Southern Methodist University, Roy was an untiring source of encouragement to my work. He once drove

---

[1] Robert L. Foster, "Shepherds, Sticks, and Social Destabilization: A Fresh Look at Zechariah 11:4–17," *JBL* **126** (2007): 735–753.

[2] Robert Foster, "Undoing the Future: The Theology of the Book of Zechariah," *HBT* **34** (2012): 59–72.

the 45 minutes or so from Ft. Worth to Dallas to visit me in my home and hear more about my working theory on hermeneutics. Though I expressed my gratitude to him on several occasions, I regret that I could not offer him this tribute during his years living among us. I am grateful for the opportunity to honor Roy's memory, a fine scholar whose life's work was deeply involved in the prophets and biblical theology, and who was equally a gentleman to me and to so many. זיכרונו לברכה.

Abbreviations

AB	Anchor Bible
ABRL	Anchor Bible Reference Library
BAR	*Biblical Archaeology Review*
BETL	Bibliotheca Epheremidum Theologicarum Lovaniensium
BHQ	*Biblia Hebraica Quinta.* A. Shenker et al., eds., Stuttgart: Deutsche Bibelgesellschaft, 2004–
BibInt	*Biblical Interpretation*
BS	Biblical Studies
BZAW	Beihefte zur Zeitschrift für die alttestamentliche Wissenschaft
CC	Continental Commentaries
CSCD	Cambridge Studies in Christian Doctrine
FAT	Forschungen zum Alten Testament
GUS	Gorgias Ugaritic Studies
HALOT	*The Hebrew and Aramaic Lexicon of the Old Testament.* Study edition. Ludwig Koehler, Walter Baumgartner, and Johann J. Stamm. 2 vols. Leiden: Brill, 2001
HBT	*Horizons in Biblical Theology*
HCOT	Historical Commentary on the Old Testament
HdO	Handbuch der Orientalistik

HSM	Harvard Semitic Monographs
IBT	Interpreting Biblical Texts
JBL	*Journal of Biblical Literature*
LAI	Library of Ancient Israel
LHBOTS	Library of Hebrew Bible/Old Testament Studies
NCB	New Century Bible
NEA	*Near Eastern Archaeology*
NICOT	New International Commentary on the Old Testament
NIDB	*New Interpreter's Dictionary of the Bible*
OTL	Old Testament Library
OTT	Old Testament Theology
SBLRBS	Society of Biblical Literature Resources for Biblical Study
SBLSymS	Society of Biblical Literature Symposium Series
SBLWAW	Society of Biblical Literature Writings from the Ancient World
SBT	Studies in Biblical Theology
SNTSMS	Society of New Testament Studies Monograph Series
THOTC	Theological Old Testament Commentary
VT	*Vetus Testamentum*
VTSup	Supplements to Vetus Testamentum

CHAPTER 1

Prophets to a Remnant

Tucked in at the very end of the prophetic books, at the very end of the Christian Old Testament, the Books of Haggai and Zechariah are two of the more neglected texts of the Old Testament. The relative obscurity of their message to most readers of the Hebrew Bible (or Old Testament) parallels the relative obscurity of the original audience of these two books to their Persian overlords, the people residing in the small district of Yehud, a small portion of the previously larger state of Judah, at the southernmost reach of the empire. Yet, these two books are at great pains to convince their audiences that these people, their capital city Jerusalem, their Temple, and their god, YHWH, have a significance on the world stage all out of proportion to their role within the empire.[1]

---

[1] The practice in previous volumes of the Old Testament Theology series is to translate the divine name, Y-H-W-H, also known as the Tetragrammaton, as "Yahweh." However, there is another convention in scholarship, which I follow here, to leave out the vowels and use only the consonants, YHWH, as here. This originates with a variety of Jewish scholars in their attempt to show respect for the divine name, which is imitated by some Christian scholars as well. I will use this shorter convention because I see my own work in conversation with a variety of scholars, including Jewish scholars and, out of respect for them and for the divine name, I utilize only the consonants.

2 THE THEOLOGY OF THE BOOKS OF HAGGAI AND ZECHARIAH

PROPHETS AND PEOPLE IN THE "MIDDLE TERRITORY"

The Books of Haggai and Zechariah each begin by invoking the Achaemenid Dynasty and perhaps its best-known ruler, Darius I. The editors who crafted these prophetic materials into coherent books wanted their audiences to see the activities of YHWH and the people of YHWH in light of, and sometimes in contrast to, Persian rule. Both prophetic books continuously use the phrase "YHWH Sabaoth," often translated as "LORD of hosts" in English, which communicates in part that YHWH reigns over the hosts of heaven. However, the emphasis of this title for both the Books of Haggai and Zechariah is that YHWH, who brought the "hosts" of Israel out of Egypt (e.g. Exod 6:26; 7:4; 12:17, 41, 51), reigns over Persia just as YHWH ruled over Egypt. And just as YHWH settled the Exodus people in the land of Canaan, YHWH has returned the exiles to their land, and one day soon the nations of the Persian Empire will bring their wealth to honor YHWH at Zion (Hag 2:4–9, 20–23; Zech 2:6–12; 8:20–23; 14:12–19), just as Israel's "plunder" of the Egyptians helped them honor YHWH in building the Tabernacle. The prophetic proclamation of YHWH Sabaoth intends to evoke from the original audiences that the God who delivered them out of Egypt has now come to the aid of the descendants of Israel in the Persian period.

In contrast to the strong claims about YHWH Sabaoth ruling the nations and the promise that the wealth of the nations will come to Zion, the great Persian kings Darius I and Xerxes I seem not even to know of the small province of Yehud, the geographical descendant of the much larger, preexilic territory of Judah. In the published lists of the nations that Darius and Xerxes claim to have conquered or ruled, neither king mentions Yehud, though their lists of nations run from Greece in the West to Egypt in the South to the Indus Valley in the East and modern Southern Uzbekistan/ Western Tajikistan in the North.² Yehud is simply one of ten districts that make up the larger Persian satrapy, Ahar-nahara, "Beyond the River," with Yehud not even among the most important districts given the prominence of the central ruling site, Damascus, as well as the coastal city of Sidon and the inland province of Samaria.

Egyptologist Steven Ruzicka offers some insight into the worldview of Yehud's Persian overlords, observing the competition for control of the Levant between the Persians and the Egyptians, a struggle replicating earlier struggles between Egypt and Assyria, and then Babylon. This ongoing struggle leads Ruzicka to observe that the region of Syro-Palestine, in which one finds Yehud, is, as he calls it, "middle territory," land that served as both a buffer from direct action of Persia against Egypt or vice versa, and land that each kingdom desired to subject for exploitation of its resources.³ Yehud certainly experienced exploitation of its resources by the Persians as part of the satrapy, "Beyond the River," a subject of explicit concern in Zechariah 9–14. These same chapters also reflect the fears of Yehudites during the Egyptian revolts against Persia and Persia's efforts to subdue Egypt, as Yehud served as a launching pad for the Persian assault on Egypt. Yehud also had a role to play on the world stage in the

---

[2] Xerxes I apparently did not conquer any nations per se, though he subdued a few rebellions at the change of the throne. Though Xerxes repeats formulas from the inscriptions of Darius I in his *daivā* inscription, Xerxes does not claim to conquer the nations he lists but calls them "the countries of which I became king" (Pierre Briant, *From Cyrus to Alexander: A History of the Persian Empire*, trans. Peter T. Daniels [Winona Lake, IN: Eisenbrauns, 2002], 553).

[3] Steven Ruzicka, *Trouble in the West: Egypt and the Persian Empire, 525–332 BCE* (New York: Oxford University Press, 2012), 4.

Persian economy. But it was a bit part while the major players on the stage, the Persian rulers, did not even mention Yehud in any known record.

By contrast, various biblical authors of the Persian period saw the hand of YHWH in the machinations of empire in ways out of proportion to the imperial (lack of) interest in Yehud. In 539 BCE the first Persian king, Cyrus II, produced the famous Cyrus Cylinder. The Cylinder declares that Marduk instructed Cyrus to repatriate Mesopotamian peoples to their homelands and to restore their sanctuaries, resettling their gods in their rebuilt temples. The author of the Book of Ezra apparently appropriated their knowledge of this conventional Persian policy and, failing to mention that Cyrus acted in this way toward other nations and their gods, declared that Cyrus' provision for the exiled people to return to their homeland and to restore their Temple came at YHWH's behest (Ezra 1:2–4).[4]

The Book of Ezra and the Books of Haggai and Zechariah, all view Jerusalem and the Temple devoted to YHWH Sabaoth as the key site for YHWH's future activities, which will make Jerusalem central, not marginal, in their known world. Yet, this emphasis on the centrality of Jerusalem and YHWH's Temple is not only dissonant with the perspective of the Persian rulers, it also does not reflect the experience of the audience of these books. Archaeological evidence indicates that, though Jerusalem remained stable from the time of the city's destruction at the hands of the Babylonians in 586 BCE until the time of Nehemiah's

---

[4] See Amélie Kuhrt, "The Cyrus Cylinder and Achaemenid Imperial Policy," *JSOT* 25 (1983): 83–97; Bob Becking, "'We All Returned as One!': Critical Notes on the Myth of the Mass Return," in *Judah and Judeans in the Persian Period* (ed. Oded Lipschitz and Manfred Oeming; Winona Lake, IN: Eisenbrauns, 2006), 3–18.

return to the city in 445 BCE, the city was sparsely inhabited, a fact reflected in Neh 7:4, "the city was large and spacious; there were few people in it and no houses being built."[5] Charles Carter, basing his work on the data previously collected by Kenneth Hoglund, argues that the number of returnees to Persia was much smaller than the numbers claimed in Nehemiah.[6] Though the city would still have been viewed as an important cultic center, the place with the remains of the foundation of Solomon's Temple, Jerusalem was not the central administrative site in Yehud until after the return of Nehemiah, who rebuilt the city's walls as part of the Persian effort to fortify its southern boundary in response to the strengthening rebellions of the nation of Egypt.[7]

In other words, during the times reflected in the Books of Haggai and Zechariah, including those portions of the Book of Zechariah that belong to dates later than Darius I but predating the arrival of Nehemiah (Zech 9–14), Jerusalem remained sparsely populated and regionally insignificant. As suggested in the work of Oded Lipschits and his colleagues, the prominence of the lion seal impressions at Ramat Rahel during the middle Persian period (late 6th to mid-5th century BCE), indicate that Ramat Rahel, not Jerusalem, served as the administrative center for Yehud for over a century.[8]

---

[5] David Ussishkin, "The Borders and Size of Jerusalem in the Persian Period," in *Judah and Judeans in the Persian Period* (ed. Lipschitz and Oeming), 147–166.

[6] Charles E. Carter, *The Emergence of Yehud in the Persian Period: A Social and Demographic Study* (LHBOTS 294; Sheffield: Sheffield Academic Press, 1999).

[7] John W. Betlyon, "A People Transformed: Palestine in the Persian Period," *NEA* 68:1–2 (2005): 7.

[8] Oded Lipschits, "Persian Period Judah: A New Perspective," in *Texts, Contexts, and Reading in Postexilic Literature* (ed. Louis Jonker; FAT 2/53; Tübingen: Mohr Siebeck, 2011), 187–211.

Jerusalem, formerly the prominent city of the region, languishing in secondary status to the formerly less prominent city, Ramat Rahel, has a parallel in the relationship between Sidon and Tyre during the Achaemenid Period. During Babylon's onslaught of the Levant, Nebuchadnezzar engaged in a protracted siege eventuating in the capitulation of the Tyrians and the deportation of its elite to Babylon, with the result that Tyre lost its significance in the region even before Alexander the Great destroyed the city. Sidon, on the other hand, was not besieged by the Babylonians and so took on a more prominent role in Phoenicia, a role previously played by Tyre.[9] The relationship between Ramat Rahel and Jerusalem appears much the same as with Tyre and Sidon. Jerusalem was destroyed and its elite deported by Nebuchadnezzar while life in Ramat Rahel went along fairly undisturbed. And thus, Jerusalem, like Tyre, found itself in a secondary role in the district of Yehud, rising to greater prominence only in the latter period of the Achaemenid rule and more so during the Seleucid era.

With the prophetic rhetoric about Yehud and Jerusalem's significance in the eyes of YHWH Sabaoth – in spite of their struggles and relative insignificance under Persian rule – it comes as no surprise that the visions of the Jerusalem Temple in the Books of Haggai and Zechariah disproportionately amplify the significance of the house of YHWH on the world stage. Although the opening of the Book of Ezra claims that a mass of people returned to Jerusalem during the days of Cyrus with the specific

---

[9] Vadim S. Jigoulov, *The Social History of Achaemenid Phoenicia* (London: Equinox, 2010), 166; cf. J. Brian Peckham, who thinks that the elite returned to Tyre after Nebuchadnezzar's death (*Phoenicia: Episodes and Anecdotes from the Ancient Mediterranean* [Winona Lake, IN: Eisenbrauns, 2014], 370).

aim of rebuilding the sanctuary in Jerusalem, the Books of Ezra, Haggai, and Zechariah agree that some twenty years later the temple site had been cleared but the work of rebuilding remained largely unfinished. Nevertheless, the Books of Haggai and Zechariah envision a future where the Temple becomes the concern of peoples far away from Jerusalem (Zech 6:12–15), with a splendor even greater than Solomon's Temple (Hag 2:6–9), while YHWH provides special protection for the Temple against future enemies (Zech 9:5–8). The dearth of evidence from the biblical text about the exact date of the completion of the Second Temple indicates, in fact, that the Temple did not achieve a glorious state in either its structure or in the eyes of the audiences of the Books of Haggai and Zechariah. The Temple would only achieve such great status centuries later with the coming of Herod I in the 1st century BCE.

In other words, the theology of the Books of Haggai and Zechariah addresses the apparent insignificance of Yehud, Jerusalem, and the Second Temple on the world stage based in the belief that YHWH Sabaoth exercises power over the nations, beginning with YHWH returning the Jewish exiles to their homeland and to Jerusalem for the express purpose of rebuilding the Temple. The assurances of God's authority over the nations and YHWH's deep concern for those living in Yehud and Jerusalem were meant to strengthen the people to pursue the aims of the prophetic discourse: to trust in YHWH for their future, to rebuild the sanctuary of YHWH, and to pursue the moral demands made by YHWH in the Torah and the former prophets. The fact that the divine order of the world proclaimed by the prophets remains an unknown secret outside of Yehudite circles was a problem that the prophets who followed in the Zechariah tradition (i.e., those who produced

Zech 9–14)[10] would continue to deal with, especially at the intersection of the grandiose visions of Haggai and Zechariah and the continued struggles of the community before the time of Nehemiah.[11]

Ehud Ben Zvi argues that the people in the province of Yehud did not experience the land as one of existential risk in the way that previous generations did during the era of Assyrian and Babylonian dominance with their devastating military campaigns that destroyed cities in Northern Israel and Southern Judah and sent thousands of exiles from their homeland. Zvi bases this claim in part on this very point, that the province of Yehud was marginal to the Persian Empire, unable to pose a legitimate threat to the Persians, and so unlikely to draw the sustained military attention of the armies of Persia.[12] While Yehud may not have experienced any profound sense of threat during the reigns of

---

[10] Many biblical scholars divide the text of the Book of Zechariah into two sections, First Zechariah (chs. 1–8) and Second Zechariah (chs. 9–14), though some further divide the book into Second Zechariah (chs. 9–11) and Third Zechariah (chs. 12–14). Because of my own emphasis on the final form of the book (see below), I will avoid using these terms, though, as the language indicates here, I believe the last portion of the book developed in the hands of disciples of the original prophet, Zechariah.

[11] The language of "unknown secret" comes from Ehud Ben Zvi, "On Social Memory and Identity Formation in Late Persian Yehud," in *Texts, Contexts and Reading* (ed. Jonker), 139–140.

[12] Ibid., 106–107. Briant notes that the interest in Yehud ascribed to Cyrus is really just an "optical illusion" based on the imbalance of evidence, namely the textual evidence of the Books of Ezra and Nehemiah versus a lack of similar, Persian texts. He goes so far as to claim that, even as Nehemiah fortified the walls of Jerusalem, "there is nothing to prove that Susa or Persepolis considered Judah a bulwark of Persian dominion against fickle and unruly Egypt" (*From Cyrus to Alexander*, 585–586). While I do not wish to overestimate the importance of Yehud even after the return of Nehemiah and the rebuilding of Jerusalem's walls, I argue below that it seems safe to presume that the rebuilding of the walls functioned within the larger Persian

Darius and Xerxes, the latter chapters of the Book of Zechariah indicate that the people experienced some existential anxieties, including both internal divisions and also a complex of worrisome concerns about neighbors near and far: Damascus, Tyre, Sidon, Ashkelon, Gaza, Ekron, Ashdod, Greece (Javan),[13] Assyria, and Egypt (chs. 9–10), with the threat of chariots and horses in Ephraim and Jerusalem (9:9–10). How might one account for the sense of threat expressed in these oracles?

The anxiety apparent in the texts of Zechariah 9–10 and the wide range of important cities and countries named in these chapters reflect the instability in the region during the first decade or so of the reign of Artaxerxes I. As Artaxerxes came to power in 464 amid political confusion due to the murder of Xerxes I, Inaros of Egypt declared himself king and invited the Athenians to join him in expelling the Persians from the Levant. Cities on the coast like Tyre, Sidon, Gaza, Ashkelon, and Ashdod were cities that Artaxerxes fortified and where he built a larger fleet to hold at bay the Athenian navy. Still, in the first major Persian campaign to put down the Egyptian revolt in 459/458, the Persians lost to the Egyptians, losing up to one-quarter of their army and suffering the death of Achaemenes, the satrap of Egypt, who was killed in the battle of Papremis. Only in 456/5 did the Persians, under Artabazus and Megabyzus, take the Egyptian capital Memphis and destroy most of the fifty Athenian ships meant to reinforce the Egyptian fleet.[14] The anxieties expressed and addressed in Zechariah 9–14 make good sense in light of the regional uproar

strategy to shore up their southern boundary against the threat of Egyptian revolt and incursion.

[13] On Javan as a reference to the Greeks as such, see *HALOT*, 1:402.

[14] For an excellent summary of the Egyptian revolt and the Persian response, see Ruzicka, *Trouble in the West*, 29–32.

and the likelihood that Persian armies marched through the Levant to Egypt, while reports swirled about the Persian defeat at sea.

In this light, it is likely that the mission of Nehemiah in the 440s to rebuild the walls of Jerusalem was part of a larger Persian strategy to maintain stricter control of Palestine and to mobilize conscripted armies from the area to battle Egypt, should the need again arise.[15] Given that worries over internal strife and (potential) external onslaught against Jerusalem are intimated throughout the Book of Zechariah, it seems that Nehemiah's mission in the 440s is the *terminus ad quem* of the book. Certainly rebuilding of the walls of Jerusalem, representing more direct interest of the Persians in the goings-on of Yehud, along with the building of small fortifications at major crossroads in the Levant, at industrial installations, and in the middle of cities, towns, and villages, would have provided the people with a greater sense of security for their future.[16]

The long-term struggle of Yehud, Jerusalem, and the Temple in their subject status within the Persian Empire, along with the heightened anxieties about their future in the midst of an international conflict, thus serves as the backdrop to the unfolding theological response found in Zechariah 9–14. The disciples in the Zechariah tradition that edited the book knew the prophecies about the return of YHWH to the people (Zechariah 1–6) and the demands for justice made upon the people (Zechariah 7–8), and likely also knew the bold promises to Zerubbabel and his

---

[15] See Betlyon, "A People Transformed," 7; I appreciate the private conversation with Baruch Halpern for the observation that building up fortifications would aid in the conscription of an army among local peoples.

[16] See Betlyon, "A People Transformed," 7.

contemporaries recorded in the Book of Haggai (2:6–9, 19–23). The prophetic material collected in Zechariah 9–14 had both to account for the reasons why the grand promises in Zech 1:7–6:15 did not come to full fruition and also to offer hope to people who continued to put their faith in YHWH Sabaoth, whose power among the nations had been promised to benefit them. It is worth noting that the final chapter in the Book of Zechariah continues to acknowledge the realistic fears of the people concerning the inner strife of Yehud and the potential that the nation will suffer greatly in the midst of the conflicts between Persia, Egypt, and Greece. The theological promises made in the earlier portions of the book then become eschatological in chapter 14, looking forward to a time in the indefinite future that will end subjection and the threat of devastating conflict, when YHWH finally fulfills the good promises made through Haggai and Zechariah and the prophets who went before them.

SOCIAL DIVISIONS IN THE YEHUD COMMUNITY

In terms of the social context within Yehud, and in Jerusalem in particular, the reading offered here places a great deal of emphasis on four specific passages in the Book of Zechariah: 1:1–6, 7:8–14, 8:16–17, and 11:4–17. Each of these passages, in their own way, points to the divisions that exist between the minority elite of Yehud and the majority subsistent class, so that the messages of these prophets address both groups but place the burden for change upon Yehud elites.[17] In fact, the Book of Zechariah develops around the demand of YHWH upon the elite to do

---

[17] For a good discussion of the increased stratification experienced in Yehud in the Persian period see Samuel L. Adams, *Social and Economic Life in the*

justice for the sake of the people's future in the land and the ultimate failure of Yehud's leadership in this regard, so that the promise of God's abundant care is constantly left to the future.[18]

Zechariah 1:1–6 is not explicitly a call to justice, but highlights the fact that the prophet's demands of the elite in the days of Darius were consonant with the message of the prophets before the exile:

> Do not be like your ancestors, who, when the former prophets called unto them saying, "Thus says YHWH Sabaoth: turn, I pray, from your evil ways and your evil deeds," did not listen and so did not draw near to me, declares YHWH. (1:4)

The visions recorded in Zech 1:7–6:15 are clearly not about the people's return to YHWH but, rather, affirm the ways that YHWH returns to the people. In chapters 7 and 8, the prophet enumerates YHWH's demand for the people to return to YHWH by doing the justice that God demands. Zechariah 7:9–10 summarizes the message of the former prophets in order to lay their demands on the elite of Yehud: judge with true judgments; act with faithfulness and compassion toward your sister and brother; do not exploit the widow, orphan, alien, or poor; and do not plot evil against one another. Zechariah 8:16–17 reiterates and refines this message for the current generation to whom YHWH promises blessings: speak truthfully to your neighbor, judge with fairness and truth, do not plan evil in your hearts against your neighbor, and do not give false testimony.

Second Temple Period (Louisville, KY: Westminster John Knox Press, 2014), 77–80, 103–125, 130–145.

[18] See Robert L. Foster, "Undoing the Future: The Theology of the Book of Zechariah," *HBT* 34 (2012): 59–72.

The importance of these texts becomes apparent when we give attention to these imperatives in Zechariah 1–8. Rhetorical texts like the prophetic books build their arguments in support of the imperatives. The prophets of ancient Israel – and the prophetic books bearing their names – wanted the people to *do* – or not do – certain things. If we want to understand the aim(s) of the rhetoric of the prophetic material, we must look at the imperatives foremost, over and above the indicative material.[19] Noticing these imperatives allows us to distinguish, for example, the direction of the Book of Haggai from the Book of Zechariah. The imperatives of Haggai exhort the audience to build the Temple, to stop neglecting the house of YHWH and their obligation to bring honor to the name of YHWH. The Book of Zechariah, on the other hand, exhorts the people to return to YHWH, which chapter 7 clarifies as obeying the message of the former prophets about taking care of the widow, orphan, alien, and poor; and which chapter 8 defines as defending the rights of the widow, orphan, alien, and poor in the court.

Zechariah 11:4–17 also includes imperatives but these are directed to the prophet, beyond the usual "say such-and-such to the people." The prophet performs dramatic actions, breaking two

---

[19] If rhetoric is, as Aristotle claims, "the art of persuasion," then the aim of rhetorical analysis is to determine the persuasive aims of the author. Scholars of the biblical text, and the prophets in particular, have sought to determine this in a variety of ways. See, for example, Karl Möller's use of a variety of modern rhetorical theorists to determine the rhetorical aims of the Book of Amos (*A Prophet in Debate: The Rhetoric of Persuasion in the Book of Amos* [LHBOTS 372; Sheffield: Sheffield Academic Press, 2003]). I am arguing that, grammatically speaking, the most direct form of address is the imperative. If we want to determine the persuasive aims of a book, primacy of place should be given to the grammatical form that most explicitly states the authors'/editors' demands.

staffs, which represents the breaking of the covenant with all the peoples and the family ties that join Judah and Israel (11:11, 14).[20] The background to these dramatic acts lies in the continued exploitation of the poor of the land so that they suffer because of the greed of the governors and the elite in the days before Nehemiah.[21] The structure of the Book of Zechariah indicates that the delay in the fulfillment of the visions of the prophet Zechariah – and, indirectly, the failure of the promises enumerated in the Book of Haggai – lies at the feet of the elite, who have not returned to YHWH and so guarded the rights of the oppressed but, instead, exploited the majority poor for their own gain.[22]

The theological concerns of the Books of Haggai and Zechariah are, thus, twofold. On the one hand, the promises of an exalted Yehud, Jerusalem, and Temple remain a secret to all except those who have heard the promises proclaimed by the prophets because the land, city, and Temple remain subject and at-risk. Both of the Books of Haggai and Zechariah want their audiences to know that YHWH Sabaoth is the also the Great King over all the earth and that the Temple, Jerusalem, and Yehud are the center of YHWH's rule in the world. On the other hand, the division between the majority poor and the minority rich of the preexilic period persists in postexilic Yehud. The Book of Zechariah, in particular,

---

[20] David Stacey helpfully discusses texts like Zech 11:4–17 in terms of "prophetic drama," also known as "sign-acts," because this description emphasizes the way that prophets' actions dramatize the message that YHWH communicates to the people (*Prophetic Drama in the Old Testament* [London: Epworth, 1990]).

[21] See Robert L. Foster, "Shepherds, Sticks, and Social Destabilization," *JBL* **126** (2007): 743–746.

[22] Foster, "Undoing the Future."

wants the audience to see that the promises of the Great King, YHWH, of future glory for the Temple, Jerusalem, and Yehud, depend on the people, and the elites in particular, turning from the sin of unjust exploitation and working for justice for the oppressed. Otherwise, the promises will continue to be pushed off into the indefinite future.

PERSONAL PERSPECTIVES IN PERFORMING BIBLICAL THEOLOGY

The following chapters will therefore situate the theologies of the Books of Haggai and Zechariah between the two poles of the position of Yehud in the Persian Empire and the struggles of the poor under the demands of the Yehudite elite. Still, the method behind the interpretation presented here primarily emphasizes the texts as blends of narrative and rhetoric, though plenty of historical and cultural analysis is employed in order to illuminate imagery and allusions to cultural context. The choice to see narrative and rhetoric as primary, and historical and cultural analysis as secondary, stems from my vision of biblical theology as an enterprise that deals with the final form of the books incorporated into the canon, emphasizing the *biblical* in "biblical theology."[23] Consequently, while I will not always make

---

[23] Some scholars argue that biblical theology of the Christian Scriptures should prioritize the Septuagint (LXX), as the tradition through which the New Testament developed was the LXX, especially given that the New Testament primarily quotes the Old Testament from some portion of the Septuagint tradition (see, e.g., Martin Hengel, *The Septuagint as Christian Scripture: Its Prehistory and the Problem of the Canon* [OTS; Edinburgh: T&T Clark, 2002]). While this is not the place to get into a lengthy discussion of the canon, it is apparent from the earliest full canon list known to us, Athanasius' Festal Letter 39, that the Old Testament referred to in the letter was not

this explicit, the research behind this book began with concerns for things like plot conflicts and characterization in narrative and the use of imperatives (and interesting places where the text lacks an imperative), parallelism, and the like in rhetoric.

On the other hand, my understanding of the *theology* of "biblical theology" sees this enterprise as a descriptive endeavor. Consequently, I will spend much of my time highlighting the explicit theological claims and implicit theological assumptions encoded in the narrative and rhetoric of these two books. I am particularly interested in how the theological claims of the text are used to forward the argument of these two books.

Even so, as a practicing Christian and former pastor I am interested in what people of faith do with the theological claims and assumptions explicated in this book. In particular I am interested in theological ethics within a Christian framework as informed by the work of biblical theology. Consequently, each of the following chapters will end with a section entitled "Biblical Theology and Theological Ethics," which will contain four parts on *divine motivation, doubts, divine command*, and concluding thoughts on *prophetic witness* (though in at least one instance, a unit does not have all four elements). "Divine motivation" builds

---

the LXX, at least in so far as Athanasius excludes many of the additional books found in many LXX traditions. Furthermore, though the text quoted by the New Testament writers was the LXX, scholars have observed that the LXX text quoted in the Gospel of Matthew or Paul's letters does not look like any known LXX traditwion but often appears to be a Greek text corrected in order to better agree with a Hebrew *Vorlage*. In other words, even the developing LXX tradition prioritized the Hebrew (see M. J. J. Menken, *Matthew's Bible: The Old Testament Text of the Evangelist* [BETL 173; Leuven: Leuven University, 2004], 280, 282; Christopher D. Stanley, *Paul and the Language of Scripture: Citation Technique in the Pauline Epistles and Contemporary Literature* [SNTSMS 74; Cambridge: Cambridge University Press, 1994], 42–46).

on Linda Zagzebski's work on divine motivation theory and explicates the virtues and actions of God evidenced in the text that might serve as a positive model for Christian ethics in the *Imitatio Dei*.[24] "Doubts" is a short section in each chapter that reminds us that the biblical text witnesses to key figures resisting God's professed designs in the world – for example, Abraham, Moses, Jeremiah, and so forth – and offers my own commentary about, for example, the presentation of God's violence or the portrayal of women that we have good reason to doubt serve as continuing models for faithful ethics.[25] "Divine command" theory is likely the ethical theory many of us are most familiar with, though under this heading I will discuss prescriptive materials as well as ethical ideas found in the indicative material. Finally, after discussing theological ethics derived from the texts under these three rubrics, each chapter will close with comments on the "prophetic witness," offering some brief thoughts on how these ethical claims and ideals in the Books of Haggai and Zechariah might shape the practice of faith communities, including and especially, given my own location, the Christian church. These final sections do not articulate a robust ethical theory and so should be taken for what they are: formative ethical reflections. Also, though I take my cue from the fact that this book contributes to a series entitled "Old Testament Theology," a title for this corpus of biblical literature that reflects the Christian tradition, I hope these thoughts may still resonate with Jewish readers,

---

[24] See the full articulation of the theory in Linda Trinkaus Zagzebski, *Divine Motivation Theory* (Cambridge: Cambridge University Press, 2004).

[25] The title "Doubts" reflects the influence of Robert Davidson's important work, *The Courage to Doubt* (London/Philadelphia: SCM Press/Trinity Press International, 1983).

secular theorists, or any others who might have interest in what might be called an effort at "public theology."

Finally, given this concerted effort at ethical reflection, I should admit that I read these prophetic texts through the lens of the Civil Rights Movement in the United States and the many African American preachers and theologians who have shaped my perspective by their proclamation and dramatic action, not least of which are Martin Luther King, Jr. (1929–1968) and James Cone (1938–2018). Those looking back on the Civil Rights Movement have described the activity of that prophetic proclamation as "speaking truth to power," to which I would add the corollary of "offering hope to the powerless." I believe that my view of the prophets as speaking truth to power and offering hope to the powerless has roots in the prophetic books themselves. But, I would be remiss not to admit that my predilection for what I see in the text is also born from interaction with a variety of forms of liberation theology.

CHAPTER 2

I Am with You

The Book of Haggai

The Book of Haggai unfolds across four narrative episodes (1:1–1:15a; 1:15b–2:9; 2:10–19; 2:20–23), marked in the text by the date when the prophet Haggai came forward to make each of the four proclamations during the reign of Darius I (1:1; 1:15b; 2:10; 2:20). While this series of narratives tell of Haggai's interaction with the remnant of Israel and their leaders, several key imperatives indicate the persuasive aim of the book: "Go up to the hills and bring down trees and build this house" (1:8) and "Be strong, Zerubbabel . . . be strong Joshua . . . be strong all people of the land . . . and act!" (2:4). Several more imperatives punctuate this collection of stories (1:5, 7; 2:15, 18), but these serve to exhort the audience to introspection as a means to motivate them to fulfill these two, primary imperatives. In which case we can fairly summarize the purpose of the Book of Haggai as to encourage the book's audience to fulfill Haggai's commands, to be strong and to finish the work of building the Temple to YHWH. The explicit theological claims and implicit theological assumptions of the book intend to motivate its original audience to achieve this aim, perhaps not too long after Haggai's prophetic ministry.

YHWH OF HOSTS: A TROUBLING PRESENCE

Scene one of the Book of Haggai (1:1–15a) opens quite simply with a marker of the time when Haggai delivered his message (the first day of the sixth month of the second year of Darius), a designation of the recipients of his message (Zerubbabel the governor and Joshua the high priest), and a basic description of Haggai's role as prophet (he delivers the word of YHWH).

The theological claim opening the book is in the description of Haggai as a prophet: "a word from YHWH was in the hand of Haggai the prophet" (1:1). The people in the days of Haggai possessed some sense of YHWH's work through prophets, especially remembering the threats from the prophets Isaiah, Jeremiah, and Ezekiel of the Temple's destruction, devastation of Jerusalem, and exile of the people. The medium of the delivery, "by the hand of the prophet," indicates that the prophecy was written (see Jer 36:9–32). Though the collocation is rare in the Hebrew Bible, this vision of the prophecy coming by the hand of Haggai links this passage, at least for informed audience members of the Book of Haggai, to the great, preexilic prophets of Isaiah and Jeremiah (Isa 20:2; Jer 37:2; 50:1). So, for the audience of the Book of Haggai this opening line evokes a sense of the power of YHWH and YHWH's word that, in their communal memory, was a force of desolation. In this light, the opening of Haggai may have induced the fear of YHWH. After all, words uttered previously to the exiles via Isaiah and Jeremiah led to Northern Israel and Judah and Jerusalem's demise. Yehud, the small district "Beyond the River" and of no account to the Persians, certainly could not afford to have YHWH as their enemy (again).

There is also, of course, the claim that the book records the word of YHWH. This seems like a rather obvious point but it must be remembered that the people returning to the land of Yehud had religious options. The god who presumably endorsed and supported the military and building projects of the Persian kings was named Ahuramazda. In one inscription published by Darius' son, Xerxes I, the king claims that (a) it is by Ahuramazda's favor that Xerxes ruled the empire and (b) those who want to live a happy life and be blessed in death should worship Ahuramazda at the proper time and with the proper ritual.[1] Interestingly, Ephraim Stern notes that no clay figurines of other gods are found in the former regions of Judah or Samaria dating from the Persian Period.[2] But there are certainly cult sites and figurines in the surrounding Levant and their variety indicates local as well as Egyptian, Greek, and Persian influences.[3] So, this message through Haggai from YHWH does not emerge in a vacuum. Other gods are on offer in the region and certainly from Persia. But the book claims that the one addressing the people and its leadership via the prophet Haggai is the God of Jerusalem, Judah, and Israel's past, the same God of the earlier prophets like Isaiah and Jeremiah.

In the very next portion of the narrative, the narrator appends an adjective to the name of YHWH that clarifies YHWH's identity: "Thus says YHWH *Sabaoth*" (1:2a). The earliest references in the Old Testament canon to YHWH Sabaoth occur in the Book of Exodus, which evokes a specific "host" consisting of a particular number of people in the days of the Exodus. According to the description of the tenth plague in Egypt and the people coming

---

[1] XPh§4d in Amelie Kuhrt, *The Persian Empire* (London: Routledge: 2010), 305.
[2] Ephraim Stern, *Archaeology of the Land of the Bible, Volume II: 732–332 BCE* (ABRL; New York: Doubleday, 2001), 488, 490.
[3] Ibid., 479–513.

out of the land, YHWH led a purported 600,000 men out of Egypt, plus women and children, so close to one-and-a-half million people (Exod 12:37–42).

The God who led the great host of Israel out of the land of Egypt long ago now addresses the people under Persian rule. The invocation of the Exodus in "YHWH Sabaoth" lends a more positive outlook to the message coming in the Book of Haggai, drawing on the communal memory of the Exodus event. Furthermore, the fact that the same God who addressed and delivered a great host out of Egypt now addresses the small population of people living in early postexilic Yehud those hearing these words a new perspective on their situation.[4] Perhaps the narrator lets the implied audience in on part of the "unknown secret" that Zvi refers to in the writings of this period.[5] The God who cares for Israel is the same God of the Exodus whose power benefits the people, rather than sending them into exile as in the days of the former prophets.

The conflict that drives this opening narrative comes in the contrast between the perspective of the people of the land and YHWH Sabaoth. The people claim that "The time has not yet come to build the house of YHWH" (Hag 1:2b) while YHWH

---

[4] Israel Finkelstein estimates a low figure for Yehud's population, around 12,000 ("The Territorial Extent and Demography of Yehud/Judea in the Persian and Early Hellenistic Periods," *Revue Biblique* 117 [2010]: 45). Oded Lipschits, who thinks that the territory of Persia extended further than Finkelstein allows, holds that the population was closer to 30,000 ("Demographic Changes in Judah between the Seventh and the Fifth Centuries B.C.E.," in *Judah and the Judeans in the New-Babylonian Period* [ed. O. Lipschits and J. Blenkinsopp; Winona Lake, IN: Eisenbrauns, 2003], 364). Either way, the number of people in Yehud at this time paled in comparison to the number of people the Exodus narrative states came out of Egypt.

[5] See Chapter 1, n. 11.

I Am with You: The Book of Haggai

wants to know, "Is this the time for *you* to dwell in your roofed houses while this house lies ruined?" (Hag 1:4).[6] Part of YHWH's outrage at the people's question is hinted at in another part of the people's communal memory of the days when an original contingent returned from Babylon to Yehud. The opening section of Ezra claims that at the beginning of the reign of Cyrus, the first Persian king authorized Sheshbazzar and a group of Israelites to return to their homeland with the express purpose of rebuilding the Temple of YHWH and to make offerings to God. According to the Book of Ezra these people did not leave empty-handed but received back the vessels of gold and silver that Nebuchadnezzar had pilfered from Solomon's Temple, as well as the goods and beasts necessary to carry out their cultic obligations (Ezra 1:2–11). The dating of this first narrative in the Book of Haggai indicates that the prophet delivered his message some twenty years after this original return to the land. How much longer do the people think they will need before acting on their original reasons for coming back to the land?

While the people put off building the House of YHWH, the prophet speaking for YHWH observes that the people live in "roofed houses" themselves. The Hebrew root, *spn*, occurs only five other times in the Old Testament, notably three times in describing the completion of the roof of the Temple that Solomon built.[7] Thus, the odd idea that the people live in "roofed" houses (what other kind of houses do people reside in?) may not simply

---

[6] I have italicized *you* to indicate the presence of the second-person plural pronoun *'attem* that makes the address more emphatic, more accusatory.

[7] See the discussion of the noun and verb built on the root *spn* in Martin J. Mulder, *1 Kings Vol. 1: 1 Kings 1–11* (trans. John Vriend; HCOT; Leuven: Peeters, 1998), 248; Marvin A Sweeney, *I & II Kings: A Commentary* (OTL; Louisville, KY: Westminster John Knox Press, 2007), 112.

refer to their houses being finished, with a roof over their head, but may also evoke the relationship between the incomplete Temple in the days of Haggai and the completed Temple in the days of Solomon. It seems that the prophet accuses the people of giving priority to their own home building when, given the commission in the days of Cyrus, the priority belonged to the building of the Temple.

The problem seems to lie in the way the people take care of themselves but fail to honor YHWH. The temple/house in the ancient Near East symbolized heaven on earth, the dwelling of God in human community, with the people's service intended to elicit divine benevolence. People often sought to build elaborate and massive structures to communicate the special nature of the temple space, ensuring unconscious reverence and awe on the part of the people.[8] The communities who built temples intended for them to be functional and therefore not too dissimilar from the most opulent structures they knew, the royal residences.[9] It proves as no surprise, then, given the sacral function of temples and their implicit role in eliciting reverence and awe for the god who dwelt therein, that the prophet's words addressed the state and priestly leaders within the district of Yehud, Zerubbabel the governor and Joshua the high priest (1:1). Political leaders, mostly kings, ensured that temples were built in the ancient Near East and the high priest should care most about the proper means to honor their god. This narrative implies that for twenty years the people failed in the most basic way to honor YHWH. But, as we

---

[8] Michael B. Hundley, *Gods in Dwellings: Temples and Divine Presence in the Ancient Near East* (SBLWAW 3; Atlanta, GA: Society of Biblical Literature, 2013), 131–133.
[9] Ibid., 135.

will see later, this did not stop them from seeking God's benevolence. The proper relationship between honoring God and receiving God's benefits was broken at its foundation.

The prophet claims that the people should have known that something had broken down. Haggai exhorts the people to consider their paths (vv. 5, 7). The people in the prophet's days knew that things had not gone well for them for some time:

> You sowed much but brought in little
> Ate but were not satiated
> Drank but could not get drunk
> Put on clothes but had no body for them
> And the one receiving a wage receives it in a pierced bag[10] (1:6)

The people should have known something was wrong with crop failures and garments falling off emaciated bodies and not enough alcohol to drink away their problems.

Apparently, the people could not put two-and-two together and see that it was YHWH who brought these troubles into their lives. The prophet arrives to underscore this reality to the people:

> You sought for the abundant [harvest] but – look – little! And whatever you brought to this house *I* blew it away. (1:9)
> *I* called for a drought upon the earth and upon the mountains and upon the grain fields
> And upon the sweet wine and upon the oil and whatever springs forth from the land
> And upon the human beings and upon the beasts and upon all the labor done by hands. (1:11)

These are words of a prophet who stands in the tradition of Isaiah and Jeremiah, delivering words from YHWH asserting that the

---

[10] I owe the nice turn of phrase "the one receiving a wage" to my colleague, Tyler Kelley.

devastation the people experience comes because YHWH acts as their enemy. YHWH is YHWH Sabaoth, the God who brought Israel out of the land of Egypt. But YHWH is also the God who sent a word by the hand of the prophets Isaiah and Jeremiah before the downfall of Northern Israel and Southern Judah. Since the loss of crops and the effects upon the people did not lead to the realization that the people were failing at a basic level to reverence their God, YHWH sends the prophet Haggai to make the message clear.

The problem is not that the people did not think that YHWH possessed the power to act. As Haggai saw it, the people brought offerings to the House of YHWH (v. 9a).[11] Bringing offerings to the site of the former Temple seems like the proper protocol for receiving divine favor.[12] But the prophet confronts the people with the idea that such gifts do not override the basic concern to provide a built space that denotes the people's proper reverence and awe of YHWH. And so Haggai confronts the people's desire for divine benevolence without basic, proper reverence by declaring that the traumatic experiences in the land were, in fact, acts of divine punishment.

When Haggai calls upon Zerubbabel and Joshua and the people to consider their ways, he utilizes a familiar metaphor. A "path" (*derek*) generally connotes "that which is trodden underfoot."[13] As a metaphor for "well-trodden" activities of the people, it connotes

---

[11] I take the noun phrase *habbayit* as a reference to "this house," i.e., the site of the House of YHWH that the text says lies in ruins.

[12] Hundley, *Gods in Dwellings*, 131, notes the importance of following the proper protocol when accessing the divine space of a temple site.

[13] Philip J. King and Lawrence E. Stager, *Life in Biblical Israel* (LAI; Louisville, KY: Westminster John Knox Press, 2001), 178.

something more like a "custom."[14] In the context, this demand to "consider your paths" includes their regular religious behavior, which they expected to yield divine benevolence and instead yielded divine punishment, and which went widely unnoticed until the prophet arrived on the scene. The role of the prophet in this case, then, is to interrupt this customary practice, at least for a time.

It seems that Haggai arrived with these words of divine advice without solicitation by either Zerubbabel or Joshua.[15] That is, the prophetic word arrives, ironically, as an act of unsolicited divine benevolence, offering the people direct instruction on how to rectify their troubled circumstances: "Go up to the mountains and bring down trees and build this house and I will place my favor on it and I will be glorified, says YHWH" (v. 8). If and when the people carry out this basic act twenty years in the making, then the basic elements associated with a temple will emerge. YHWH will be glorified, that is, receive the awe and reverence implied by the magnificence of the structure itself. And YHWH will place favor upon the house, that is, act benevolently rather than punitively.

Many of the prophets in the preexilic period offered their own imperatives to help rectify the circumstances that presaged exile, often dealing with idolatry and injustice. But at the climax of this opening narrative in the Book of Haggai, the narrator offers an observation rare among the prophets: Zerubbabel, Joshua, and all

---

[14] Ferdinand E. Deist, *The Material Culture of the Bible: An Introduction* (Biblical Seminar 70; Sheffield: Sheffield Academic Press, 2000), 236.

[15] It was customary for prophets to offer divine advice to authorities in times of crisis, though the authorities often sought out this advice; see Martti Nissinen, *Ancient Prophecy: Near Eastern, Biblical, and Greek Perspectives* (Oxford: Oxford University Press, 2017), 216.

the remnant of the people *obeyed* the summons of YHWH and the people feared before the face of YHWH (v. 12). The narrator's reference to the people's fear may simply refer to the fact that the people considered their ways and found sufficient motivation to act on the prophet's words in light of the clear signs of divine punishment that they experienced. But to say that people feared YHWH does not necessarily mean that they were simply afraid of YHWH and wanted to get on YHWH's good (benevolent) side. For example, Shiphrah and Puah, the midwives in the opening of the Book of Exodus, feared God, which seems to mean that they honored God above Pharaoh, because they refused to obey Pharaoh's command to kill the baby boys of Israel (Exod 20:15–22). Later in the story of the Exodus, when the people stood on the other side of the Sea of Reeds with the bodies of the Egyptians lying dead on the shore, the narrator states that the people feared YHWH and trusted (*'mn*) in YHWH and Moses (Exod 14:30–31). Certainly, in the Exodus narrative, there must have been an element of being afraid after seeing God devastate the Egyptian armies in the sea. But there was also an element of trusting YHWH and Moses, because the people could see that when YHWH promised salvation and a future through Moses, they could trust his message.

So, it seems that, in the case of the Book of Haggai, "fear" implies that the people were afraid as they came to see that YHWH exercised power to devastate the land. But "fear" also implies that the people chose to honor YHWH and to trust the message through Haggai (1:12) that YHWH would favor them in the rebuilt Temple (1:8). Their trust and obedience lead to further theological motivation as YHWH kept sending messages through Haggai to the people summarized in the narrative as "I am with you" (v. 13). This reiterated claim may have proven necessary after the experiences of the previous season of sufferings in the land. After all, Haggai had just revealed to the people that failed harvests, starvation, and tattered garments were the result of YHWH's acting against the people.

The narrative goes on to say that the divine motivation "stirred up" the spirit of Zerubbabel and Joshua and the remnant of the people to come and work on the House of YHWH (v. 14). As this first scene comes to a close, the narrative echoes the story in Exodus 35 in which YHWH commands the people to bring out their riches to build the Tabernacle and everyone with a willing spirit (*rûaḥ*) acts in accordance with the message delivered by the hand of Moses (35:21, 29).[16] The narrator in Haggai 1 wants the implied audience to understand the moment that the remnant of Yehud obeyed the word of YHWH and YHWH strengthened their spirit as reminiscent of the days of the Exodus. In the Exodus narrative, not only did the people respond with their spirits but the Book of Exodus ends with YHWH's glory filling the Tabernacle (Exod 40:34–38; cf. the "glory" that YHWH will receive in the rebuilt Temple in Hag 1:8). As YHWH enabled the people in the days of Moses to fulfill the vision of the Tabernacle given to Moses, so through Haggai the people and their leaders experience the stirring of YHWH to keep working on the Temple. This stirring up of the spirit also recalls another communal memory of when YHWH stirred up the spirit of Cyrus to send those captive in Babylon back to Jerusalem to rebuild the Temple (Ezra 1:1) and the people who chose to return to the land to carry

---

[16] The list of connections include the reference to the spirit of the people (Exod 35:21; Hag 1:14), the message (Exod 35:4; Hag 1:13), acting on the message (Exod 35:39; Hag 1:14), and the fact that this command came "by the hand of" Moses/Haggai (Exod 35:29; Hag 1:1).

out the rebuilding (Ezra 1:5). Finally, in the days of the prophet Haggai, the leadership and people of Yehud commit to fulfilling the implicit promise made in the days of Cyrus to rebuild the Temple of YHWH.

Even though Haggai 1 reports that the people took up the rebuilding process with renewed energy, the book as a whole does not report that they actually completed the project. Thus, it seems that the scribes who produced the Book of Haggai wrote to persuade the people of Jerusalem and Yehud in that same or subsequent generation to finish the work so long delayed. This opening narrative offers its persuasion on one level by asking the audience to envision the work of rebuilding the Temple as part of a New Exodus, with YHWH Sabaoth having returned a remnant to the land and now stirring up the people's spirits just as YHWH did in the days when the people brought their gifts for the building of the Tabernacle. In like manner, YHWH would receive glory in the new Temple as YHWH filled the Tabernacle with glory, as reported in Exodus 40.

But the New Exodus is not the only theological motivation that the opening narrative offers to the book's audience. The book also reminds the people that Haggai was a prophet much like Isaiah and Jeremiah, whose promises of devastation came true. The narrative portrays Haggai speaking ex post facto but his prophetic discourse similarly imbibes words of judgment and punishment, which the audience of the Book of Haggai need to heed as a warning before something worse happens.

The initial solution lies in simply fearing YHWH and obeying the directive of God delivered by Haggai to do the work. The people want to experience YHWH's favor but Haggai 1 reminds the audience that the offerings the people brought to the old site of God's house did not yield divine benevolence. Why? Because the people neglected a more basic way of reverencing YHWH by rebuilding "this house" for YHWH. In the end, the advice of the Book of Haggai remains much the same as that of the prophet Haggai: if the people want to receive God's benevolence, they must show proper reverence and build a house that glorifies the God of Israel.

I WILL FILL THIS HOUSE WITH GLORY

The Book of Haggai dates the second narrative just a little over a month-and-a-half after the first and keeps the governor, high priest, and remnant in view as the audience of the prophet's oracles (2:1–2). Now that the people have made a good start at rebuilding the Temple, a new conflict comes to light. YHWH, via Haggai, recognizes that the people who returned from exile and were alive when the Babylonians overthrew the city and destroyed Solomon's Temple look at the beginnings of this new Temple and it seems like nothing in their eyes (2:3).[17] It is the contrast between the meager beginnings and the glorious memories of the former House of God that the prophet addresses.

When the people looked at the new Temple and reflected on the recent problems that the land and its people faced, something more than the house's lack of grandeur likely troubled them. Temples in the ancient Near East and their glory were meant to provide a home for the people's god, a place where heaven and earth met "so that the powers of heaven could be brought to bear

---

[17] Given that the Babylonians destroyed the First Temple some sixty-seven years before this oracle, the people who would have seen the Temple in its former glory would have to be well into their seventies; see Carol L. Meyers and Eric M. Meyers, *Haggai, Zechariah 1–8* (AB 25B; Garden City, NY: Doubleday, 1987), 49.

on the people's behalf to bring security in an otherwise insecure world."[18] The splendor of Solomon's Temple apparently made the people feel immensely secure, so much so that the Book of Jeremiah indicates that Jeremiah preached a sermon simply meant to disabuse the inhabitants of Jerusalem of the notion that the presence of the glorious Temple guaranteed their security (Jer 7). One of the theological implications of this conflict in Hag 2:3 is that YHWH knows that the underdeveloped Temple site in the days of Darius I would evoke distrust in YHWH, with a lack of grandeur simultaneously communicating to some a (continued) lack of divine presence.

Haggai meets this doubt and fear with a trifold imperative: "Be strong Zerubbabel! ... Be strong Joshua! ... Be strong all people of the land!" followed by the command "Work!" (v. 4). YHWH does not leave the people in doubt but responds and seeks to motivate their efforts by drawing further on the Exodus narrative: "I am with you ... which is the word that I covenanted with you when you came up from Egypt; and my spirit is standing in your midst. Do not be afraid!" (v.5). In Exodus 6, YHWH addresses the people through Moses in order to convince them to follow Moses out of Egypt, even though Pharaoh clearly opposes the idea. In this speech, Moses affirms that YHWH remembers the covenant (*bryt*) with Abraham and promises to bring them out (*yṣ'*) of the land of Egypt and give them the land of Canaan as their possession (Exod 6:2–8).[19] In Haggai, YHWH Sabaoth, who brought the hosts of Israel out of Egypt, also brought the former exiles back to

---

[18] Hundley, *Gods in Dwellings*, 134.
[19] See the discussion of the way Exodus 6 refers back to the covenant with Abraham and his descendants in Donald E. Gowan, *Theology in Exodus: Biblical Theology in the Form of a Commentary* (Louisville, KY: Westminster John Knox Press, 1994), 86.

their homeland (2:4). This prophecy on the lips of Haggai, then, roots the experience of the people in Jerusalem and Yehud in the postexilic period even further back, back to the original covenant God made with Abraham to give him and his descendants the land of Canaan (Gen 15:18–20). If the new Temple, which is literally just getting off the ground, seems like nothing in the eyes of some, the prophet offers them a new vision, to see this time as the renewal of the covenant made with Abraham and as part of the New Exodus that brought the people back to the Promised Land.

What the people do not realize, staring at a Temple mount and barely making progress on their building project, is that the spirit of the God of Abraham and Moses and the Exodus stands in their midst. This is the hidden secret that not even the people of the land or Joshua or Zerubbabel can see. A glorious temple was meant to convey the meeting of heaven and earth and to mediate the divine presence. And though YHWH demands a Temple be built to glorify, to reverence, God, paradoxically the lack of a glorious Temple does not indicate YHWH is absent. The troubles in the land, the presence of the prophet and the prophetic word, and the response of the people are all signs of YHWH's presence. Therefore, YHWH commands the people, "Do not fear!" (Hag 2:5c). This command, which serves as a basic element in prophetic oracles of salvation, reminds the people that they have experienced a salvation from captivity in Babylon like the salvation from captivity in Egypt.[20] Surely the people's presence in the

---

[20] Marvin A. Sweeney, *The Twelve Prophets: Volume Two* (Berit Olam; Collegeville, MN: The Liturgical Press, 2000), 547, makes the observation that "fear not" is a basic element in prophetic (and priestly) oracles of salvation.

land from which they were once exiled is a sign of YHWH's presence among them!

But YHWH is not done offering words of assurance to the people of the land and their leaders. The people should be strong and work and not fear *because* YHWH will make the heavens and the earth, sea and dry land, and the nations tremble (2:6–7). When YHWH makes the nations quake all the costly things of those nations will come to Jerusalem and fill the House of YHWH with glory, in what seems a reversal of Nebuchadnezzar taking the costly vessels of the Temple to Babylon during the reign of Jehoiachin (Hag 2:7; 2 Chr 36:10). After all, all of the silver and gold of the nations belongs to YHWH, according to the prophet (Hag 2:8).

These images of YHWH making the heavens and earth and the nations tremble and bringing the costly vessels and silver and gold to the House of YHWH in Jerusalem evoke YHWH as the Great King who conquers nations and plunders them. As the various reliefs of the Neo-Assyrians indicate, plundering a city was part-and-parcel of its capture.[21] Moreover, the ravaging of the countryside could be seen as an event of cosmic proportions, where the earth quaked (Ps 60:2). This cosmic element reverses the way that YHWH controlled heaven and earth and caused the crops of Yehud to fail (Hag 1:10–11). Now YHWH promises to conquer and plunder the nations all the way into their countrysides and to bring their wealth to Jerusalem and to the new Temple. YHWH the Great King who conquered Egypt and defeated Pharaoh and plundered the Egyptians (Exod 11:1–3; 12:33–36) will do the same

---

[21] Othmar Keel, *Symbolism of the Biblical World: Ancient Near Eastern Iconography and the Book of Psalms*, trans. Timothy J. Hallet (Winona Lake, IN: Eisenbrauns, 1997), 106.

for the people in the coming days by plundering the nations, likely a reference to all the nations subject to the King of Persia. The King of Persia certainly felt that he deserved the wealth of the nations, as can be seen in the tribute reliefs in Persepolis where representatives bring their wealth to the king's grand palace.[22] But YHWH promises to conquer – or perhaps, better, subdue – the nations given the claim to already own the silver and gold of the nations and bring the treasures that the King of Persia considered his own to the new Temple.

So, YHWH will shake the nations and bring their costly vessels to Jerusalem, "And I will fill this house with glory" (Hag 2:7). Obviously, to "fill this house with glory" includes references to the riches of the nations coming into the Temple. But the proclamation likely implies more than just these riches from the nations. To "fill this house with glory" echoes the language at the end of the Book of Exodus when, after the people finished the Tabernacle structure, the glory of YHWH descended, filling the Tabernacle so that not even Moses could enter (40:34–35). Generations later, the glory of God filled the Temple completed by Solomon's workers so that the priests could not enter (1 Kgs 8:10–11). The narrative in Haggai 2 continues to draw out the image of the New Exodus as the people express understandable sadness over the Temple mount that cannot compare to the glorious days of Solomon. YHWH promises that days lie on the horizon when the Temple they build will be filled with the glory of YHWH, just as YHWH's glory filled the Tabernacle and, later, the Temple of Solomon.

---

[22] See the images and discussion in Donald M. Wilber, *Persepolis: The Archaeology of Parsa, Seat of the Persian Kings* (rev. ed.; Princeton, NJ: The Darwin Press, 1989), 75–84. See also Michael J. Chan, *The Wealth of Nations: A Tradition-Historical Study* (Tübingen: Mohr Siebeck, 2017).

As the narrative comes to an end, Haggai offers one last vision to the people of the glorious days that lie ahead: "And in this place, I will give *shalom*" (Hag 2:9). In this final promise the prophet continues to assert that YHWH is the Great King *in this place*, as opposed to the king of Persia, who viewed himself as the Great King who grants peace from his royal city and palace. As Pierre Briant notes, especially in the Behistun inscription, Darius I articulated that the subjection of the conquered peoples listed there both expressed imperial power but also the *Pax persica*, as Darius restored imperial order.[23] Haggai assures the people of Yehud and their leaders that YHWH will subject the nations of the empire, bring their wealth to the Temple, and that the new Temple will be the site from which peace emanates, not from the palace in Persepolis or one of the other capital cities of Persia.

This second narrative in the Book of Haggai intends to motivate the book's audience to finish the work begun in the early days of King Darius I. The reminiscence on the discouragement felt by those who saw the work before the people completed the foundation (see 2:10-19 for the completion of the foundation) likely indicates the discouragement of those who first read and heard the Book of Haggai. How could this remnant in a small district within the vast Persian Empire build a Temple that could compare to the great Temple of Solomon, much less the great building projects of Darius I or Xerxes I?

The inferior nature of their building project raised the question of the beneficence of YHWH. If the people's hardships meant that they often could not even feed themselves sufficiently, how could

---

[23] Pierre Briant, *From Cyrus to Alexander: A History of the Persian Empire*, trans. Peter T. Daniels (Winona Lake, IN: Eisenbrauns, 2002), 171.

they expect YHWH to provide them with riches enough to build a Temple worthy of their God? In this second narrative, the theological motivation continues to arise from the vision of a New Exodus. This story affirms to the book's audience that they are already in the midst of the New Exodus. Just as YHWH fulfilled the covenant promise to Abraham and Abraham's descendants by bringing Israel out of Egypt, so YHWH brought the remnant of the people out of Babylon and returned them to the Promised Land and to the city of Jerusalem. And when YHWH exhorts the people "Fear not!" YHWH affirms that they have already experienced the salvation of YHWH.

The task at hand is to finish the work so that the story as recorded in the Book of Exodus may be completed. The people need to finish the work so that the glory of YHWH may fill this house just as it filled the Tabernacle at the end of the Book of Exodus and just as the glory filled Solomon's Temple upon its completion. According to the Book of Haggai, YHWH wants the people to understand YHWH's desire to make this happen and that YHWH will ensure that the House reflects the glory of their God. YHWH promises to act as the Great King who subdues the nations and exacts from them plunder and tribute so that the Temple is truly glorious. In the end, the promise is that one day soon Jerusalem and the Temple mount will serve as the center for peace in their known world as the Great King, YHWH, reasserts benevolent rule not only for Jerusalem and Yehud, but for all the nations of the earth. YHWH's intervention at this point, like YHWH's intervention in the days of the Exodus, occurs because YHWH has a special relationship with these people, because YHWH made a promise to their ancestors, a solemn covenant, that YHWH acted upon long ago and now acts upon once again.

FROM THIS DAY, BLESSING

Within the flow of the Book of Haggai, there is a two-month break before the prophet comes to the people with another message from YHWH Sabaoth. The prophet arrives in time for celebrating that the foundation of the Temple is finally finished. Haggai brings a word of good news, though the blessing that YHWH promises moving forward is initially contrasted to the troubles the people experienced before the time they finished laying the Temple's foundation (2:10-19).

The word of YHWH to the people on this day begins with a report on the actions of Haggai at the prompting of YHWH. Sometime recently God instructed Haggai to go and seek a *torah*, an "instruction," regarding holy things and unclean things.[24] The first instruction reports on the *torah* of holy meat offered in thanksgiving or fulfillment of a vow, which the person offering was allowed to partake in eating (Lev 7:14-18). The *torah* in Lev 17:19 makes it clear that the flesh of the sacrifice loses its holiness if it comes into contact with anything unclean.[25] The second

---

[24] Many people commenting on this verse translate *torah* as a "ruling," i.e., a decision or a judgment in a legal sense; e.g., David R. Hildebrand, "Temple Ritual: A Paradigm for Moral Holiness in Haggai II 10-19," *VT* **39** (1989): 161; Tim Meadowcroft, *Haggai* (Readings; Sheffield: Sheffield Phoenix Press, 2005), 180-181; Meyers and Meyers, *Haggai, Zechariah 1-8*, 55. Given that the prophet commands the people, "consider from this day backward/forward" (2:15, 18), so that the people are instructed by this analogy and its explanation, it seems that Haggai is not asking for a judgment, as if the question he raises would be disputed. Rather, YHWH commands the prophet to seek instruction from the priest about the holy and profane, clean and unclean, which is an important part of the priests' duties (Lev. 10:9-11). The implication is that the answers to the prophet's questions are obvious, just as the experiences of the past and the promises of the future are also obviously instructive to anyone who gives them due consideration.

[25] Meadowcroft, *Haggai*, 181; Meyers and Meyers, *Haggai, Zechariah 1-8*, 55.

instruction that Haggai seeks concerns the rather obvious case of a person made unclean by a corpse and whether this makes whatever they touch unclean. The priest's answer combines the general knowledge that any person who is unclean and touches something else makes that something else unclean (Lev 7:19–21) with the specific *torah* that affirms that touching a dead body makes a person unclean (Num 19:11–22). Thus the person who becomes unclean by touching a corpse makes whatever they touch unclean by default.

No doubt people familiar with some of the basic sacrifices in Israel, like those described in Leviticus 7, and with a general knowledge that corpses make people unclean, knew that the holy meat does not communicate holiness to other objects, while unclean humans, especially those made unclean because touching a corpse (Num 19), do make other objects unclean. The point of Haggai's exchange with the priests is not the remedial instruction from the priests on holiness and uncleanness. Rather, Haggai reports on his two queries and the stark contrast of the answers he received, which he and his audience would have expected, in order to describe the stark contrast that the people will experience between life prior to and life after completing the Temple's foundation.

For the third time in the Book of Haggai the prophet commands the people to "reflect" (2:15). The fact that Haggai will issue this command a fourth time in 2:18 makes this instruction a sort of leitmotif within this short book. Haggai's instruction is that the people should not have needed a prophet to come and command them to rebuild the Temple. If the people had simply placed this knowledge in their heart (*śîmû-nāʾ ləbabkem*), and considered the poor return on investment from their crops (v. 16), they would have known that offering sacrifices at the site of a nonexistent

Temple did not make them holy in the sight of YHWH any more than holy meat can make anything it touches clean.

But they also should have known that whatever they offered to YHWH at the Temple site, without attempting actually to build a Temple that would honor God, would be considered by YHWH as unclean (v. 14). Moreover, the analogy with the uncleanness communicated by a dead body functions to accentuate the problem. The *torah* about touching corpses states that the person who becomes unclean by touching a dead body and *fails to cleanse themselves* defiles the Tabernacle and will be cut off from the people of Israel (Num 19:13). The failure of the people's crops in the days of Haggai was meant to warn the people that, if they continued to fail to build the Temple, and so metaphorically fail to cleanse themselves, they would be cut off from YHWH. The fact that a prophet had to come and tell them that their crops' failing was a sign of their being defiled before YHWH points to a basic failure to take to heart this previous instruction – *torah* – from YHWH.[26]

Further comments from YHWH via Haggai reinforce the fact that YHWH was speaking/acting but the people failed to listen. The prophet uses a harsh word as YHWH claims, "I struck you," a metaphor that comes from battle, as in Samson striking a thousand men with a donkey's jawbone (Judg 15:16) or Ahithophel's plot to pursue David and strike him dead (2 Sam 17:2). YHWH acted violently against the people, apparently so violently that some of them died. YHWH goes so far as to claim that "before

---

[26] See the argument in Robert L. Foster, *Wrestling with God and World: The Struggle for Justice in the Biblical Tradition* (Dallas, TX: Journey Publications, 2013), 64–65, that the appearance of a prophet upon the scene clearly indicates that something is fundamentally wrong in Israelite society.

me, you were not" (2:17b).[27] This conclusion seems quite harsh but also seems to be the point of the interrogation of the priests in 2:12–13. YHWH does not choose just any situation of uncleanness but a circumstance that obviously makes a person unclean and, if a person fails to cleanse themselves, results in that person being cut off from Israel. "And so before me, you were nonexistent." The people kept coming to offer their sacrifices but YHWH did not acknowledge their existence because their failure to attend to building the Temple made them perpetually unclean in God's sight.

But all of this harsh treatment at the hands of YHWH lies in a time "from this day backward" (2:15a). YHWH wants the people to put these events behind them, learning their lessons, and focus on what lies ahead. If the time before the people finished the foundation of the Temple entailed "blight and mildew and hail" (2:17), the future holds the promise of the grains and (grape) vines, fig trees, pomegranates, and olive trees (2:19).[28] Basically, Haggai

---

[27] Many commentators think Hag 2:17 relies on Amos 4:9, which also has YHWH attacking with blight and mildew, and concludes, "yet you did not return to me." However, Hag 2:17 is a verbless clause, so one would have to infer the idea that the people did not return to YHWH, based on previous knowledge of the Amos passage (so Sweeney, *The Twelve Prophets*, 552; James D. Nogalski, *The Book of the Twelve: Micah–Malachi* [Macon, GA: Smyth & Helwys, 2011], 791). I think it is better to view the narrative as showing Haggai adapting formulaic prophetic speech to his own purposes (so David L. Petersen, *Haggai and Zechariah 1–8: A Commentary* [OTL; Philadelphia: Westminster Press, 1984], 92). I have taken the subject ʾēlay as perceptual, with the implication that when the people came to sacrifice they essentially still did not come "before" YHWH, because YHWH ignored them.

[28] I take haʿōd as "there is yet," as in the statement that Jacob's sons make to Joseph about Benjamin when they went down to Egypt: "There is yet another brother" (Gen 43:6). The idea, then, is that the people have suffered losses in their farming but "there is yet" seed and vines and trees that will produce the

reiterates that YHWH will bless all the basic crops the people grow in order to feed themselves.[29] Haggai reiterates what the preexilic prophets held true, that YHWH exercises sole control over the productive powers of the earth (see Hos 2:8, 23).[30] Just as YHWH could strike the crops so that they yielded less than the people needed to sustain themselves, so "from this day forward" YHWH promises to bear up the land's harvest. The people ought to place this promise in their hearts (reiterated twice in 2:18) and contemplate YHWH's promises for their future.

The final word offered by YHWH through the prophet in this narrative is as emphatic as it is broad: "I will bless" (2:19b). Translators and commentators often add the pronoun "you" to the end of the phrase, "I will bless you." But, the pronoun is actually absent from the text; the phrase simply declares, "I will bless." Certainly, it seems that "you" is implied but its absence is all the more striking in a passage where the 2nd-person plural suffix forms an important part of the rhetoric: "consider in *your* [pl.] hearts" (2:15); "I struck *you* [pl.] with mildew ... all the works of *your* [pl.] hands ... and so before me, *you* [pl.] were not" (2:17); "Consider in *your* [pl.] hearts" (2:18). The passage ends with "From this day on, I will bless" (2:19), however, not "I will bless the work of your hands" or "I will bless your fields" or even, more simply, "I will bless you." Just an extravagant, unrestricted declaration: "I will bless."

---

foods that they need for sustenance, which YHWH will ensure happens "from this day forward."

[29] See the summary of "Cultivation and Production of Edibles" in King and Stager, *Life in Biblical Israel*, 93–106.

[30] Othmar Keel and Silvia Schroer, *Creation: Biblical Theologies in the Context of the Ancient Near East*, trans. Peter T. Daniels (Winona Lake, IN: Eisenbrauns, 2015), 37.

This phrase extends the assurance that YHWH gave through the prophet several times previously, "I am with you," meaning, "I am on your side." Moreover, the simple phrase "I will bless," on its own at the end of the sentence, likely encompasses more than just the blessing of the harvest but also the blessing of the wealth of the nations that YHWH promised to bring to the Temple in order to fill it with glory. "This day" marks an important turning point for the people, for the land, for the Temple, for YHWH. From now on, "I will bless."

This third major narrative in the Book of Haggai moves away from the promise of a New Exodus as it seeks to persuade the people to finish building the Temple. Instead, it offers an extended *torah*, an instruction the audience of the book is also to place in their hearts and consider. If they neglect to finish building the Temple they know that YHWH will treat them as unclean, work against them, and treat them as if they do not exist. But, if they finish the work of the Temple, they will experience the beneficence of their God, who will sustain them in their sowing and reaping and who will also simply, profoundly, bless.

This narrative does not lose sight of the image of YHWH as the Great King, which emerges in the strong contrast between "to strike" and "to bless." As Briant observes, Darius I styled himself as absolute monarch over his lands, the universal authority, in a way that struck Greek writers as extreme.[31] This universal authority meant that a person could easily fall into disfavor with the king by their failures and be dishonored by the king or even suffer execution if the king thought they had committed crimes warranting such punishment.[32] On the other hand, finding favor with the king by performing admirably in one's duties could mean

---

[31] Briant, *From Cyrus to Alexander*, 302. [32] Ibid., 319, 322.

accruing all kinds of honors, including sitting at the king's table and receiving the king's provision or, perhaps, even using the king's bounty at one's own table, as with many governors within the empire.³³ This section of the Book of Haggai presents YHWH in a similar light, withholding from the people when they dishonor God by failing to build the Temple but promising a bounty when the people honor God by finishing the first step toward completing the new Temple. The power of YHWH to strike or to bless ought to motivate the people, perhaps especially because, unlike the Persian king, YHWH's promise to bless does not seem to discriminate at all according to a person's rank under YHWH's rule.

YHWH'S ENGRAVING

The final narrative of the Book of Haggai (2:20–23) reports a second message that the prophet delivered on the day when the foundation of the Temple was completed. This time Haggai directs his words to Zerubbabel. This short narrative is the final representation of the prophet within the book intended to motivate the book's audience to finish building the House to YHWH Sabaoth.

On the same day that YHWH promises to unreservedly bless, the prophet offers another vision of YHWH boldly acting beyond the borders of Yehud:

> I will shake the heavens and the earth and I will overturn the throne of the kingdoms and destroy the strength from the kingdoms of the nations. And I will overturn charioteers and their chariots and horses and their riders will go down, a man by the sword of his brother. (Hag 2:22)

---

³³ Ibid., 314.

Perhaps the most striking image among these several, short descriptions of YHWH's violence against foreign armies is that "I will overturn the *throne* of the kingdoms." The singular "throne" implies that YHWH will overturn the throne of Darius, who rules over multiple kingdoms. Apparently, YHWH as the Great King, the singular authority in the heavens and the earth, will brook no competition. King Darius I prided himself on the way he subdued the nations of his empire with his armies.[34] Now, in this latest word from Haggai, YHWH promises to overturn the visible implements of the warring empire: "And I will overturn charioteers and their chariots and horses and their riders will go down" (Hag 2:22b). Once again the text echoes Exodus language, as both the songs of Moses and Miriam praise YHWH because "horse and rider he has tossed into the sea" (Exod 15:1, 21). Just as YHWH subdued the great ancient Near Eastern empire of the past, Egypt, so YHWH promises to subdue the great ancient Near Eastern empire of the present, Persia.

As the Great King, YHWH, promises to overthrow the king of Persia and also to exalt Zerubbabel to greater prominence. Many commentators translate the final promise in 2:23 as, "I will place you like a signet, for I am with you, declares YHWH Sabaoth." Thus, for example, Carol and Eric Meyers take the Hebrew word *ḥôtām* as "signet," interpreting the phrase to mean "I will set you as a signet on my finger/hand," in parallel with Jer 22:24.[35] In this view, Zerubbabel would serve as the unique imprint of YHWH's rule in the world.

However, the strong thread of echoes of the Book of Exodus throughout the Book of Haggai point in another direction, leading

---

[34] See, e.g., DNa in Kuhrt, *Persian Empire*, 502–503.
[35] Meyers and Meyers, *Haggai, Zechariah 1–8*, 69.

me to translate this phrase as "I will place you as an engraving." In Exodus 28, in YHWH's instructions about preparing the garments that Aaron and his sons will wear as priests, YHWH commands Moses to have a crown made for Aaron's turban. Upon that crown the artisans should inscribe, "like the engravings of a seal" (*ḥôtām*) the phrase, "Holy to YHWH," and Moses should set (*śym*) the crown on the turban with blue lace. As a result, Aaron will take on any guilt that the people incur in making their holy offerings to YHWH, so that YHWH may accept them (28:36–38). In the final preparations for the Tabernacle, before the glory of YHWH fills the Tabernacle, Moses carries out these instructions (Exod 39:30–31).

This final proclamation to Zerubbabel in the Book of Haggai marks a final reversal promised in the book. Prior to the people finishing the foundation for the Temple, YHWH rejected their sacrifices as unclean (1:9; 2:14). But from the twenty-fourth day of the ninth month in the second year of Darius, so this prophecy implies, YHWH will accept the people's offerings, because YHWH will set (*śym*) Zerubbabel as an inscription (*ḥôtām*) among the people that will remind YHWH of the special relationship with the people of Yehud and Jerusalem as people "holy to YHWH." The final affirmation from YHWH in the Book of Haggai is spoken to Zerubbabel: "you, I have chosen" (2:23). YHWH has made a choice via Zerubbabel to accept the sacrifices of the people and, in the flow of the book, to subdue nations, bring their wealth to Jerusalem, fill the Temple with glory, renew their harvest, and make Jerusalem the center of peace in the world. This is a quite amazing "hidden secret," and the people are reminded of this great secret whenever they see their governor Zerubbabel in their midst. When they see Zerubbabel they also see YHWH's engraving and know that YHWH has chosen them, their city, their district, and accepts them as "holy to YHWH."

So the final appeal merges the discourse of the Great King with the discourse of the New Exodus, though the emphasis on the New Exodus seems predominant. According to the Book of Haggai, the audience to whom it appeals should finish rebuilding the Temple because YHWH, the Great King, is also a mighty warrior who will bring down the throne of Darius, and bring an end to his rule over Yehud and Jerusalem. This image of YHWH as the Great King simultaneously reminds the people of God's work in the past to deliver Israel out of slavery in Egypt by throwing chariots and charioteers, horse and rider, into the sea.

More subtly, if no less profoundly, this final story selects a unique image from among those available in the stories of the Book of Exodus: the engraving of the crown placed on the head of Aaron. In the Book of Exodus, more than a third of the book deals with the preparations and building of the Tabernacle, the sanctuary of YHWH in the midst of the tribes of Israel where they would come to offer God sacrifices, seeking God's beneficence. The Book of Exodus makes it clear that, even shortly after being saved from Egypt, YHWH made provision for the people as they came to offer sacrifices holy to YHWH, knowing that they would often fail to hold to YHWH's standards. The engraving on the crown on Aaron's head would remind YHWH – and the people – that YHWH promised to accept the people's sacrifices (Exod 28:36–38). The Book of Haggai mentions more than once that YHWH rejected the people's sacrifices. Perhaps the audience of the book doubted whether finishing the Temple was worth it if God's beneficence was so capricious, like the capricious favor offered by the Persian King. And so the book reminds the audience that YHWH placed Zerubbabel among the people as a sign that YHWH would accept their sacrifices going forward, with the implication of receiving YHWH's beneficence. Perhaps at the time the scribes produced the book, Zerubbabel was a person still fresh in their memories, though perhaps he was still alive. Either way, the people could draw on the memory or the image of Zerubbabel and remember YHWH's commitment to accept their offerings, which would encourage them to keep building knowing God's intention to bless.

BIBLICAL THEOLOGY AND THEOLOGICAL ETHICS

Divine Motivation

The Book of Haggai does not reference any virtue of YHWH Sabaoth. So, whatever ideas we might glean from the book toward theological ethics based in the *imitatio Dei* come from the book's description of YHWH's actions. One important action of YHWH in the text occurs when YHWH "stirs up" the spirit of Zerubbabel, Joshua, and the people to do the work of building the Temple. YHWH demands that the people really turn to the work that supposedly constituted a major reason for their return to the land, but YHWH does not leave them to their own devices. Rather, God empowers them for this task. And if the people feel discouraged because, with just the foundation completed, the new Temple site cannot compare to the grandeur of Solomon's Temple, Haggai encourages them by telling them that YHWH is with them, that is, on their side. In fact, YHWH's siding with them and placing YHWH's spirit in their midst shows God's covenant commitment to the descendants of Abraham, which is God fulfilling God's own commitments many years after the fact. What makes these actions possible, however, is God's previous action of the New Exodus as YHWH liberated the people from their captivity in Babylon and brought them home. YHWH is the Great King who saves the exiles and settles them once again in the Promised Land.

The book also promises that YHWH will take further actions in the future. YHWH will place YHWH's favor on the Temple, that is, bestow what the people need when they come seeking YHWH's beneficence in the Temple. God will go beyond the community's basic needs for rain and crop growth and will shake the nations so that the Temple is enriched and, one assumes given the imagery, the people are enriched as well. YHWH will also grant peace to the people, assuring them of security in the small district in the "middle territory" that has been caught up in the wars of three consecutive empires. All these things plus other unnamed benefits are likely what constitute God's generic commitment to "bless" the people in the future. Finally, God will make Zerubbabel God's engraving, which means that YHWH will accept their offerings rather than reject them.

Doubts

We will have other occasions in the present volume to deal with the biblical image of the divine warrior and the question of its validity in theological ethics. For the moment, I want to raise a doubt concerning the images in Haggai 1 of God punishing Israel by withholding rain and sending pestilence so that the people starve to the degree that their cloaks hang loosely on their emaciated bodies (1:6, 11). Surely this is one of those disturbing portraits in Christian Scripture of a vengeful God with the power and will to inflict great harm on humans.[36] This portrait is possibly even more troubling because the question of loyalty to God in this passage does not have any discernible connection to

---

[36] Ronald E. Clements, "Prophecy, Ethics, and the Divine Anger," in *Ethical and Unethical in the Old Testament: God and Humans in Dialogue* (ed. Katharine J. Dell; LHBOTS 583; New York: T&T Clark, 2010), 92.

some moral obtuseness on the part of the people, if that is presumed to be a major (and typical) reason for God's anger being directed to Israel's disloyalty.[37] Especially given the questionable nature of the moral outcome – we would not sanction any other moral being inflicting similar harm on others, even if we understood the anger of feeling rejected – it seems best to understand these human emotions ascribed to God as provisional guides to the God–human relationship.[38] And, given the ease with which the authority of the Bible, much less literature with such primal power as the prophets, can be abused to impose one's will on others, it seems that one of the criteria for discerning the proper appropriation of the text is itself moral: Does it promote an abuse of power that harms others?[39] While the notion of divine anger has an important role to play in Christian moral formation, if this leads Christians to exert their own power to the harm of others, this raises doubt about whether we have discerned the best interpretation of Scripture. While I think it is important to ask whether what makes God angry in Scripture makes us angry, I would argue that we need to reevaluate any interpretation that gives explicit or implicit justification for harming others, especially in the name of God.

Divine Command

While the Book of Haggai contains imperatives, these do not command people to ethical action (in Chapter 9 we will briefly discuss the importance of not too readily dividing the ritual from

---

[37] Clements highlights this defense in his discussion (ibid., 93).
[38] Ibid., 100.
[39] On the possible abuse of Scripture and prophecy and, therefore, the need for discernment, see R. W. L. Moberly, *Prophecy and Discernment* (CSCD; Cambridge: Cambridge University Press, 2006), 12–13.

the ethical as a part of forming the whole ethical person). However, we should note the one human ideal in the text, though the ideal lies in the future and is clearly an act of YHWH: Zerubbabel will become YHWH's engraving in the midst of the people. With the background of the Book of Exodus in mind, we see Zerubbabel enacting the ideal of bearing the sins of the people so that they may have a right relationship with God.

Prophetic Witness

One of the major ideas that has emerged in the variety of liberationist theological writings since the 1960s is that the prophets, among others, demand that the church act to liberate others from oppressive situations. The implied theology behind much of the Book of Haggai's message is also rooted in the Exodus narrative and the fact that the people have experienced a New Exodus. It seems to me that the church that understands the implicit theology of Haggai will then commit itself to new efforts of liberation. For example, white churches and Christians in the United States know that African Americans have gone through various epochal moments of liberation, first in the emancipation from chattel slavery and then later in the various benefits of voting, education, and economic opportunity – among other benefits that resulted from the Civil Rights Movement. The Book of Haggai's grounding in a New Exodus theology reminds white Christians like me to engage in the next liberation effort, like the Black Lives Matter movement, and to continue to fight for racial justice because one liberative act is never enough.

Part of that New Exodus imagery entails taking on the sins of others in order that they might experience God's liberative blessings. What comes readily to mind to me is the modern imbalances of incarceration for people of black and brown skin in the United States. It is easy for churches to preach morality, for example, with regard to drugs. But a church shaped by the vison of the New Exodus will absorb some of the stigma of being "formerly incarcerated," welcoming those who have found their way out of an oppressive system as people created in the image of God, whom God desires to favor, to provide for and even enrich. If the church is not the place where people find a second chance because the church decides to overlook the individual's past, where else will such people experience liberation?

CHAPTER 3

Return to YHWH

The Introduction to the Book of Zechariah

We do not know much about the biography of Zechariah son of Berechiah, son of Iddo. The Book of Zechariah does not concern itself much with the person as with the fact that Zechariah is "the prophet" who, during the reign of Darius I of Persia, received words from YHWH. What we know then is that Zechariah was one of those figures recognizable in Yehud as a practitioner of a form of "intuitive divination" whose utterances were believed, at least by those who recorded them, to be inspired by YHWH, the God of Israel.[1]

In line with other prophetic books, this recognition of Zechariah as a messenger inspired by YHWH serves as the theological starting point for the material that follows. The theology of the Book of Zechariah relies on the expectation that the original community who received the book would agree that the words of Zechariah from the past have implications for the audience in the present. The pregnant question, as with all prophecy, is whether or not the audience who receives this collection of prophecies will acknowledge its value, veracity, and applicability.[2]

---

[1] This definition of a prophet derives from Martti Nissinen, *Ancient Prophecy: Near Eastern, Biblical, and Greek Perspectives* (Oxford: Oxford University Press, 2017), 31.

[2] Ibid., 22.

This question of whether and how the audience will receive this book that derives from a prophetic figure in the past is, in part, what distinguishes the Book of Zechariah from the Book of Haggai. The Book of Haggai seems intended to motivate the audience in the lifetime of Haggai the prophet to finish building the Temple in accordance with Haggai's original exhortations. The Book of Zechariah, while dating its collections to the early years of the reign of Darius I, actually emerges much later, during a period of war between Persia and Egypt and other regional and not so regional (=Greek) powers, likely in the 450s BCE, some sixty years after the latest date of Darius recorded in Zechariah 7:1.[3]

So, the scribes who crafted the narrative and rhetorical message of the Book of Zechariah make the theological assumption that the words of YHWH through Zechariah some sixty years ago have important implications for their audience. However, the scribes placed the earlier prophecies in conjunction with others generated within the tradition associated with the prophet Zechariah, which automatically reinterprets the words of the original prophet.[4] The striking feature of this reinterpretation is that the original prophecies that indicated so much promise for the lives of the inhabitants of Jerusalem and Yehud in Zechariah's days have apparently not come to fruition and, according to the Book of Zechariah, will not come to fruition in the foreseeable future.[5]

---

[3] See the discussion in Chapter 1.
[4] Nissinen, *Ancient Prophecy*, 147, makes this important point that the literature of the prophets is the production of communities that "adopted, interpreted, and reinterpreted prophetic message for their own purposes."
[5] I developed this basic argument, which serves as the foundation for this substantive expansion, in Robert L. Foster, "Undoing the Future: The Theology of the Book of Zechariah," *HBT* 34 (2012): 59–72.

All of this means that the Book of Zechariah deals with the theological problem of why the words of YHWH through a prophet in the past did not come to fruition. Based on the traditions of the Torah, some may have wondered if Zechariah was a false prophet because his words of promise did not come true (Deut 18:15–22). Others may have been tempted to believe that YHWH did not have the strength to accomplish the promises made through Zechariah. Either way, the Book of Zechariah works to show that the fault for the promises not being fulfilled, and their postponement to the future, lies with the people of Jerusalem and Yehud and not with YHWH or YHWH's prophet.

The first memory in the Book of Zechariah is not as innocent as it may appear: "In the eighth month of the second year of Darius the word of YHWH came to Zechariah, son of Berechiah, son of Iddo" (Zech 1:1). This sentence obviously marks the date of the first oracle that the scribes included in the Book of Zechariah. But, given the trajectory of this book, it may be much more than a simple marker in the life of Zechariah, Darius, and the people of Yehud. Rather, in the corporate memory of the people of Yehud, this date in the text also tells the audience that this message that came to Zechariah occurred some twenty years after the people returned to the land under the directive of Cyrus, with orders to rebuild the Temple and renew the worship of YHWH (Ezra 1:1–4). But if, as the Book of Ezra claims, YHWH led Cyrus to return the people to their land to renew the worship of YHWH in Jerusalem, then the first commandment of the prophet intimates that something went wrong:

> And you [Zechariah] speak unto them, "Thus says YHWH Sabaoth,
> 'Return unto me,' declares YHWH Sabaoth,
> 'Because I have returned to you,' says YHWH Sabaoth." (1:3)

Why did the prophet Zechariah admonish the people in his day to return to YHWH if the people he addressed in his day had already lived in Jerusalem and Yehud for twenty years? Had the people *not* returned to YHWH in the twenty years since their return to the land? According to the Book of Zechariah, the answer to that question is, apparently, "No."

Memory becomes more complicated as the Book of Zechariah introduces the first words that we hear from the prophet: "YHWH was angry with your ancestors, really angry" (1:2).[6] The ancestors that the prophet had in mind, as the original audience of the book surely understood, were those who had gone into exile to Babylon under Nebuchadnezzar. YHWH was angry at the generations leading up to the exile, with the word anger ($qṣp$) here often denoting a retributive anger at misdeeds or failure to do good, which led (or could lead) YHWH to punish the community (e.g. Num 18:5; Josh 9:20; 2 Chr 19:10).

What made YHWH angry with the generations before the exile? According to the prophet Zechariah, YHWH's anger arose because of the evil paths and the evil deeds the people committed before the exile (1:4). The use of the metaphor "paths" is surely not coincidental. "Path" (*drk*) implies a well-trodden way, meaning many people across many generations walked the same course to the degree that it becomes a recognizable path.[7] The generations leading up to the exile did not simply commit the occasional evil

---

[6] This line uses the word $qṣp$ at the beginning and the end of the sentence. This use indicates the editors wanted to emphasize YHWH's anger, which I attempt to show in my translation while keeping the integrity of the word order.

[7] For a discussion of *drk* as "a surface trodden down by traffic," see Philip J. King and Lawrence E. Stager, *Life in Biblical Israel* (LAI; Louisville, KY: Westminster John Knox Press, 2001), 178.

deed but did so to the degree that their evil became a well-worn path. One might even say that the commission of evil deeds became "customary" for the people.[8] The theological problem in the preexilic period was the persistence of evil, even after YHWH confronted the people though the earlier prophets. The community in the days before exile resisted YHWH and provoked YHWH to anger, leaving YHWH with no choice but to act against them.

The evocation of this memory of YHWH's anger with preexilic Judah and Jerusalem implies that the current inhabitants of Jerusalem and Yehud are also provoking YHWH to anger by refusing to return to YHWH. This refusal to return offends YHWH "*because I have returned* to you."[9] The grammatical structure here is important. YHWH had already returned to the people as evidenced by their return to the land some twenty years earlier. But the people had not responded in kind by returning to YHWH. Some sixty years after the prophet Zechariah, the Book of Zechariah raises the question of whether the people ever returned to YHWH in the eighty years since their return to Yehud.

Past memories of the former prophets and their generations issue a warning. YHWH had called out to those generations, "Turn from your evil paths and your evil deeds!" But the people had refused. The Book of Zechariah reminds its audience of the terrible outcome in words that are disturbingly matter-of-fact: "Where are your ancestors now? And did the prophets live on

---

[8] Ferdinand E. Deist observes that, on occasion, *drk* denotes something so routine that it has become a custom in a culture (*The Material Culture of the Bible: An Introduction* [ed. Robert P. Carroll; TBS 70; Sheffield: Sheffield Academic Press, 2000], 236).

[9] Noting the difference in the verbs and reading the *waw* as "because"; see Foster, "Undoing the Future," 61–63.

in perpetuity?"¹⁰ Those prior generations went into exile and the earlier prophets who addressed them died. Why should the generation in the days of Zechariah or those who now hear this book deriving from his tradition think things will go differently for them if they refuse to return to YHWH? According to this oracle, the generation that went into exile had to admit that YHWH dealt with them just as their paths and their deeds deserved (1:6).

Implied in this memory is that YHWH acts consistently across generations. If YHWH became angry with previous generations and sent them into exile, the audience of the Book of Zechariah should not be surprised at YHWH expressing anger toward those who returned from exile. The demand was for the people to return to YHWH. But the audience will have to wait for a description of what YHWH wanted when the prophet commanded the people to return. For now, the next portion of the book offers an elaborate set of visions of how YHWH returned to the people.

BIBLICAL THEOLOGY AND THEOLOGICAL ETHICS

Divine Command

Understandably, modern interpreters read the command "Return to me" as a command to repent. For those who attend to the Book of Zechariah as Scripture, it is important to recognize that God calls for repentance. Christian history is full of injustices enacted by the church that require repentance, like sexism, anti-Semitism, and racism. In fact, when people continue to perpetuate sexism or

---

[10] Many translations have "do the prophets live *forever*?" I have translated the word *'ôlām* as "perpetuity" because of my doubts that people in ancient Israel had the conception of "eternity" that people do in the present. See James Barr, *Biblical Words for Time* (2nd ed.; SBT 33; Eugene, OR: Wipf & Stock, 1962), 123–124.

anti-Semitism or racism, we have reason to question whether they have actually returned to God.

Divine Motivation

The model of God in terms of ethics lies in the claim, "I have returned to you." God's claim in this phrase is that the ability of the people to return to God arises from the fact that YHWH returned to them first. Those who would imitate God must move with generosity toward others before ever making a responsive demand of them. Certainly an important part of any community of faith's prophetic witness will include calling people to repentance for failing to do justice. But, in imitation of God, one might well ask if the Christian church has a reputation of initial generosity, of showing care for those in need, before ever making demands of them. One suspects the worst.

God's generosity does not deny God's anger with sin. God's anger arises because of injustice in the land, as we will see later in Zechariah (7:7–14). The people stubbornly refused to respond to YHWH's demands for justice. As important as it is to ask whether the church acts with generosity before making demands on behalf of God, we should also ask whether we are angered by the stubborn refusal to do justice, whether by the church or by the rulers of the world.

Prophetic Witness

Prophetic witness lies in living in the paradox of generosity and anger, turning to people in kindness while demanding repentance. There seems to be a logical sequence here, however. The community of faith that makes demands of others, especially, without first showing a God-like generosity will likely fail to establish the moral authority for its preaching. Moreover, a church that itself is not living out its repentance for sins and fails to show anger at the complicity of the church in perpetuating sin, will also fail to have moral authority when it demands (angrily?) repentance from others. The prophetic witness of the church demands anger about and repentance from its own sin before expressing any anger at the sins of others.

CHAPTER 4

YHWH Has Returned to You
Zechariah's Vision

The scribes who assembled the Book of Zechariah reiterate that the prophet Zechariah received a word from YHWH (1:1 and 1:7b), but the next series of oracles (1:7–6:15) portray Zechariah as an ecstatic prophet, who receives a series of visions and who is taken on a series of "spirit journeys."[1] This series of visions elevates the status of the prophet but not because of the ecstatic experience itself. Rather, the prophet's ecstatic experiences imply that YHWH granted the prophet access to the divine court, not only to see its goings on, but also to serve as the divine messenger to the people. Just as entering the king's presence in Persia was restricted, likewise the access to the divine court was not granted to just anyone. The scribes of the Book of Zechariah seek to assure the audience that Zechariah's words are the words of a divine courtier, an authorized messenger who brings YHWH's word.[2]

---

[1] On prophet and ecstasy, see Martti Nissinen, *Ancient Prophecy: Near Eastern, Biblical, and Greek Perspectives* (Oxford: Oxford University Press, 2017), 183–191.

[2] The restricted access to the king and the role of messengers to other portions of the empire are briefly discussed in Pierre Briant, *From Cyrus to Alexander: A History of the Persian Empire*, trans. Peter T. Daniels (Winona Lake, IN: Eisenbrauns, 2002), 260–261; Lloyd Llewellyn-Jones, *Kings and Court in Ancient Persia 559–331 BCE* (DDAH; Edinburgh: Edinburgh University Press, 2013), 33–35.

The message that the prophet delivers assures the audience that YHWH, who rules the nations, will act on the world stage for the sake of Jerusalem and Yehud, choosing Jerusalem again (1:17), dwelling in its midst (2:14), and ensuring that the city and the Temple are rebuilt (1:16). At the time that the scribes published the book, these lofty visions had not come to fruition. Eventually, the book will reveal the indictment from the Great King against the leaders in Yehud that prevented the immediate fulfillment of these visions. But, for now, the visions show what YHWH promises before the indictment of sin, telling what could have been, if only the people had listened to Zechariah's call to return to YHWH.

YHWH, GOD OF COMFORT AND MOTHERLY COMPASSION

This long series of visions begins rooted in the historical plane: "On the twenty-fourth day of the eleventh month – the month of Shebat – in the second year of Darius" (1:7a). Though the book will move shortly into the heavens, the editors show the audience the correspondence between heaven and earth, much like the correspondence between the administrative center of the empire and its provincial centers.[3] These heavenly visions were meant to impact the people of Jerusalem and Yehud at a concrete moment in time. Sixty years after the fact, these visions of the good things of YHWH in the divine court, unfortunately, only accentuate the people's failure to return to YHWH even though YHWH had returned to them.

---

[3] Briant, *From Cyrus to Alexander*; Llewellyn-Jones, *Kings and Court in Ancient Persia*.

Zechariah's first vision begins by describing riders on variously colored horses who roamed the earth and found all at peace, the *Pax persica* (1:8–11). As with other empires, the Persian world at "peace" did not mean all the areas of the empire experienced prosperity. The vision of the world at peace elicits a troubled cry from one of the angels in the heavenly court: "YHWH of hosts, just how long will you not have motherly compassion toward Jerusalem and the cities of Judah, which you have been angry with these seventy years?" (Zech 1:12).

This short plea offers insight into the feelings of discontent with YHWH that Jerusalem and the cities of Yehud experienced in the days of Zechariah. The angel appeals to YHWH Sabaoth, which, as we observed earlier, designates the God of Israel who brought the "host" of Israel out of Egypt. But this God, who also brought the exiles back to Jerusalem and Yehud, had not acted in the way that the angel or the people felt was consonant with YHWH's special relationship with the descendants of Israel. The angel expects motherly compassion from YHWH. Somewhere along the way God should have looked at the people to whom God had given birth and been moved to renew her care for them.[4] Instead, from the angel's perspective, YHWH harbored anger against the people for seventy years. Because of this anger, YHWH let the Temple lie in ruins (Zech 1:16) and kept the land from yielding a harvest consonant with the idea of a land "flowing with milk and honey" (1:17).

---

[4] Following Beth LaNeel Tanner's suggestion that we read *rḥm* as "motherly compassion" in relation to God in light of the fact that the term also refers to a mother's "womb"; see, e.g., Beth LaNeel Tanner, "Psalm 69," in Nancy deClaissé-Walford, Rolf A. Jacobson, and Beth LaNeel Tanner, *The Book of Psalms* (NICOT; Grand Rapids: Eerdmans, 2014), 556.

YHWH does not chastise the angel for voicing this protest. Rather, the angel's plea moves YHWH to offer the angel good and comforting words (1:13). The word "to comfort" (*nḥm*) occurs in several contexts where one person offers comfort to another at the death of a loved one (e.g. Gen 37:35; 2 Sam 10:2). However, in relationship to YHWH, this word can also mean something like regret or repentance, as when YHWH regrets having made humanity (Gen 6:6–7) or having anointed Saul as king (1 Sam 15:11, 29, 35). Perhaps, then, this report of YHWH's words to the angel implies more than comfort but also that YHWH regretted what Israel suffered for seventy years on account of YHWH's anger. Either way, the description of YHWH, the king in the heavenly court, comforting the angel/regretting past actions, makes a striking image. Kings, as the inscriptions of Darius I indicate, are victorious in battle, builders of great projects, just in rulings, possessed of physical and intellectual qualities beyond compare.[5] YHWH the Great King, however, expresses vulnerability and sorrow over the way his anger brought suffering to the people.

YHWH's next words, given through the angel to the prophet, clearly demonstrate YHWH's repentance from the anger of the past:

> I have great anger against these nations who are at ease. I was only a little angry but these have aided each other for evil. Therefore, thus says YHWH, "I will return to Jerusalem with motherly compassion." (1:15–16a)

The anger (*qṣp*) that YHWH expressed against Judah and Jerusalem, sending them into exile (1:2), is the same anger (*qṣp*) that

---

[5] See the succinct discussion of these qualities in Briant, *From Cyrus to Alexander*, 210–216.

YHWH now expresses toward those who carried out YHWH's punishment because they strengthened each other's resolve to do evil. Assyria's violence against North Israel was bad enough, but Babylon, because of their concerns to keep Egypt from controlling the Levant, inflicted even more violence, utterly destroying cities in order to keep the Egyptians from benefitting from the cities of the Levant.[6]

YHWH apparently regrets selecting the Babylonians to carry out divine punishment and promises to turn to the people of Jerusalem and the cities of Yehud with motherly compassion (1:16). And in the same way that YHWH comforted the angel, YHWH promises to comfort Zion (1:17b). YHWH also promises to choose the city of Jerusalem once again (1:17c), recalling the days of Solomon, when YHWH agreed to choose the city and the Temple as the place where YHWH would dwell (1 Kgs 8:44, 48). Behind the promise to choose Jerusalem once again, then, lie intimations of Jerusalem's future greatness, which will benefit the cities of Yehud (1:17a).

At the heart of the angel's plea, and so at the heart of the Book of Zechariah's theology of intercession, is the implication that YHWH can be moved. The cry of the angel moved God not only to comfort the angel but also to rebuke the Babylonians and to promise a return to glory for Jerusalem. YHWH returned to the people because an angel asked YHWH to do so. The fact that the plea moved YHWH Sabaoth should move the people to respond to YHWH's call to return.

---

[6] Lawrence E. Stager, "The Fury of Babylon: The Archaeology of Destruction," *BAR* 22 (1996): 59–69, 76–77.

A WALL OF FIRE, AN INDWELLING PRESENCE

For the emotions expressed by YHWH to have meaning, they must lead to concrete actions. The second vision recorded in the Book of Zechariah (2:1–17), which is actually three smaller visions of unequal length (vv. 1–2, 3–4, 5–17), offers a description of the consequences of YHWH's anger and motherly compassion. As it turns out, the acts prompted by YHWH's anger against the nations receive much less attention (2:1–4) than the acts prompted by YHWH's motherly compassion toward Jerusalem and the cities of Judah (2:5–17).

The first part of the vision reports that Zechariah saw four horns representing the nations that scattered Judah, Israel, and Jerusalem (2:1–2). The horn metaphor likely envisages two rams or goats, relying on local knowledge of the way the largest and strongest goats intimidate other goats through lunges or body butts in order to express dominance for mating season.[7] So the two nations in question were the "dominant males" of the region who inflicted damage in their domination – namely, Assyria and Babylon. But these beasts meet their match as four farmers come and domesticate them and cut off their horns. This latter image implies that YHWH raised up Persia to subject Assyria and Babylon.[8]

---

[7] "Horn" (*qrn*) can refer to rams, goats, or, on one occasion, a wild ox (see Deut 33:17). For the discussion of the way that male goats express their dominance over other male goats, see Allen S. Gilbert, "The Native Fauna of the Ancient Near East," in *A History of the Animal World in the Ancient Near East* (ed. Billie Jean Collins; HdO 64; Leiden: Brill, 2002), 11.

[8] Several issues make these four verses difficult to decipher. One has to do with whether the "four horns" represent the totality of the military might of nations who have afflicted Judah, Israel, and Jerusalem, which would include Persia (so Carol L. Meyers and Eric M. Meyers, *Haggai, Zechariah 1–8*

As important as it was to show that YHWH returned to the exiles by domesticating their former oppressors, the dominant theme in this second vision is not God's anger but God's compassion for the exiles, those who "could not raise their head" (2:4) under Assyrian and Babylonian dominance. In fact, one could say that YHWH's anger rose from YHWH's motherly compassion; because YHWH felt sorry for the exiles' suffering, YHWH acted to deliver them from their oppressors.

Displacing Assyria and Babylon from world dominance was only one act motivated by YHWH's motherly compassion for the exiles. The angel of YHWH made their plea for motherly compassion *for* Jerusalem and the cities of Judah. The text tells the audience that just as quickly as the prophet Zechariah looked up to see four horns and then to see four smiths, Zechariah then saw a young man going by with a measuring line (2:5). The prophet, fully immersed in the vision, does not hesitate to ask the young man, "Where are you going?" The young man replies that he is going to take measurements for the new Jerusalem (v. 6). Just as the young man leaves the scene an angel appears who directs another angel to run after the young man and tell him not to

---

[AB 25B; Garden City, NY: Doubleday, 1987], 136) or are two sets of horns of two different beasts (Mark J. Boda, *The Book of Zechariah*, NICOT [Grand Rapids, MI: Eerdmans, 2016], 160). Since 2:2, 4 refer to these as the nations that *scattered* Judah, Israel, and Jerusalem it seems more likely that these horns represent Assyria and Babylon, as Persia never "scattered" the Israelites. The second difficulty concerns the question of what exactly *ḥārāšîm* (2:3) refers to. Boda well notes that one can take the form in question as a participle of the root "to plow," which would then be "those who are plowing," i.e., farmers (Boda, *Book of Zechariah*, 164). By implication, these "farmers," representing Persia, have shorn the horns of the Assyrians and Babylonians so that they can no longer harm any peoples, especially the peoples of Yehud.

bother. The city of Jerusalem will be so stuffed full of humanity and beasts that they will not bother with building a wall (vv. 7–8).

Zechariah's proclamation that the city would need no walls because of the great number of people and beasts dwelling in and around Jerusalem would have been astounding at a time when the city lacked walls because of a lack of resources and so few inhabitants. However, the prophet adds to the astonishing nature of the vision by reporting YHWH's promise to be "a surrounding wall of fire" for Jerusalem and "the glory in her midst" (2:9).

City walls, of course, provide the protection needed to ensure a bustling city life. The best-preserved fortification in the Levant from the Persian period is at Tel Dor, which had a thick fortification wall of an offset-inset design (i.e., with projecting and receding sections that provided a better view and more control of the wall line against battering rams, scaling ladders, and sapping).[9] YHWH wants the people who hear the prophet's word to imagine a wall beyond anything they knew, a "wall" that not only would protect them but would consume enemies who tried to invade them.[10] Zechariah promises that the fire of God that once felt threatening to Israel would now threaten violent nations coming against Jerusalem. On the other hand, just as YHWH had once

---

[9] For a discussion of the Tel Dor fortification walls, see Ephraim Stern, *Archaeology of the Land of the Bible, Volume II: The Assyrian, Babylonian, and Persian Periods 732–332 BCE* (ABRL; New York: Doubleday, 2001), 464–466, with subsequent reports online at the "Tel-Dor Excavation Project" (http://dor.huji.ac.il/index.html; accessed February 22, 2019). This description of offset-inset walls and their benefits comes from Philip J. King and Lawrence E. Stager, *Life in Biblical Israel* (LAI; Louisville, KY: Westminster John Knox Press, 2001), 234.

[10] For YHWH as a consuming fire (or who sends out consuming fire), see Exod 24:17; Num 11:1; 16:35; Deut 4:24; 2 Kgs 1:10–14.

descended in glory in the midst of Jerusalem to fill the Temple built by Solomon, so that even the priests could not enter (1 Kgs 8:11; 2 Chr 7:1–2), YHWH would come to dwell in the midst of the city and mark the city – and its people – as belonging to YHWH.

Visions of something new (a wall of fire) and old (glory in the midst of Jerusalem) were not enough for the prophet to convey God's motherly compassion and sorrow. Immediately following the vision of fire and glory the prophet reports emphatic cries of sorrow: "'Woe! Woe! And flee from the land of the North,' says YHWH, 'though I swept you there'" (2:10) and "Woe Zion! I will return those dwelling in Daughter Babylon" (2:11). Waldemar Janzen has argued that the woe-cry, born from the funerary lamentation, "must be characterized as a marker of pain, the direction of which is determined by the addressee named subsequently."[11] Unlike many woe-oracles in the prophets, these cries by the prophet Zechariah did not express God's grief over the sins of North Israel and Judah. Rather, they express YHWH's sorrow for the way YHWH let anger get in the way of showing motherly compassion for the exiles (1:13). The people of Israel must return home from exile in order to prevent YHWH's heart from breaking over the punishment that went on for too long. The grief that the angel expressed (1:12) was subsequently voiced by YHWH via the voice of the prophet.

These visions of fire and glory and the proclamations of YHWH's deep sorrow that call the people back to the land and to Jerusalem were still not enough. By the time Zechariah prophesied, people had already returned to Yehud and begun to dwell in

---

[11] Waldemar Janzen, *Mourning Cry and Woe Oracle* (BZAW 125; Berlin: Walter de Gruyter, 1972), 82.

Jerusalem but the Temple still lay in ruins and, as the prophet Haggai observed, many harvests yielded insufficient returns. Zechariah responded to these realities by promising an astounding reversal of fortune that, when it came to pass, the people would know that YHWH had sent him (2:13). Those nations – Assyria and Babylon – who had once taken the people of Israel, Judah, and Jerusalem into exile as spoils (2:12), would become spoil for those whom they had used as slaves (2:13).

By the time the scribes of the Book of Zechariah assembled the prophecies that make up the book, such claims presented a theological problem. Apparently, the authority of Zechariah's words required the tradition to offer an explanation for the apparent failure of his grand visions, especially since Yehud was by then caught up in the wars of the Persians against the Egyptians and Greeks. Was Zechariah a false prophet or did YHWH's word fail?

The book offers no immediate answer, though it will directly address the question of true and false prophets later (13:1–6). For the moment, the text continues to focus on Zechariah's vision of the return of YHWH to the people. The strongest claim in this second vision narrative occurs at the end: YHWH commands Zion to rejoice and sing because YHWH will come dwell in their midst, with further, astounding consequences for Jerusalem (2:14).

From the perspective of the prophetic tradition, the real problem that faces this city of rubble and rabble is the absence of YHWH. The visions of Ezekiel prior to the exile described the glory of YHWH departing the Temple, a seeming prerequisite to the overthrow of the city and razing of the Temple (Ezek 10). The prophet Zechariah promises that YHWH will dwell again in the midst of Zion and that this will draw peoples from many nations to come to the city to become part of the people of God

(Zech 2:15). Once again, the prophet makes the bold claim, "And you will know that YHWH Sabaoth sent me unto you."

Even the extraordinary assertion that YHWH will cause the nations to become part of the people of God is not the whole of the claim in 2:15. The verb used for the nations' joining themselves to YHWH, *lwh*, occurs infrequently in the Hebrew Bible, in one place referring to the intimate bond Leah desires to have with Jacob (Gen 29:34) and in another place to the way that the Levites should join with the Aaronite priests in ministering to YHWH at the sanctuary (Num 18:2, 4). The prophet is not envisioning a simple alliance between the people of Jerusalem and the people who come to the city from other nations, merely residing in the city while conducting business. The prophet's use of "to join" implies possibly the intermarriage with foreigners, once forbidden by Torah but now allowed because these foreigners become YHWH's people, or it implies that they will join regularly in the worship of YHWH at the Temple, or perhaps both these things.

As this narrative closes, it indirectly claims YHWH Sabaoth as chief above all gods, including the great god of Persia, Ahuramazda. The imperial propaganda at Apadana Hall in Persepolis includes sculptures of peoples from various nations processing, bearing gifts and tribute to Darius I, intended to show the solidarity of the king and his subject peoples.[12] This sort of propaganda extended far beyond the bounds of Persepolis, down

---

[12] Matt Waters, *Ancient Persia* (Cambridge: Cambridge University Press, 2014), 142–145. See the images and discussion in Donald N. Wilber, *Persepolis: The Archaeology of Parsa, the Seat of the Persian Kings* (rev. ed.; Princeton, NJ: The Darwin Press, 1989), 73–83. Note also Brent A. Strawn, "'A World under Control': Isaiah 60 and the Apadana Reliefs from Persepolis," in *Approaching Yehud: New Approaches to the Study of the Persian Period* (ed. Jon L. Berquist; Semeia Studies 50; Atlanta, GA: Scholars Press, 2007), 85–116.

into Egypt, where the Behistun Inscription extolled the greatness of King Darius, listing the nations whom he subjected and who paid him tribute and claiming, "These are the people that came to me. By Ahuramazda's will I was the king of them."[13] Devotees of Ahuramazda proclaimed him as the one who brought "happiness to humankind." But this happiness really pertained mostly to the Persians and, especially, the Persian elite and the imperial representatives in the satrapies, not subject peoples like those in Yehud. The theology of the nations in Zechariah 2:15–17 offers the unexpected: joy to the people residing in Jerusalem because YHWH Sabaoth, God of all the nations, joins peoples of other nations to the people of Jerusalem.

"And you will know that YHWH of hosts sent me unto you" (2:15c). This reiteration of prophetic acclamation only reinforces the need for the scribes to publish this book. The Book of Nehemiah witnesses to the fact that by 445 BCE the city of Jerusalem was still experiencing troubles, without walls to fortify it (Neh 1:1–3; 2:1–3), not to mention that YHWH did serve as a wall of fire surrounding the city. Nehemiah also laments that the people of Yehud and the city of Jerusalem are, nevertheless, still slaves even in their own land because they must send the abundance of the land in tribute and taxation to the king of Persia (9:36–37). And Nehemiah rebukes the people of Yehud and Jerusalem for giving their daughters and sons in marriage to people from Ashdod, Ammon, and Moab (13:21–31), a far cry from Zechariah's vision of nations joining themselves to Jerusalem and becoming the people of God. This strong contrast between the realities in the

---

[13] For the translation, see Bruce Lincoln, *"Happiness for Mankind": Achaemenid Religion and the Imperial Context* (Acta Iranica 53; Leuven: Peeters, 2012), 110.

days of Nehemiah and this particular vision of the prophet Zechariah demands some resolution. But the Book of Zechariah does not come to this resolution immediately. The audience must wait while the book continues to articulate the memory of Zechariah's visions of YHWH's return.

GUILT REMOVED

The Book of Zechariah indicates that the prophet endured a protracted state of ecstasy as the visions continue to unfold. The prophet remains in the heavenly court but the scene shifts to YHWH Sabaoth sitting in the court of justice. This third vision, and the one which follows, turns away from Jerusalem at large to focus one of its key figures and institutions in this third vision, Joshua and the high priesthood. The return of YHWH to Jerusalem and Yehud brings beneficence to Joshua and, in the next vision, to Zerubbabel. Yet, in focusing on Joshua and Zerubbabel, the book does not lose sight of the people. What benefits the high priest and the governor will also benefit the people.

YHWH, the Great King, has returned to Jerusalem and, like any king in the ancient Near East, as the Great Judge, YHWH hears cases brought before God's court. The prophet Zechariah is brought into the court by the angel of YHWH to witness a bit of courtroom drama. Joshua the high priest stands in the court of YHWH, before the angel of YHWH, while *haśśāṭān*, "*the* Satan" (or *the* Accuser), stands at Joshua's right making accusations against the high priest (3:1).

The narrator does not enumerate the nature of the accusations that "the Satan" brings against Joshua. But the narrative gives some indication of the transgressions that have landed the high priest in court in its reference to Joshua's filthy garments (3:3-4). Given the book's opening word that invokes the preexilic prophets, perhaps the description of Joshua's filthy garments intends to draw the audience's attention to the Book of Isaiah, since that prophet condemned the prophets and priests of his day for being a bunch of drunkards (Isa 28:1–22). Walking into the residence of the priests and prophets was like entering into a frat house the morning after a party gone horribly wrong; there is not a spot in the place that is not covered in vomit and excrement (ṣ'h). The priests and the prophets are so drunk that, when they try to render judgments on behalf of the people, their words are nothing but gibberish: "Thus, command to command, command to command; line to line, line to line; a little here, a little there" (Isa 28:10).

Anyone devoted to the words of the preexilic prophets would have been scandalized and saddened by the vision of Joshua the high priest standing before YHWH in a garment covered in excrement (ṣ'h; Zech 3:3-4). This is the high priest, after all; did he get so drunk that he could not control his bowels? How could the high priest possibly render true judgments on behalf of the people? "The Satan" not only has Torah on his side – the law forbade "for generations in perpetuity" the priests from drinking wine or any intoxicant (Lev 10:9) – but Joshua has made "the Satan's" prosecution of the offense all that easier by the proof of the violation that stains his garments.[14]

Joshua stands before YHWH as someone clearly guilty of violating Torah. And yet, instead of accepting "the Satan's"

---

[14] I owe this observation of the prohibition against priests drinking wine to Tyler Kelley.

accusation, YHWH rebukes the Accuser (v. 2).¹⁵ "Rebuke" (g'r) implies that Satan's accusations are somehow improper, in the same way that Jacob and Joseph's brothers found his dreams of them bowing down before Joseph improper (Gen 37:10) and Boaz warned his field hands against charging Ruth with improperly seeking to glean in Boaz's fields (Ruth 2:16). In what world would "the Satan's" accusation against Joshua as unfit to serve as high priest be improper since he is clearly a drunkard?

The tomb inscription of Darius I contains a number of lines where the king describes himself as a wise and just judge. The king lauds the fact that he does not maintain friendship with those who are "Lie-followers" but is a friend to those who do what is right. Yet the king also claims that, because he is not hot-tempered but keeps his wits about him, he is not moved hastily

---

¹⁵ There is some confusion in this text when v. 2 says that YHWH addresses the Accuser saying, "YHWH rebuke you!" (3:2). It is awkward, to say the least, for YHWH to address "the Satan" in the third person. This verse is apparently one of those places in Scripture where the line is blurred between YHWH and the angel of YHWH, as in Genesis 18. Yet, we should resist modifying the text so that the person speaking in 3:2 is no longer YHWH, as in the MT and LXX, but instead (by appeal to 3:1) say it is the angel of YHWH (cf. Boda, *Book of Zechariah*, 232; David L. Petersen, *Haggai and Zechariah 1–8: A Commentary* [OTL; Philadelphia: The Westminster Press, 1984], 186–187; Lena-Sofia Tiemeyer, *Zechariah and His Visions: An Exegetical Study of Zechariah's Vision Report* [LHBOTS 605; London: Bloomsbury, 2015], 128–129). Not only does this move detract from the theological freight of the passage but then creates a different problem by having the angel answer (*vayya'an*) himself in 3:4, rather than having the angel standing next to Joshua (3:1, 3) answer YHWH's defense of Joshua by having the filthy clothes removed. In other words, the text is difficult as it is – who is "he" in every case is complicated – but taking the person confronting the Accuser in 3:2 as an angel of YHWH only introduces new problems. I suggest we stick with the original problem.

by accusations brought before him. Rather, if a person proves that they are willing to cooperate with the king's will, that person will receive a reward.¹⁶ As Amélie Kuhrt summarizes, the king "judges services rendered according to the potential of the individual, and is ready to reward loyalty."¹⁷

Perhaps in like manner, YHWH, the Great Judge, does not regard Joshua in terms of the violation of a particular law but sees that Joshua wants to serve YHWH loyally, if given the chance. YHWH then rebukes "the Satan," not for falsely accusing the high priest, but for failing to see Joshua's potential, the loyal service that Joshua might yet render to YHWH. YHWH does not deny the guilt of Joshua. Rather, YHWH acknowledges Joshua's guilt and takes away the stained garments, clothes him in clean robes, and places a pure diadem on his head (vv. 4–5).

The theological implication of the first part of this vision (3:1–5) is that the return of YHWH occurs, not because of the uprightness of the people but in spite of their guilt. Even the high priest stands before YHWH an obvious drunkard and in violation of Torah. But in motherly compassion and in sorrow for the troubles the exiles experienced under Assyria and Babylon, YHWH returned. YHWH's motherly compassion made it possible to begin again, starting with the high priest.

---

¹⁶ DNb§§7–8f; see the translation in Briant, *From Alexander to Cyrus*, 212.
¹⁷ Amélie Kuhrt, "The Achaemenid Persian Empire (c. 550–c. 330 BCE): Continuities, Adaptations, Transformations," in *Empires: Perspectives from Archaeology and History* (ed. Susan E. Alcock et al.; New York: Cambridge University Press, 2001), 109. Kuhrt argues that the fact that this inscription is identical to an inscription extolling Xerxes (though the Xerxes inscription, XNb, adds a line) indicates that this is a central tenet of Persian kingship (ibid., 107).

YHWH Has Returned to You: Zechariah's Vision 77

But removal of guilt is not a license to keep going as before. The Just King still demands loyalty:

> If you will walk in my path and if you will guard my charge
> Then you will also execute judgment in my house and also guard my court
> and I will give to you pathways between these standing here.
>
> (3:7)

The conditional nature of the promise to Joshua – "if you will walk in my path ... then you will execute judgment in my house" – hints at a potential trouble in the oracle that opens the Book of Zechariah (1:1–6).[18] When the postexilic community failed to "return" to YHWH, even though YHWH had returned them to their land, the prophet declared that the postexilic community was acting similarly to their ancestors who did not "return" to YHWH when YHWH called. Furthermore, just as that previous generation continued in their evil paths and suffered YHWH's judgment, the generations after the exile, by persisting in their path, stood in jeopardy of suffering similar judgment (1:4–6). This charge (*'wd*, 3:6) to Joshua, then, functions like a warning, as when Moses warned people not to come onto Mount Sinai (Exod 19:23) and Samuel warned the people about the troubles they would experience under the rule of a king (1 Sam 8:9). If Joshua wants to serve as high priest, he must walk in God's path (3:7) not in the evil paths of his preexilic ancestors (1:6). Just here we also get a hint from the editors of the book about why the amazing promises in chapter 2 failed to come to fruition. Joshua, and those with him and the generations after him, failed to walk in the path of YHWH.[19]

---

[18] Taking the second *waw* in the sentence as a conditional. On the conditional *waw* see Bill T. Arnold and John H. Choi, *A Guide to Biblical Hebrew Syntax* (Cambridge: Cambridge University Press, 2003), 147–148.

[19] Notice that Zech 3:7 is the only place apart from 1:4, 6 that uses the word "path," though 9:13 uses a verbal form of *drk*.

For the moment, the vision continues to focus on the potential that may come from Joshua's loyal obedience. If Joshua keeps to God's path, "I will give you pathways [*mahləkîm*] between these standing here" (3:7d). "These standing here" implies the angels, "the Satan," and the prophet in the heavenly court. If Joshua proves loyal to YHWH by offering judgments in line with Torah, YHWH will grant him access to the heavenly court, similar to Zechariah and the prophets in the preexilic generations (e.g. 1 Kgs 22; Isa 6; Jer 23). Joshua will attain a status on par with Moses and Samuel, serving both as priest and prophet, an astounding turnaround for this scandalized high priest.

But this promise of elevated status was just the beginning of the vision of potential benefits stemming from YHWH's return to the high priest. Not only would YHWH elevate Joshua, the "neighbors" (*rēaʿ*) sitting at Joshua's table are a sign that YHWH will bring forth "the Branch" (3:8). This narrative has hinted at the possibility of the negative judgments against the preexilic community coming against the postexilic community. But now the text invokes the possibility of experiencing the fulfillment of preexilic promises. The Book of Jeremiah recorded YHWH's promise to bring forth from the line of David a just "Branch," who would do justice in the court and in the community (Jer 23:5; 33:14–15). If Joshua proves to be a loyal priest, with those sitting as his table following suit, the promises that YHWH made to Jeremiah could come to fruition.

Yet one more symbol of a better future comes in the form of a stone placed in front of Joshua with seven eyes upon which YHWH will make an engraving that symbolizes YHWH's removal of the land's guilt in a single day (3:9). What this image meant to its original audience remains elusive.[20] Perhaps the easiest part to decipher is the exclamation, "Lo, I will have engraved its engraving," meaning that YHWH claims to be responsible for engraving the eyes on the stone. But what the seven *pairs of eyes* (*ênāyim*) refers to proves particularly opaque. A tantalizing link comes from the final two oracles of Balaam who, when the Spirit of God came upon him, claimed that in his state of ecstasy he fell to the ground but his two eyes (*ênāyim*) were uncovered (*glh*; Num 24:4, 16), that is, wide open to the revelation from YHWH. If the vision recorded in Zechariah 3 connotes something similar by the seven pairs of eyes engraved on the stone, then perhaps YHWH claims that Joshua will have unprecedented access to visions from YHWH, in fact the whole counsel of God, if we may understand seven to represent "wholeness, totality."[21] In this case, the visions that Joshua receives will be so powerful and effective that it will lift away the guilt of the land in a single day.

All of this dramatic language – the rebuke of "the Satan," the changing of Joshua's soiled garments, and the promises to elevate the high priest to the status of a prophet, for Zechariah's generation to experience the Branch's arrival, for Joshua to gain extraordinary vision, and for the cleansing of the land's guilt – has a practical outcome. "'In that day,' declares YHWH Sabaoth, 'one person will call to their neighbor to rest under a vine or to rest under a fig tree'" (3:10). What YHWH will accomplish via the dramatic deeds envisioned in chapter 3 is to create a place for the beautiful ordinary, where a person may say to her neighbor,

---

[20] For a good summary of the various scholarly opinions, see Tiemeyer, *Zechariah and His Visions*, 139–145.
[21] M. Eugene Boring, "Seven, Seventh, Seventy," in *NIDB* 5:198.

"Come, sit with me in peace under the vine or under the fig tree and rest." The vision of Zechariah 3 is not about placating an angry God, who, in fact, has clearly eschewed anger and instead extended great motherly compassion, but to provide a place of peace for the ʿam hā ʾāreṣ, the people of the land.

FINISHING THE HOUSE OF YHWH

The Book of Zechariah shows the prophet in such a protracted state of ecstasy that an angel must come and essentially awaken him from the allure of his most recent vision (4:1). In the narrative, the angel then asks Zechariah what he sees and the prophet lists off several items: a gold lampstand with a bowl and seven branches of light, and two olive trees, one on the right and one on the left of the lampstand (4:2–3). But what any of these items represent the prophet cannot say (4:4–5).

Apparently the angel decides not to satisfy the prophet's curiosity about these items and instead answers Zechariah's puzzlement with a word for Zerubbabel, governor of Judah:

> "Not by might nor by power but by my rûaḥ,"
> says YHWH of hosts.
> "What are you, O great mountain?
> Before Zerubbabel you will become a plain
> and he will place the head stone with shouts of 'Beautiful! Beautiful!' to it." (4:7)

Most modern English translations render rûaḥ as "Spirit/spirit" (so RSV, NRSV, NIV, CEB, NJB). Translating the word with a capital "S" – "Spirit," as in the NIV, NRSV, RSV – implies, in a Christian theological context, the third person of the Trinity, the Spirit who is God three-in-one, in addition to the Creator and Savior. But rendering rûaḥ in this way, as a personal spirit in some sense, detracts from the import of the exhortation delivered to Zerubbabel.

As the Book of Haggai confirms, Zerubbabel played a significant role in laying the foundation of the Temple. The word of YHWH to the prophet Zechariah intends to affirm to Zerubbabel that he would also finish the work (Zech 4:9a). Yet the strength to complete the work would not come from human beings but from the *rûaḥ* of YHWH. The vision of the Valley of Dry Bones in Ezekiel 37 illuminates the intended effect of YHWH's *rûaḥ* on Zerubbabel and the people. In Ezekiel 37, YHWH commands Ezekiel to prophecy to the "dead bones" of hopeless Israel, which come together and are covered with sinews and flesh (Ezek 37:1–8). Into these bodies that Ezekiel's prophetic words have brought together, Ezekiel prophesies the breath (*rûaḥ*) of YHWH, which then brings them to life (Ezek 37:9–10). The subsequent interpretation of this arresting vision is that YHWH will bring Israel out of their hopeless situation in exile – so bad that the prophet pictures it as a valley of dead bones (!) – and will revive the people and resettle them in the land of Israel (37:12–14). This revivification, in turn, echoes the original story of creation where God formed the first *'ādām* out of dust and breathed the breath of life into the first human.

Of course, the people of Israel were not literally dead in the days of Ezekiel. But in the exile the people of Israel felt completely devastated, as if their bones were completely dried up (Ezek 37:11).[22] Zerubbabel and the people in the days of Zechariah were not dead either but they lived in a time where laying the

---

[22] Brent Strawn, "Commentary on Ezekiel 37:1–14," *The Working Preacher*, December 10, 2017, www.workingpreacher.org/preaching.aspx?commentary_id=3320.

foundation of the Temple seemed like "a day of small things" (4:10a), of little worth in a little-known district "Beyond the River," which did not even have a Temple worthy of their God. According to the Book of Haggai, some people, when they saw the completion of the Temple's foundation, remembered the glory of Solomon's Temple and felt that what they beheld in postexilic Yehud was nothing in comparison (Hag 2:3). As the Book of Ezra relates the story, the older generation who had seen the glory of Solomon's Temple wept aloud at the site of the foundation, even while those younger shouted for joy (Ezra 3:10). One can imagine that Zerubbabel and the people living in the days of Zechariah felt discouraged and, given their lack of resources, wondered how they would ever complete the Temple, much less build anything worthy of the name of YHWH.

According to the Book of Zechariah, YHWH did not rebuke the people for looking at the Temple foundation and despising "the day of small things" (4:10) any more than YHWH condemned Joshua in the previous vision. Instead, YHWH continued to express motherly compassion and offered a word of encouragement, promising to transform this people, moving them from fatigue, fear, and sorrow to rejoicing with shouts of "Beautiful! Beautiful!" The day would come, under Zerubbabel's leadership, when the people would no longer look back with sad longing for the glory of the old Temple. Rather, they would see that YHWH had breathed into them new life and built a new, glorious Temple of such beauty that it would elicit shouts of joy (4:7, 10).[23]

---

[23] The word *ḥēn* often refers to the favor a person experiences with God or humans but this term can also refer to the attractive qualities that make a person favorable (see Boda, *Book of Zechariah*, 297).

For the third time in this series of reports of the prophet's visionary experience the text asserts, "and you will know that YHWH Sabaoth sent me unto you" (4:9). Zerubbabel's completion of the Temple was meant to confirm that YHWH indeed had returned to the people. But, in fact, the Hebrew Bible does not contain a report of Zerubbabel bringing the Temple to completion. According to the Book of Ezra, opposition from the "adversaries" of Yehud made the people afraid to finish their work (Ezra 4:4). And, though the Book of Ezra claims that the prophecies of Haggai and Zechariah spurred on the people to finish building the Temple, this would have to have occurred over the long term if, as Ezra 4:14 claims, the people did not actually complete the Temple until the sixth year of Darius II, around 417 BCE, more than 100 years after the date given for Zechariah's visions! The audience of the Book of Zechariah, sometime in the 450s, would have heard the assertion, "and you will know that YHWH of hosts sent me to you" and recognized that Zerubbabel, in fact, did *not* finish the Temple. The book continues to prime the audience for an explanation about why these promises did not come true. But for now they must continue to wait while still other promises are envisioned.

The vision finally returns to the lampstand, its lamps, and the olive trees standing on either side. YHWH explains the seven lamps as "the eyes of YHWH that roam in all the earth" (Zech 4:10c). In light of the more expansive phrase in 2 Chr 16:9, "the eyes of YHWH are roaming in all the earth to give strength to those whose hearts are wholly unto [YHWH]," the image of the seven eyes that roam the earth reinforces the assertion that YHWH's *rûaḥ* strengthens Zerubbabel and company to finish building the Temple.

Zechariah, however, still wants to know the meaning of the two olive trees standing beside the lampstand (4:12). The angel explains, "These two are 'sons of oil'" (4:14). What "sons of oil" means is not readily apparent but perhaps similar phrases in the Old Testament can illuminate its meaning.[24] The phrase "son of strength" (*bny ḥyl*; e.g., Deut 3:18; 2 Kgs 2:16; 2 Chr 26:7, 9) indicates that the men in question have the strength to provide a needed service while "sons of wickedness" (*bny 'wlh*; e.g., 2 Sam 3:34; 7:10) indicates that the men referred to perpetrate evil. Thus, "sons of oil" likely refers to those who offer the provision that comes from oil. Given the direct link to the lampstands, it seems that these "sons of oil" provide the olive oil that fuels the sanctuary lamps, that is, the lamps in the presence of YHWH.[25] Given that the visions of chapters 3 and 4 address two persons in particular, Joshua the high priest and Zerubbabel the governor, the convoluted metaphorical concept seems to imply that there is a symbiotic relationship between the work of YHWH to strengthen the people and the work of Joshua and Zerubbabel to carry out their tasks. As Joshua and Zerubbabel prove faithful to their task as "sons of oil," providing oil for the seven lampstands, the seven eyes of YHWH that roam the earth will continue to provide strength to the people. Not by might nor by power but by the breath of YHWH – but also not without the faithful service of Joshua and Zerubbabel.

---

[24] For a summary of the variety of scholarly perspectives on what this phrase means and who these two "sons" are, see Tiemeyer, *Zechariah and His Visions*, 159–165.

[25] Olive oil was used in a wide variety of ways, including as fuel for sanctuary lamps (see King and Stager, *Life in Biblical Israel*, 97).

THE RETURN OF YHWH: A CURSE UPON THIEVES AND LIARS

Not all of Zechariah's visions were of fantastic promises and the possibility of hope on the near horizon. YHWH, who acts with motherly compassion, is still the God of the preexilic prophets, who offered more words of judgment than of hope. YHWH setting things right for the people's future meant rebuilding Jerusalem and its Temple and restoring its priestly and political leadership. It also required YHWH to clean house. If the *Pax persica* mostly benefitted the elites of the empire and their representatives in the provinces, then those bent on using their positions for self-aggrandizement readily enough exploited the courts for their own gain. It was one thing for YHWH to forgive a drunken high priest for not being able to perform his duties properly. It would be another thing for YHWH to allow injustice to persist in the land.

Zechariah's fifth vision of a flying scroll, twenty cubits long and ten cubits wide (5:2), reflects God's promise to overthrow one unjust mechanism in the courts: the use of bribes. The angel of YHWH explains to Zechariah the meaning of the scroll he sees:

> "This is the curse upon the face of all the land because of all the thieves so that it is as if they are without blame and those who swear as if they are without blame. I have sent it out," declares YHWH,
> "and it will come to the house of the thief and the house of the one who swears falsely in my name
> and it will settle in the midst of his house and will completely destroy its beams and its stones." (5:3–4)

The Book of Isaiah describes those who take bribes as thieves and condemns the princes of the people who are "accomplices with thieves, all of them lovers of a present and pursuing bribes; they do not judge for the orphan and the lawsuit of the widow never reaches them" (Isa 1:23).

The princes who serve as judges of the people allow the elite to exploit widows and orphans, accepting bribes so that the their cases never come to the court, likely meaning that these "thieves" (the elite) seize the property of the widow and orphan as the princes line their pockets.

The ugly truth that Zechariah exposes is that the courts were so perverted in his days that these "thieves" and false witnesses went about "as if they are without blame" (5:3). Those with the power to exercise justice make a mockery of it not simply by accepting bribes but also by creating a system that normalizes corruption. Part of the prophet's role is to let the corrupt elite know that the eyes of YHWH that roam the earth also see the corruption in the court and that YHWH intends to do something about it.

What makes the situation even more offensive to YHWH is the fact that those who corrupt the courts of justice "swear falsely by my name" (5:4b). And this is happening "upon the whole face of the land" (5:3a). There is not one place throughout the land of Yehud where this corruption – in the name of YHWH – does not persist. In the Persian Empire, as with other ancient Near Eastern empires, the king's duties included ensuring that judges ruled justly and removing them if they proved corrupt.[26] In fact, on several occasion the Persian king executed royal judges who rendered justice for money.[27] YHWH, as the Great King, now moves to ensure that the injustice that reigns in courts throughout

---

[26] Pierre Briant, "Social and Legal Institutions in Achaemenid Iran," in *CANE* 1:524.
[27] Ibid.

Yehud comes to an end and that the houses built by riches taken from the poor are destroyed (5:4).

The fact that YHWH sends a curse against those who corrupt the courts and rob the poor may have also brought to mind the promise in the Book of Deuteronomy that those who think they will be safe even though they walk in the stubbornness of their heart will suffer the curses written in Deuteronomy and God will blot out their name from under heaven (Deut 29:10). In the days of Zechariah, YHWH apparently pledged to execute this judgment throughout the land, which would serve as a warning to the rest of the people to return to YHWH and not walk in the paths of wickedness like their ancestors.

REMOVING WICKEDNESS FROM THE LAND

For the return of YHWH to be complete, YHWH must not only eradicate unjust practices within the courts. YHWH must also go to the root of the problem and remove wickedness from Yehud. In the sixth of Zechariah's visions (5:6–10) he sees a pair of winged women come to take "Wickedness" away to the land of Shinar. Shinar is in Southern Mesopotamia and is mentioned in Dan 1:2 as the land to which Nebuchadnezzar removed the vessels from the Jerusalem Temple, placing them in the sanctuary of his god. In the description of this sixth vision, Zechariah beholds an ephah coming forth, which the angel describes as "their eye in all the land" (5:6). Someone lifts the lid from the ephah, revealing a woman inside whom the angel calls, "Wickedness" (5:7–8). Quickly, the angel shoves "Wickedness" back into the ephah, replaces the stone lid, at which point the pair of winged women come and remove "Wickedness" to Shinar in order to build her a house there bearing her name (5:9–11).

This singular eye seems deliberately to contrast with the seven eyes of YHWH in the earth. YHWH's seven eyes strengthen those completely devoted to YHWH, in this case Zerubbabel and the people to finish building the Temple. An intriguing possibility for the reference to "their eye in all the land" comes from the number of Greek sources in the fifth and fourth century BCE that refer to an official known as "the king's Eye."[28] According to the *Cyropaedia*, among the duties of the king's Eye was to ensure that a satrap's land was cultivated and the taxes paid.[29] One of the problems that the Book of Zechariah will identify as contributing to the delay in fulfilling Zechariah's glorious visions is the greed of Yehud's governors who took advantage of the king's food allowance, which meant, of course, managing the king's land and taxes for their own benefit (see Chapter 7 in the present volume). Perhaps then, in Zech 5:5-11, the prophet references the king's Eye, the official whose enforcement of the king's economic system and taxation was experienced as "Wickedness" in Yehud.[30]

---

[28] Briant, *From Cyrus to Alexander*, 343-344.
[29] See the translation in ibid., 343.
[30] The Old Greek has *adikia auton* "their injustice," which aligns with the text of the Syriac Peshitta (see the apparatus in *BHQ 13: The Minor Prophets*, ed. Anthony Gelston [Stuttgart: Deutsche Bibelgesellschaft, 2010], 126), which Petersen follows (*Haggai and Zechariah 1-8*, 254, 256). Boda interprets this passage as the "all seeing eye" of Wickedness personified as a divinity and an evil entity that "soon will be localized to its place of origin, Babylon" (*Book of Zechariah*, 346). I agree with Tiemeyer (*Zechariah and His Visions*, 225-226) that the woman Wickedness is not to be seen as a divine figure, especially because I believe "their eye" refers back to the people who pervert court justice and because the two women with wings who carry Wickedness away are also not deities per se, though certainly celestial beings of some sort. Meyers and Meyers retain the reading in the MT, translating it as "appearance" but do not offer an explanation of how "appearance" functions in this visionary report (*Haggai, Zechariah 1-8*, 297-298). Sweeney sees "their eye" as a reference to the Persian authorities who rule Judah from Babylon

For the people of Yehud to return to YHWH, YHWH must remove this "Wickedness" from the land, both to ensure that the people do not persist in evil paths like their ancestors (1:4) and also to allow the widow, orphans, and other poor to flourish in the land. If this understanding of the reference to "Wickedness" is correct, the combination of the two visions in Zechariah 5 announce, if indirectly, that YHWH will ensure justice in the court (*mšpṭ*) and in society (*ṣdqh*). The emergence of the fullness of justice in the land would surely signal that YHWH returned to Yehud and its people.

YHWH'S ANGER FULLY PACIFIED

In the seventh and final vision of this series (6:1–8), images from the first vision (1:8–11) resurface as the prophet describes four chariots with a driving horse, each of a different color, going in all four directions of the wind (6:1–5). The chariots and their horses present themselves "before the lord of all the earth" (6:5), a clear reference to YHWH.

The image of the four winds as horse-drawn chariots sent out by YHWH builds on images familiar from the court of the King of Persia who had chariots at his disposal to carry out his bidding.[31] That these chariots in the vision range the whole earth in every direction implies that, ultimately, all events that occur in the Persian Empire fall, not under the purview of Darius I, but under

---

(Marvin A. Sweeney, *The Twelve Prophets*, vol. 2 [Berit Olam; Collegeville, MN: The Liturgical Press, 2000], 620). The fact that the Old Greek refers to *adikia*, injustice in the social realm, seems to lend itself to my proposed interpretation, making the effect of the "eye" explicit.

[31] See David F. Graf, "The Persian Royal Road System," *Achaemenid History* **8** (1994): 167–189; Waters, *Ancient Persia*, 111–113.

the purview of the "lord of all the earth," YHWH. This vision simultaneously places Jerusalem and Yehud at the center of the world, since YHWH has once again chosen to take up residence in Jerusalem.

But as the angel of YHWH releases three of the four chariots to wander the earth (6:6–7) the real concern of the vision comes into focus:

> Then he cried out and spoke unto me, saying,
> "Look at the ones going into the land of the north.
> They have pacified my spirit in the land of the north."
> (6:8)

The final line of the angel's speech echoes an assertion made several times in the Book of Ezekiel that YHWH will punish Jerusalem by sending its inhabitants to Babylon until YHWH's anger is fully satisfied (*nwḥ*, as in Zech 6:8c; see Ezek 5:13; 16:42; 21:22; 24:13). Zechariah's vision apparently claims that the time of YHWH's punishment is complete and the anger of YHWH is fully satisfied.[32] And so Zechariah's visions come full circle. YHWH reaffirms what was stated in the first vision: in motherly compassion and sorrow YHWH has turned away from the anger expressed in exiling Judah and North Israel (Zech 1:12–17) and that the people's punishment has come to an end. The future of YHWH lies in the midst of the people of Jerusalem, where YHWH dwells and rules as the Great King. The question that

---

[32] My translation of *nwḥ* follows *HALOT* 1:679. Meyers and Meyers rightly note that 5:11 uses the Hophal form of *nwḥ*. However, their move to take the Hiphil of *nwḥ* in 6:8c in line with the Hophal of 5:11 and, thus, translate 6:8c as "*they have placed* my spirit in the north," seems to miss the force of the Hiphil and thus, the link between 6:8c and the passages in the Book of Ezekiel (Meyers and Meyers, *Haggai, Zechariah 1–8*, 329).

remains now is, How will the people respond to the visions? And will they return to YHWH as YHWH has returned to them?

A FINAL, DRAMATIC ACTION: THE BRANCH, THE PRIEST, AND PEACE

Zechariah eventually came out of his visionary state, out of the glories of the heavens and into the world of Jerusalem. The Book of Zechariah does not mark off this "word of YHWH" by introducing another date in the reign of Darius. Apparently the scribes who wrote the Book of Zechariah want the audience to closely associate "the word" delivered in 6:9–15 with the vision cycle.

YHWH instructs Zechariah to go to Heldai, Tobiah, Jedaiah, and Zephaniah, recently returned from exile and of some wealth, take from them silver and gold, and on that same day go to the house of Josiah son of Zephaniah and make some crowns (6:9–11a). YHWH tells Zechariah to place one of the crowns on the head of the high priest Joshua (6:11b), whom the audience met earlier (Zech 3).[33] All of this leads to an interpretive word:

> Thus said YHWH of hosts: "Behold a man, 'Branch' is his name and he will 'branch out' from his place and build the Temple of YHWH. And he will build the Temple of YHWH and he will bear majesty and he will sit and rule upon his throne and there will be a priest upon his throne and there will be a counsel of peace between the two of them." (Zech 6:12–13)

Of all the visions in the heavens, the prophet's dramatic action affirms the third vision, which saw the restoration of Joshua son of Jehozadak to his role as high priest and led to an affirmation

---

[33] The singular pronominal object is often omitted in Biblical Hebrew and can be supplied from the context, as here (Meyers and Meyers, *Zechariah 1–8*, 353).

that Jeremiah's promise of a coming Branch would be fulfilled (3:1–8). Since the prophet performs a dramatic action, it symbolizes, not that Joshua the high priest is "Branch," but, rather that the visible reality – Joshua with a crown on his head – symbolizes an unseen reality, the coming of "Branch," who will build the Temple.[34]

The audience of the Book of Zechariah already knows that YHWH promised that Zerubbabel would finish building the Temple for YHWH (Zech 4). So it seems that the scribes want to convey to the audience that Zerubabbel was the prophesied "Branch" without saying so explicitly. According to Zechariah's explanatory oracle, this "Branch" sitting on his throne would also have a priest sitting on his own throne, with a counsel of peace between them (6:13b–c). Bringing these two together – "Branch" and priest – implies that Zechariah wanted to confirm that, in his lifetime, YHWH would fulfill promises made through Jeremiah of a Branch that branches out from the line of David and a never-ending line of priests issuing from the tribe of Levi (Jer 33:14–26).

Carol Meyers and Eric Meyers observe that the "counsel of peace" that the prophet says will exist between "Branch" and the priest implies more than an amicable relationship between Joshua and Zerubbabel. The word "counsel" (‛ṣh) often occurs in reference to the counsel of YHWH (e.g. Isa 19:17; Jer 32:19; Ps 33:11).[35] Given this added implication, it seems that the "counsel of peace" builds on the earlier image of Joshua and Zerubbabel as "sons of oil," providing oil for the seven lampstands, the seven eyes of YHWH

---

[34] For the idea that the dramatic action emphasizes an unseen reality, not the reality of the action, see David Stacy, *Prophetic Drama in the Old Testament* (London: Epworth Press, 1990), 260.

[35] Meyers and Meyers, *Zechariah 1–8*, 362.

that roam the earth. Together, the governor and the high priest facilitate YHWH's work for peace in Jerusalem and in Yehud. Joshua has access to the heavenly court of YHWH by which he can reveal the whole of God's will for the people. Zechariah has the breath of YHWH giving him and the people power to finish YHWH's work of building the Temple to honor YHWH and grant the people access to YHWH's beneficence.[36] Surely these persons and their work will make for peace.

Dramatic actions performed by the prophets occurred because the prophets knew that words were not powerful enough or clear enough for their audience to get the point.[37] Moreover, prophets employed dramatic action in order to convey through a mundane reality an unseen reality that was usually large scale.[38] It seems that the editors of the Book of Zechariah included this drama to drive home the point in the visions concerning the exaltation of Joshua and Zerubbabel in the days of Zechariah, which simultaneously would symbolize the elevation of Jerusalem and Yehud. The fact that this narrative uses the images of crowns does not necessitate the elevation of Zerubbabel to kingship; the most exalted courtiers of the king wore crowns, though ones slightly shorter than the king's.[39] But the crowns of silver and gold do symbolize that Joshua and Zerubbabel have received a great honor (see Esth 8:3 and the crown given to Mordecai by the king). And, the large-scale reality emphatically unveiled here is that YHWH intends, in the days of Zechariah, to bring to an

---

[36] The temples in the ancient Near East were understood to grant access to the god and to the benefits that the god provided; see Hundley, *Gods in Dwellings*, 131–136.
[37] Stacey, *Prophetic Drama in the Old Testament*, 267.   [38] Ibid., 260.
[39] Llewellyn-Jones, *Kings and Court in Ancient Persia*, 60–61.

end the seventy years of exile, symbolized by the coming of the Branch and restoration of the high priest.[40]

For the fourth time in the book, the prophet states, "and you will know that YHWH Sabaoth sent me unto you" (v. 15). In the immediate context, this exclamation affirms that people from far away will come and build the Temple, likely a reference to the people from other nations that join themselves to the people in Jerusalem (2:15). However, as noted previously, if the Book of Ezra reports things correctly, this promise of a rebuilt Temple did not come to fruition in Zechariah's days (Ezra 4). Furthermore, though Zechariah promised that the exaltation of Joshua and Zerubbabel would bring peace to Jerusalem and Yehud, in the days when the scribes produced the Book of Zechariah, Yehud found itself caught up in the wars of Persia with Egypt and Greece.

These considerations make the very last phrase in chapter 6 so significant: "if you will truly listen to the voice of YHWH your God" (6:15c). According to the Book of Zechariah, YHWH acted in the days of Zechariah to restore the people and to transform their lives from ones of struggle into lives of joy and peace. But, again, how did the people respond? Did they return to YHWH? Before the exile, prophets warned the people of impending doom and no one responded. The prophet Zechariah delivered bold promises to the people but eighty or so years later Jerusalem and Yehud hardly reflected their glorious visions. Which implies that the people failed to return to YHWH. The audience awaits

---

[40] Notice that the angel in 1:12 appeals to YHWH to reverse the curse YHWH placed on the land seventy years earlier, which seems like a clear reference to the seventy years of exile in the Book of Jeremiah, both foretold to occur and *to come to an end* (Jer 25:11–12; 29:10).

for the book to spell out just exactly how the people failed to truly listen to – to obey – the voice of YHWH. But they will not have to wait long.

BIBLICAL THEOLOGY AND THEOLOGICAL ETHICS

Divine Motivation

At first it might seem disappointing that this long section of the Book of Zechariah names only one virtue that applies to God: motherly compassion (1:12). But, given how early the narrative introduces God's motherly compassion, it seems that this virtue serves as the foundation for all the good promised in the subsequent visions. If motherly compassion signifies God's motherly devotion to her people, rather than holding herself at a distance, then the number and extravagant nature of the visions, plus the final dramatic action, show God's extravagant devotion to her children.

The visions offer a wide array of God's actions on behalf of the people. One of the more interesting combinations of responses is God's anger at the nations who took the punishment of the people too far and God's regret for letting anger go too far. God expresses emotions like humans and, like humans, sometimes feels an appropriate amount of anger and sometimes, regrettably, allows anger get out of control. This regret then leads to sorrow, to God's cry of woe for the people's suffering as God experiences pain in God's own being.

This combination of regret and sorrow over anger that went beyond the bounds means that, in an important way, when God "returned" to the people, God repented of letting anger get out of control. But if repentance means turning away from a previous path and returning to the correct one, then God *must* perform deeds in keeping with God's repentance. Thus, God comes to dwell in the midst of the people and to protect them. God restores good leadership to the people, even advocating for Joshua in order to give him a chance to become the leader God perceives he might be. This restoration of leadership simultaneously envisions the fulfillment of promises in the Book of Jeremiah of the Branch that will branch forth, with both the Branch and the high priest elevated in status. This restored leadership is also God's way of enriching the people and granting them peace in their land, allowing people to celebrate the beautiful mundane, enjoying peaceful community in their vineyards and fields. And from restored leadership will come a beautiful Temple that will elicit joy from the community.

At some level, these visions of restored leadership and peaceful living arise because God deals with the sins of the people. God not only removes the guilt of Joshua the high priest but also the guilt of the people. God also promises to put an end to bribery and corruption in the courts while also removing social injustices from the land. Thus, this series of visions implies that God addresses two sides of the sin problem, enabling people to live free from sin and its impact in terms of injustice but also to live free from the guilt of past sin.

Doubts

One of the disturbing images of God dealing with sin occurs in 5:5–11, which personifies Wickedness as a woman. And, while the passage also includes two winged women who carry away sin, their feminine presence does not take too much edge off this image of wickedness given that (a) this is the only time we see women taking an active role in the book and (b) the focal point of the vision is on Woman Wickedness, not the celestial female beings. The fact that Woman Wickedness is carried away to Babylon and represents the "one eye" – the presence of a leading, foreign official – implies that this woman is a Strange Woman, like the one in Proverbs who poses a threat to foolish young men (e.g. Prov 2:18–19). The threat of the Strange Woman recurs throughout the Old Testament.[41] But, even when Woman Wisdom and Woman Folly are pitted against each other in the Book of Proverbs, both images play off the element of seduction.[42] It seems that the imagery of Woman Wickedness in Zech 5:5–11, who must be immediately thrust back into the ephah as soon as the angel shows her to Zechariah, relies on this stereotype of the dangerous female seduction of men. And while the relationship of desire for wealth to sexual desire is a common one, in light of the long history of sexism, the sexual exploitation of women, novels like the *Scarlet Letter* (that remind us how often women take the blame for sexual misconduct while their male counterparts go free), and the modern #MeToo movement, I would argue that personifying temptation in terms of female seduction is precisely something we should *not* be doing in contemporary theological ethics. In fact, our actively countering such a perspective seems to comprise a crucial part of the prophetic witness of the church.

Prophetic Witness

In addition to denouncing the way that Christianity and the larger culture have often reduced women to sexual objects and then placed blame on women for seducing men, another element of

---

[41] See the discussion in Gail Corrington Steele, *The Strange Woman: Power and Sex in the Bible* (Louisville, KY: Westminster John Knox Press, 1997), 101–119.
[42] Ibid., 105.

prophetic witness would include taking seriously the portrait of God as a woman who shows motherly compassion by referring to God as female more often. Certainly God as Father, presenting God as king who exercises sovereign control and wars against enemies, has received more than its fair share of explication. If we simply looked for the places where the Old Testament used the imagery of motherly compassion and incorporated feminine language and imagery in our theological writing, preaching, teaching, and communal discourse, it might change our worldview and invite us to an ethic that is less violent and more compassionate.

The prophetic witness of the church might then pair this discourse of God as mother and God's motherly compassion with an ethical practice of peacemaking. While Zech 1:7–6:15 contains some violent imagery, one of God's ultimate objectives for the community of Jerusalem and Yehud is peace. In fact, the world of Fair Zion will draw nations so that they become a people belonging to God (2:15). There are enough people who "are for war." What would happen if communities of faith committed themselves wholeheartedly to peace? The threat of nuclear war grows as more nations develop nuclear arms and the news reports daily of incessant warfare. It is crucial, now as always, to have a counter-witness to our worst tendencies as humans, and to actively practice peacemaking in order to show the best ideals of the God attested in Scripture.

We will have another chance to address the ethical concern for court justice and social justice in the next chapter as these come into explicit focus in Zechariah 7–8. Hence, it seems best to close with a consideration of how the church might profess its regret for actions that have gone beyond the bounds of God's ideals. Christians ought to regret and repent of the history of the church's crusades and the violence done in the name of God among the nations. Christians must regret and repent of the anti-Semitism that contributed to the greatest tragedy we can name in our time in history, and regret and repent of any way that continues to provoke modern anti-Semitism. White churches in the United States must regret and repent of the way they bought and sold slaves, participated in Jim Crow and lynching, opposed the Civil Rights Movement or told African Americans to wait for justice, and for continued opposition to Black Lives Matter. Christians should regret and repent of their history of opposition to the LGBTQ community and the way that this has produced grotesque images of what I call "happy hatred" on the part groups like the Westboro Baptist Church. The list could go on and on but perhaps even this brief-but-sobering listing will stimulate our imagination for further possibilities for the prophetic witness of regret and repentance.

CHAPTER 5

Love Truth and Peace

When Zechariah initially steps down out of heaven at the end of chapter 6, the audience of the book has no idea where he lands. What the narrative does say is that the prophet proceeded to the house of Josiah son of Zephaniah to perform the dramatic action of crowning Joshua the high priest. In the following chapter, the narrative seems to place Zechariah in the Temple, as part of the regular Temple personnel of priests and other prophets (7:3). Envoys from the otherwise unknown figures of Sharezer and Regem-melek arrive from Bethel with a question to lay before YHWH (v. 2). According to the narrative, YHWH chooses to give an answer through Zechariah (vv. 1, 4).[1]

The term that the narrative uses to describe the reason for their query, *ḥlh*, means something like "to seek the favor" (of YHWH).

---

[1] While the Near Eastern context affirms that temples serve as the natural environs of prophetic activity, it is also true that the Hebrew Bible provides practically no evidence of prophets permanently belonging to the Temple personnel (Martti Nissinen, *Ancient Prophecy: Near Eastern, Biblical, and Greek Perspectives* [Oxford: Oxford University Press, 2017], 246–248). Zech 7:1–3 is perhaps the best evidence of prophets among the Temple personnel during the postexilic era and at least suggests the interesting possibility that Zechariah was numbered among the Temple prophets, which would seem to include Haggai as well.

The particular format of the request – envoys functioning as intermediaries – is reminiscent of Moses' seeking YHWH's favor on behalf of Israel after the Golden Calf incident (Exod 32:11) and Jeroboam pleading with the man of God to seek YHWH's favor to restore Jeroboam's hand back to normal after it had been withered (1 Kgs 13:6). In both of these instances, the intermediary seeks the kindness of YHWH in spite of the people or person's failing YHWH. It seems that Sharezer and Regem-melek are doing more than simply asking for the priests or prophets for an answer to their questions. The scribes use *ḥlh* to communicate that these two individuals want YHWH to bless Bethel and make it flourish after years of struggle due to the people's failures prior to (and during?) the exile.

YHWH CALLED BUT THEY WOULD NOT LISTEN

What Sharezer and Regem-melek want to know is whether they should keep the fast during the fifth month of the year, just as they kept it throughout the exilic period (7:3). According to the dating given in the Book of Zechariah, this oracle occurs nearly two years after the date of Zechariah's visions reported in 1:7–6:8. Perhaps the community to the north of Jerusalem had heard rumors of the promises of YHWH's blessings through the prophet but found their reality failed to live up to those visions' expectations.

Zechariah answers their question with a question from YHWH: Have you fasted in the fifth and seventh months *for me* these seventy years since the exile to Babylon? It seems that the answer to this rhetorical question is, "Of course not." Just as people eat and drink for their own sakes (7:5–6), to take care of their bodily needs, so too the people have fasted these past seventy years for their own sake. The only fast YHWH commands in Torah is the "affliction" required on Yom Kippur (Lev 16:29; 23:26–29).[2] Fasting is more often born of people's natural attempt to persuade YHWH to give them relief from their troubles.

YHWH may not have commanded the people to fast but the prophet does recall some specific commands that YHWH gave to the people in the past:

> Judge with true judgment and act with steadfast love and motherly compassion,
> each person with their sisters and brothers.
> And widows and orphans, sojourners and poor, do not exploit
> And do not plan evil in your hearts, one person against their sisters or brothers. (7:9–10)

Zechariah redirects the envoys, and those whom they represent, to what seems to him to be a more pressing concern. The people did not go into exile because they failed to keep regular fast days. They went into exile because they did not look at their fellow Israelites with steadfast love and motherly compassion, refusing to listen to YHWH in the Torah or the preexilic prophets, failing to ensure justice for the oppressed, but instead actively planning harm against their neighbors.

The Book of Zechariah makes it clear from nearly the beginning that YHWH is not unmoved by those who cry out for mercy

---

[2] Notice that the term in Leviticus 16 and 23, 'nh, differs from the one in Zechariah 7 and 8, ṣwm. It seems that later traditions defined this "affliction" in terms of "fasting" from food and drink, as well as from bathing, anointing, wearing sandals, and sex (*Targum Pseudo-Jonathan* 16:29; *m. Yoma* 8:1). Richard Coggins seems to be on target when he observes that, while fasting is important to many religious communities, it seems to have been of particular concern in the Second Temple Period, which I would argue derives from the people's desire to see the land and their lives renewed (Richard James Coggins, *Joel and Amos* [NCB; Sheffield: Sheffield Academic Press, 2000], 33).

(see 1:12–13). YHWH's willingness to comfort the aggrieved does not belie YHWH's desire for the people to act faithfully, however. What happened with the previous generation is that they placed a guard by their hearts so that they would not have to listen to Torah or the words that YHWH gave through the prophets (7:12).[3] Here the Israelites and the Torah are personified as a petitioner (Torah) and the guard at the gate (their hearts). Just as a petitioner who wished to see the king went through an interrogation at the gate, and thus could be denied entrance, so the people in the days before the exile turned away Torah, almost as if they viewed the Torah as an enemy plotting against them.[4] So, when the people in turn came seeking YHWH's favor, YHWH turned them away at the gate, refusing to listen to their cries (7:13). Like the kings of Persia, the receipt of favors from YHWH depends on YHWH continuing to hold the recipient in high regard, which requires the person's faithfulness to the will of the Great King/YHWH.[5] If the people refused to obey the laws of YHWH and to accept instructions from YHWH's messengers, then they would no longer possess the land (7:15).

Zechariah's opening words are not meant to offer assurance to the envoys and those whom they represent. Rather, they function as a warning that the favor of YHWH depends less on fasting and

---

[3] I understand Torah here as some form of Hebrew Scriptures given the use of the determinate. See, similarly, Meyers and Meyers, who see the combination of *ha-tôrâ* with *ha-dĕbārîm* as possibly indicating a "working canon" of some form of the Pentateuch and some form of a collection of the former prophets (Carol L. Meyers and Eric M. Meyers, *Haggai, Zechariah 1–8* [AB 25B; Garden City, NY: Doubleday, 1987], 402).

[4] For a brief discussion of the role of the guards at the gate of the royal place, see Pierre Briant, *From Cyrus to Alexander: A History of the Persian Empire*, trans. Peter T. Daniels (Winona Lake, IN: Eisenbrauns, 2002), 260–261.

[5] Ibid., 319–324.

more on whether the people follow the instructions of the Torah to do justice and to care for the widows, orphans, aliens, and poor. Things typically do not go well for those who seek the Great King's favor but refuse to obey the Great King's laws and decrees. More than two years after the date of the oracle that opens the Book of Zechariah (1:1–6), the book tells the audience that a delegation from Bethel came to see if YHWH really had returned to Jerusalem and whether they could expect to receive YHWH's favors. The prophet's reply indicates that YHWH was still waiting to see if the people would return to their God and finally obey the Torah's demands for justice.

NOTHING IS IMPOSSIBLE FOR GOD

Momentarily the book will acknowledge the harsh realities that lay behind Sharezer and Regem-melek sending their delegation to Jerusalem. But as the narrative continues the prophet offers YHWH's assertion that these days in Yehud differ significantly from the days of Jerusalem's devastation and the exile to Babylon:

> Thus says YHWH of hosts,
> "I am zealous for Zion with a great zeal
> With a great fury I am zealous for it."
> Thus says YHWH of hosts,
> "I have returned to unto Zion and I dwell in the midst of Jerusalem.
> Jerusalem will be called 'City of the Truth'
> And the mountain of YHWH of hosts 'Mountain of the Holy One.'" (8:2–3)

YHWH's words of jealousy for Zion echo the words from the opening vision where YHWH expressed deep anger at the nations who had wreaked havoc on Jerusalem, going beyond what

YHWH intended (1:14–15).⁶ The word used here to express YHWH's feelings (*qn'*) can refer to a jealousy that a husband feels toward his wife when they suspect their spouse of having sexual relations with someone else (Num 5:11–14). Yet it can also express a zeal to do something right, as when Jehu claims a zeal for YHWH and acts to desolate the house of Ahab and to do away with the worship of Baal in North Israel (2 Kgs 10:15–28). Perhaps Zechariah used this symbol in order to communicate two things simultaneously. YHWH is zealous for Zion and wants the best for the city (8:4–15, 18–23) but is also jealous for Zion, wanting them to do the things that the Torah and the prophet tell them to do (8:16–17). This collection of Zechariah's oracles emphasizes YHWH's zeal for Jerusalem but also hints at God's jealous desires for a faithful people.

Thus, while reaffirming that YHWH has returned to Zion, the narrative adds that this return was meant to change the city so that it became "a City of the Truth" and "a Mountain of the Holy One." The several uses of "truth" (*'ĕmet*) throughout this narrative (7:9; 8:3, 8, 16 [2×], 19) make it a leitmotif of this story. The assurance of God's favor lay in the city of Jerusalem becoming a "City of the Truth," not in the practice of fasting. The failure to practice justice in the court *in truth* led to the exile of Jerusalem and Judah (7:9). And, if the people in the days of Zechariah want to experience the goodness of YHWH they need to love truth and peace (8:19) to the degree that Jerusalem earns a reputation as a "City of Truth."

The prophet's vision of Jerusalem as a "City of Truth" seems to borrow language from early in the Book of Isaiah that condemned the once faithful city for becoming a city of murderers and

---

⁶ Meyers and Meyers, *Haggai, Zechariah 1–8*, 411.

corrupt princes (1:21–23). But the prophecies of Isaiah looked forward to a time when the city and its reputation would be transformed:

> I will restore your judges as in former times
> and your counselors as at the beginning.
> After this they will call you
> A City of Justice, the Faithful City. (Isa 1:26)

Isaiah 1:26 employs the word "faithful," *ne'ĕmānâ*, not "truth," *'ĕmet*, as in Zech 8:3. Perhaps it is unwise to split hairs too finely since both terms fall in the domain of "faithfulness, trustworthiness, truth." But the slight difference between Zech 8:3 and Isa 1:26 apparently announces the key virtue that Zechariah said must be exercised within Jerusalem in order to ensure the city's future. YHWH is zealous for Jerusalem to become known as a "City of Truth."

The narrative will return to a discussion of truth and how the people must exercise it in order to ensure their experience of God's favor. But for now we must content ourselves with the additional observation that Zechariah hoped that Jerusalem would gain a reputation as a "Mountain of the Holy One." As Zion garners a reputation as a "City of Truth," inhabitants of other cities will recognize Jerusalem as the residence of YHWH, the Holy One, and will want to come to honor YHWH (Zech 8:20–23). Given the passage's reliance on the prophecies of Isaiah as it envisions Jerusalem's future as a "City of Truth," it seems likely that "City of the Holy One" also relies on language and ideas found in the Book of Isaiah.

Isaiah 10 reports the fall of Israel to the Assyrians because of their failure to ensure justice for the poor and needy, the widow and the orphan (10:1–2). But it also envisions a day when YHWH will avenge the remnant of Israel because the Assyrians went beyond God's desired punishment and instead sought to destroy nations (10:5–7, 12, 15–19). In the future, the remnant that returns will no longer lean on the nations (Assyria) that beat them but "will lean upon YHWH, the Holy One of Israel, in truth" (10:20–21). According to the Book of Zechariah, the prophet Zechariah hoped that YHWH would bless the remnant in the near future because of the people's efforts to ensure justice in the courts for the oppressed. Thus, with zeal/jealousy, YHWH wants to ensure that the remnant in Jerusalem live the truth in such a way that the nations come to see that the God in Jerusalem, YHWH, is truly "the Holy One."

But if YHWH is jealous for Zion, wanting fidelity from the city's inhabitants that will honor YHWH, YHWH is also zealous for good to come to Zion. The prophet paints a picture of future Zion, the squares of the city with the elderly finding rest and filled with children at play (Zech 8:4–5). C. H. J. De Geus argues that the Hebrew rəḥôb, "square," in this passage refers to the open space inside the interior gate of the city, serving as the heart of the town, with low benches along the wall.[7] This design of cities is still found in the Persian period, as seen in the Persian gate complex at Lachish.[8] Thus, it seems that the prophet invites the people to imagine a time when the elderly and young people, once again, spend their days in the squares interior to the inside gates to the city of Jerusalem.

---

[7] C. H. J. De Geus, *Towns in Ancient Israel and the Southern Levant* (Leuven: Peeters, 2003), 34.

[8] Ephraim Stern, *Archaeology of the Land of the Bible Volume II: The Assyrian, Babylonian, and Persian Periods, 732–322 BCE* (ABRL; New York: Doubleday, 2001), 467.

If the prophet recognized that this vision would seem impossible to the original audience (v. 6), it must have also seemed impossible to the audience of the Book of Zechariah generations later. According to the Books of Ezra and Nehemiah, by the time the scribes produced the Book of Zechariah, numerous Israelites still remained in exile and the walls of Jerusalem still lay in ruins. To imagine the elderly spending their days in the squares of the city filled with young girls and boys might seem impossible because the vision implies that the gates are rebuilt and provide safety for the elderly and the young, and that the population of Jerusalem has grown to the degree that young children can "fill" the squares.

But this vision of the future does not seem impossible in the eyes of YHWH Sabaoth (Zech 8:6). The prophet Zechariah seems to have drawn on the prophecies of Jeremiah who, in his own dramatic action, purchased a field during the days when Babylon's overthrow of Jerusalem was imminent (Jer 32:1–15). Jeremiah felt conflicted about purchasing the field, believing that nothing is impossible for YHWH (Jer 32:17) yet struggling to imagine a future for Jerusalem after YHWH's execution of judgement against the people's sins (32:23–25). But YHWH assured Jeremiah that, indeed, nothing is impossible for God (32:27). Though the people would experience exile as God's judgment (32:28–35), YHWH would bring the people back from exile and grant them once again to dwell in the city in safety (32:36–37).

Zechariah imagined that the day when YHWH would enact this vision lay just on the horizon. YHWH would indeed save the people from the lands of the east and west (Zech 8:7), returning them to Jerusalem. Moreover, these returned exiles would once again be the people of YHWH and YHWH would be their God (Zech 8:8), just as promised in the prophecies of Jeremiah

(Jer 32:38). But then Zechariah adds a provocative addendum: "I will be their God *in truth and in justice*" (Zech 8:8). The addition of these words implies that the prophet is issuing a warning to the people. Yes, YHWH will save (even more) people and bring them back to Zion. But YHWH will also act truthfully and do justice for the widow, orphan, alien, and poor (Zech 7:9–10).[9] YHWH is zealous/jealous for Zion, which means that YHWH will restore the fortunes of the people and YHWH still demands truth and justice in Zion.

The implied rebuke gains momentum as the prophet continues his proclamation. These people's hands ought to be strong because the same people seeking YHWH's favor also heard the words of the prophets only two years earlier when Zechariah exhorted the people at the founding of the Temple (8:9).[10] Zechariah then reminds the audience of the prophecies of his compatriot, Haggai, who emphasized YHWH's role in the economic hardships that the people experienced prior to laying the Temple's foundation (Zech 8:10; Hag 1:5–11). But, after the remnant laid the Temple's foundation, YHWH promised to bless them and make their agricultural efforts productive (Zech 8:11–12; Hag 2:18–19).

Zechariah apparently added dimension to Haggai's words by offering further words assuring the people that times had changed. Previously, the nations had used the names of the House

---

[9] The Book of Deuteronomy often speaks of justice (*ṣdq*) in regard to these several groups of marginalized people in Israelite society (see, e.g., Deut 24:10–18).

[10] I understand the Qal imperfect verb form here, *teḥĕzaqnâ*, as signifying obligation; because YHWH gave previous assurances through the prophets, resulting in prosperous harvests (8:10–11), the peoples' hands ought to be strong. On the imperfect as conveying obligation, see Bill T. Arnold and John H. Choi, *Guide to Biblical Hebrew Syntax* (New York: Cambridge University Press, 2003), 59.

of Judah and the House of Israel as a curse (Zech 8:13a), an idea reiterated numerous times in the prophecies of Jeremiah (Jer 24:9; 25:18; 26:6). Apparently, if people wanted to curse someone, they would say something like, "May you be like the House of Judah and the House of Israel whom Assyria and Babylon exiled!" But in the future the House of Judah and the House of Israel will become a blessing (Zech 8:13b), which results in something like, "May you be blessed like the House of Judah and the House of Israel." This affirmation that those who returned from exile would function as a blessing among the nations would draw the people's minds all the way back to Abram when God called him out of Ur of the Chaldees and promised that he and his descendants would be a blessing among the nations (Gen 12:2) – that is, that nations would bless themselves in the name of Abraham.[11] And so the prophet exhorts and rebukes those who come to seek YHWH's favor: "Do not fear! Your hands should be strong!" (Zech 8:13c).

The contrast between the immediate past and the immediate future is, perhaps ironically, what should give the people confidence about the promises of YHWH through Zechariah. In the past, YHWH planned to do harm to Judah and Israel (8:14), and those plans came to fruition. But now YHWH plans to do good to Jerusalem (8:15). If YHWH plans to do something, YHWH can and will accomplish it. The people who seek the favor of YHWH have no reason to fear YHWH's good intentions for them (8:15b). YHWH has returned to them (8:15) just as Zechariah affirmed. But the question remains, "Will the people return to YHWH?"

---

[11] For this understanding of the nations blessing themselves in relation to Abraham, see R. W. L. Moberly, *The Theology of the Book of Genesis* (OTT; Cambridge: Cambridge University Press), 141–148.

The image of the remnant's strong hands might lead the audience to expect further preaching about the need to finish the Temple. But, instead, the prophet continues to chastise the people seeking YHWH's favor and to demand from them fidelity to YHWH's ideals, to become the "City of Truth" that will ensure the future of Jerusalem and Judah:

> "These are the words that you should do:
> Speak truthfully, each person with their neighbor.
> Judge truthfully and with complete justice in your gates.
> Do not plan evil in your hearts against your neighbor and do not love false testimony
> For all these things I hate," declares YHWH. (Zech 8:16–17)

The truth that YHWH desires is truth in the court. Speaking truthfully with one's neighbor has a particular context, at the gate in the exercise of court justice. Zechariah does not mince words. YHWH *hates* when people plan evil in their hearts against their neighbors, which the parallel line defines as giving false testimony against one's neighbor.

According to the dating of the oracles in the Book of Zechariah, only two years earlier Zechariah reported a vision of the curse that YHWH pronounced against bribery in the courts, where false testimony enabled the wealthy to build great houses by robbing the poor and walking around as if they were innocent of such horrific injustices (5:1–4). In this current narrative, Zechariah reminds the people that injustice in the courts was a major factor precipitating exile (7:7–14). If the people want to experience the favor of YHWH, *these are the words* that they should put into practice. Become the City of Truth that YHWH envisions and honor the Holy One by ensuring that truth prevails in the courts. "Strong hands," then, is apparently a metaphor for the moral strength these people ought to display in order not to fail the widow, orphan, alien, and poor in Zechariah's generation.

NATIONS WILL SEEK THE FAVOR OF YHWH

The narrative finally returns to the original query of Sharezer and Regem-melek about fasting. But the way Zechariah offers his final reply only reinforces his assertion that fasting should not be the major concern for the people. YHWH does not tell the envoys and those they represent to stop fasting. Rather, YHWH simply asserts that the fasting of the fifth month – as well as the fourth and seventh and tenth months, *all* their fasts – will become festivals of joy (8:19a). YHWH is zealous for Jerusalem and the House of Judah and promises them not only tranquility (8:4–5) but also joy.

YHWH is committed to the joy of the House of Judah and the city of Jerusalem. But, the prophet reiterates, YHWH is also jealous for them, that is, they must possess a corresponding commitment to the will of their Great King: "You must love truth and peace" (8:19b). If YHWH hates injustice in the court and the lies that support such injustice, then the people must learn to love truth and peace. The prophet does not refer to "steadfast love" (ḥsd) here, the enduring commitment that the psalmists often ascribe to YHWH for the people, but rather to "love" (ʾhb) that often describes the desire a lover feels for their beloved. The people of Yehud and Jerusalem must desire truth in the court and the peace that exists between neighbors who refuse to plan evil against one another (8:17a). If the people are to experience the tranquility and joy promised by YHWH, they must contribute to it by their love of truth and peace.

Implicit in the prophet's vision of seasons of joy that will develop in the near future is an assertion of the supremacy of

YHWH over the Persian's chief god, Ahuramazda. Imperial inscriptions throughout the Persian period invoke Ahuramazda as the one who guarantees "blissful happiness for humankind," who made Darius and Xerxes and Artaxerxes king over many lands with many tongues. The Persian term for "happiness," *shiyati*, connotes prosperity and tranquility.[12] Of course, the problem with the imperial system that promotes "blissful happiness for humankind" is that it does not promote prosperity and tranquility equally for all but rather, like all imperial systems, mostly benefits the emperor and the elite, including the imperial administrators. The benefits of empire do not actually accrue to those whose labor produces the food that sits on the emperor's table and the products that fill the emperor's palaces, as well as those of the satraps, local kings, and the imperial governors.[13] The prophet Zechariah asserts that this imbalance of prosperity and tranquility is the result of corruption, a lack of truth in the courts that ensures that more wealth accrues to the wealthy at the expense of the widow, orphan, alien, and poor. The prophet envisions YHWH as greater than Ahuramazda because YHWH ensures prosperity for the *whole remnant* by ensuring justice *for all*.

When people from the nations within the Persian Empire see this great work of YHWH in Jerusalem and Yehud, they will

[12] Amelie Kuhrt, *The Persian Empire* [London: Routledge, 2010], 304, remarking on XE§1. Lincoln notes that the term is in opposition to the demonic force, "the Lie," that invaded existence, corrupting its perfection, fragmenting its unity, and led creatures to death and dissolution. Within this world, the king offers a finite measure of happiness that Ahuramazda intends for humans, but only to those who follow the divine law and perform technically perfect sacrifice (Bruce Lincoln, *"Happiness for Mankind": Achaemenid Religion and the Imperial Context* [Acta Iranica 53; Leuven: Peeters, 2012], 258–262); see, e.g., XPh§4d (Kuhrt, *The Persian Empire*, 305).

[13] See, e.g., Nehemiah 5.

apparently turn away from Ahuramazda and come to Jerusalem to seek YHWH (8:20-23). The word "to seek" (*bqš*; 8:21-22) invokes an image of peoples from various nations seeking a consultation with the king, as when the narrator in 1 Kgs 10:24 says that "the whole earth" sought the presence of Solomon to hear the wisdom that God had given him. In the final glimpse into the glorious future, the prophet tells the residents of Jerusalem and Yehud that people of other nations will come seeking the beneficence of YHWH. Within the context of the Book of Zechariah the favor which the people from the rest of the empire will seek includes tranquility for their home cities, assurances of good harvests, justice in the courts, and seasons of joy. The nations will want the favors that YHWH bestows upon the residents of Jerusalem, benefits that they do not receive when they seek the favor of Ahuramazda or the kings who, by their own estimation, rule by Ahuramazda's will.

Seeking the favor of YHWH forms an inclusio around this narrative in the Book of Zechariah (7:2; 8:21-22). According to the prophet, YHWH wants the people of Yehud to see the future that YHWH desires for them. In that future, the people will no longer fast in hopes of finding favor with YHWH because they will readily experience that favor, abundantly. As a result, nations will see the great beneficence of YHWH and turn away from Ahuramazda in order to seek YHWH in the place where YHWH dwells, Jerusalem (8:23). But the prophet is also clear that this future depends on the people acting on the words that they hear from Zechariah: ensuring justice in the courts and becoming the "City of Truth" that God desires. The threat to the future lies in the possibility that these people will act like their ancestors and place a guard by their hearts that prevents the message of the prophet from entering. The future of joy for the people of the land requires that they come to desire truth and peace. In the next chapters, the Book of Zechariah will acknowledge that Zechariah's visions of tranquility and joy did not come to fruition. But the book will make it clear that the blame lies with the people and not with their God from whom they continue to seek favor.

BIBLICAL THEOLOGY AND THEOLOGICAL ETHICS

Divine Motivation

One of the characteristics that God possesses in this section of Zechariah is jealousy or a zeal for the people of Yehud and Jerusalem (8:3). Zechariah 7–8 surely expresses God's zeal for the people to flourish but it also emphasizes the fact that God is jealous/zealous for the people to enact God's just desires. And while we might admit that jealousy, like anger, can produce violent outcomes we would wish to suppress, jealousy often emerges in faithfully committed relationships. God possesses jealousy/zeal for the returned exiles because God committed to their ancestors long ago, which also means that long ago God desired for Israel to embody God's desires in the world (see, e.g., Deut 4:1–8).

Perhaps the key elements of God's character that define God's desires in the world, according to the Book of Zechariah, are truth and justice (8:8). On the one hand, in pledging to bring (more) exiles back to Jerusalem, God promises to be their God in truth. In light of the remainder of chapter 8, "truth" signifies a commitment not to deal falsely with the people but to fulfill the promises of blessing for the city and the district. On the other hand, God commits to act with justice. While God has a general commitment to Jerusalem and Yehud, God expresses special concern for the poor, widow, alien, and orphan – those too easily exploited in court and society. This is what liberation theologians refer to as God's "preferential option for the poor" in the sense made quite clearly in the Book of Zechariah: God is committed to justice for the marginalized to the degree that, if justice fails for them, God will punish the people and even exile them rather than let unjust exploitation and violence persist.

One of the most important manifestations of God's characteristic jealousy/zeal, truth, and justice comes in the warnings of the prophets (7:7) Zechariah claims that the whole people will flourish into future generations to the degree that the community ensures justice for those lowest in society, which is simply a reiteration of the preaching of the preexilic prophets. In order to help ensure the promising future for Jerusalem and Yehud, God sends the prophet Zechariah to reinforce this basic demand. Zechariah reinforces this message with a warning about how God reacts to seeing injustice in the court and society: these are the things that God hates (8:17). God responds passionately to injustice, which for the Book of Zechariah is basically an explanation of exile. And, according to the book, God has not changed, which serves as a warning to the audience should they continue in injustice.

Nevertheless, this passage focuses much more on God's desire to make the city and district flourish. God promises to come and settle in the midst of the city of Jerusalem, to be the presence of truth and justice, and to bring the security to Jerusalem that they have lacked, in both the political and natural realms. God will protect the city so that, once again, the young and old will fill its squares (8:4–5) and God will make the land yield its produce so that all might have enough to eat (8:12). In conjunction with this last image of the fruitful land, God also promises to give these as an inheritance to the people, which implies the renewal of the promises to give each family property as their inheritance in the land (e.g. Num 33:54; 34:17–18).

Divine Commandment

Given that God is a God of justice, it is no surprise that God reiterates the demands of the former prophets to ensure just judgment (7:9). This means that the people need to speak truthfully in the court or in the gate instead of loving perjury (8:17). God promised to eliminate false witnessing in Zechariah 5 but this apparently requires that the people commit themselves to eliminating this ongoing practice. As one might expect in any society, if Jerusalem and Yehud are to flourish, the courts will need to protect the rights of all their residents.

Along with ensuring court justice, the book calls on the people to enact steadfast love and motherly compassion toward the other members in their community, including the strangers (7:9–10). This also requires that the people love truth and peace (8:19). Interestingly, Zech 7:9 is the only time the word "steadfast love" (*ḥesed*) occurs in the book. But *ḥesed* serves as an essential part of Zechariah's summary of the message of the former prophets and as another example of the way the people ought to embody one of the key virtues ascribed to YHWH (see, e.g., Exod 34:6–7; Ps 136). The people of Jerusalem and Yehud, that is, ought to imitate God's faithful love toward their own neighbors, as well as imitate God's motherly compassion (Zech 1:16). Just as God saw the people suffering in exile, heard the cry of the angel, and responded in motherly compassion by showing extravagant care for the remnant, so too the people ought to see the marginalized in their suffering, hear their cries in the court, and respond generously to ensure that these people flourish. Finally, the people ought to have a desire, even a love, for peace (8:19). In the immediate context, this means that the vision of the children playing and the elderly resting in the gates ought to be a vision that the people long for like a lover longs for their beloved. Why would anyone want less than what God imagines for Jerusalem in these chapters?

Zechariah 8:3 provides the singular ideal for the people in this section of the book. The prophet looks forward to the day when Jerusalem will be called the "City of Truth." This means that their commitment to truth in the courts, to eliminating false testimony and bribery, will be so complete that the city will gain a reputation for its commitment to truth. Perhaps this reputation will be what leads people from other nations to take hold of the garments of the people of Jerusalem and Yehud and ask to go with them to the city because "we have heard God is with you" (8:20–23).

Prophetic Witness

One of the clear implications that comes from Zechariah 7–8 is for communities of faith to embody the demand for justice in courts and society, especially on behalf of the marginalized. We might think of orphans and widows, certainly, as people still in need of aid. But, especially in the church worldwide during a global migration crisis, we can see the need for communities of faith to work for the rights and sustenance of immigrants around the world. Likewise, as someone in the United States, I can easily call to mind the long history of exploitation, violence, and death enacted on African Americans and Native Americans, including exploitation, violence, and death by great numbers of white people who identified as Christians. And that terrible history continues to this day. When we add the call of "love peace" to the demand for justice, we arrive at the basic ethic that Christians have inherited from Judaism: justice and peace. Thus, when someone as influential in the discussion of modern, theological ethics as Stanley

Hauerwas criticizes the World Council of Churches, as he did a number of years ago, for promoting "Peace with Justice" Sunday, in part claiming that these terms were too vacuous and seemed aimed at palliating a liberal consciousness,[14] a person who has read Zechariah 7–8 must protest. The prophet calls the people to ensure truth in the courts, that those on the margins might flourish and the community live peacefully. The community of faith that embraces Zechariah 7–8 as Scripture will embrace peace with justice, in no small measure in imitation of the God who is just and who creates peace.

Such a pursuit of justice and peace on the part of the church raises the question of zeal and what, exactly, the church should hate. The theologian James Cone, after looking at the white church and white theologians, called himself the "angriest theologian in America." Cone was not simply angry that (e.g.) so many white theologians, pastors, and churches failed to support the Civil Rights Movement. He was angry because our lack of engagement fostered a culture of violence and death, not just in the lynching trees of his youth, but also in the deaths of African Americans in recent years at the hands of police officers – for example, people like Eric Garner and Philando Castile.[15] For the church to engage in the call to justice and peace requires a courageous look at the true cost of injustice and resultant lack of peace and to commit to return to God and to the basic ethic that God has commanded.

---

[14] Stanley Hauerwas, *After Christendom? How the Church Is to Behave If Freedom, Justice, and a Christian Nation Are Bad Ideas* (Nashville, TN: Abingdon Press, 1991/1999).

[15] Persons whom James Cone notes in his speech, "The Cry of Black Blood," Union Theological Seminary, February 25, 2016, www.youtube.com/watch?v=P_Q768HvabU&t=371s. Accessed July 28, 2019.

That vision of peace exemplifies itself in an idyllic vision of children playing in the streets, the elderly at rest in the squares, and each person working their own plot of land, their own inheritance. If these emerge in the Book of Zechariah as a result of the presence of God in the city, we might ask about the presence of God today via contemporary communities of faith. The Catholic Church often talks about a church and its "parish," which they define as a specific community of Christian faithful within a diocese, often formed on a geographical basis.[16] If a local church looks at itself in terms of its geography, it might ask about its work for the vision of justice and peace within its geographical reach. There are a number of so-called disadvantaged communities across the United States, a phrase that too easily masks white domination that disadvantages such communities. A church who listens to the call of the prophets, preexilic *and* postexilic, now will be concerned about life in its parish, within its geographical reach, and will live presently to that bounded community, striving in partnership with its neighbors so that those disadvantaged by the system of white power may flourish, feel safe in their streets, and own their own property, just like anyone – or better: *everyone* – else.

---

[16] "Parish," in *Glossary of Catholic Terms*, United States Conference of Catholic Bishops, www.usccb.org/about/public-affairs/glossary/index.cfm. Accessed July 28, 2019.

CHAPTER 6

Victory for the House of Judah, Salvation for the House of Joseph

A historical shift occurs at Zech 9:1. The earlier narrative material purportedly came from the days of Zechariah son of Iddo during the reign of Darius I, around 520–518 BCE. But the tensions with the neighboring cities on the coast of the Levant and to the north reflected in Zechariah 9:1–11:3 gesture at the struggles in the "middle territory" during the reign of Artaxerxes I, ca. 464–455 BCE. Persia to the north and east and Egypt to the south were engaged in conflict after Egypt rebelled against Artaxerxes following the assassination of Xerxes I. The scope of the conflict expanded as the Greeks from the West joined their naval forces in the battles along the coast.

The materials that the scribes gathered in Zechariah 9:1–11:3 constitute a theological response to the historical struggles in lands traditionally belonging to Judah and Northern Israel. As the latter portion of the book continues to unfold, Zech 11:4–17 marks a dramatic break in the book's rhetoric, with symbolic actions that condemn current injustices and postpone the blessings enumerated in 1:7–11:3 into an ill-defined future, "in that day." Finally, chapters 12–14 forewarn the audience of struggles that lie ahead for the residents of Jerusalem and Yehud, though promising renewal for the city and district under a future Davidide.

The Book of Zechariah opened with a command to return to YHWH, who had returned to the people. Zechariah 1:7–6:15 sought to motivate the people to obey the opening command by enumerating the variety of ways that YHWH had returned to the people. Chapters 7–8 clearly defined "returning" to YHWH as practicing court justice and social justice. The overall trajectory of Zechariah 9–14 reports the people's failure to return, which the text blames to a significant degree on failed leadership. The scribes of this prophetic tradition labelled the prophecies of Zechariah 9–14 as a "burden" (*maśśā'*; 9:1; 12:1), like the weight of tribute borne to an enemy king (e.g. 2 Chr 17:11). The words from YHWH in the remainder of the Book of Zechariah do not bring relief to the people but place a weight upon them, just as these same words weighed down the prophet(s) who felt duty-bound to proclaim them.

At some level, the tradition about prophets and prophecy in the Old Testament required Zechariah's disciples to provide some response to the collection of oracles and visions in Zechariah 1–8, especially given the many promises of a good future for the people. Deuteronomy 18:20–22 articulates a simple criterion for determining whether a prophet is true or false: Did their prophecies come true? The scribal community that treasured the prophet Zechariah's words must have recognized the theological problem for both Zechariah and the great, preexilic "writing" prophets, Isaiah, Jeremiah, and Ezekiel. The promises within these prophecies that Israel would flourish again in their own land, postexile, did not come true. The scribal community that produced the Book of Zechariah did not believe that the fault for this failure lay with the prophet Zechariah, much less with YHWH. And so the scribes added material from the disciples of the Zechariah tradition to Zechariah 1–8 in order to explain why his prophecies "failed" and to articulate YHWH's plans to rectify this situation.[1]

As scribes added this new material they also shifted the form of address. While the first eight chapters take the form of narrative, Zechariah 9–14 contain mostly oracular material. The fact that Zech 11:4–17 returns to narration signals the important role it plays in the overall argument of the book. This shift from a collection of narratives to a collection of oracles places a greater emphasis on the preaching, which makes it even more important to attend to the most direct form of address, the imperative. The theological claims and implicit theological assumptions in this collection of oracles are in service of the persuasive aims explicated in the imperatives.

Three sets of imperatives shape the argument in Zech 9:1–11:3. These oracles command the people to "Rejoice greatly, daughter of Zion / Shout in triumph, daughter of Jerusalem" (9:9); "Ask YHWH for rain in the time of the late rains" (10:1); and "Open your doors Lebanon and fire will consume your cedars / Cry out, cypress, for the cedar has fallen" (11:1–2). Though the scribes label this section as a "burden," evidently the opening collection of oracles is not as burdensome as those of Zech 11:4–17 and 12–14.

---

[1] Nissinen observes that "there is no direct evidence of the disciples of the prophets in the Hebrew Bible" (Martti Nissinen, *Ancient Prophecy: Near Eastern, Biblical, and Greek Perspectives* [Oxford: Oxford University Press, 2017], 161). But, Nissinen also admits that his proposal of the scribal traditions that transmitted and reworked the prophetic writings is strictly conjecture (162). My own view is that prophets like Haggai and Zechariah continued to function in the earlier portion of the Second Temple period and that scribes continued to record their materials, much like Baruch purportedly recorded Jeremiah's prophecies. However, the choice to link these latter prophecies to those of Zechariah indicates that the scribes saw that the material from new prophets, at the very least, aligned well with Zechariah's prophecies.

Rather, the book reminds the audience of the command to rejoice and shout because, even sixty years after the days of Zechariah, YHWH promises a great future to those returned from exile. Unlike Zechariah 1–8, Zech 9:1–11:3 casts a vision that includes more than just descendants from the tribe of Judah. The text expands its horizons to embrace peoples who have come to settle in lands that once belonged to Northern Israel. But the future beneficence from YHWH places the demand on the people to seek YHWH and YHWH alone for their needs and not through the variety of possible, false sources of divination. This section ends by addressing peoples beyond the ancient borders of Judah and Northern Israel, warning those dwelling to the northwest while reaffirming to the returnees in "Judah" and "Joseph" that YHWH will subdue surrounding aggressors. This section attempts to persuade the people to seek YHWH alone with promises that a glorious future lies just on the horizon.

REJOICE GREATLY, DAUGHTER OF ZION

Chapter 8 of the Book of Zechariah ends with a vision of people from the nations grasping hold of the garment of individual Jews and begging to go with them to Jerusalem because they have heard that God is with them (8:23). As chapter 9 opens, the surrounding nations are not fellow travelers on the way to Zion but sources of anxiety for the people of Yehud and the lands formerly belonging to Northern Israel. In the days of Artaxerxes I, the Persians used Yehud and Northern Israel as the staging ground for their efforts to repress Egyptian rebellion, with the sea ports mentioned in Zech 9:1–8 – Tyre, Sidon, Gaza, and Ashkelon – as key fortifications against the combined sea forces of Egypt and their Greek allies. The people would have heard of the financial benefits that came to those cities as the Persians built them up (9:3). Meanwhile, further inland, the Jews increasingly found themselves surrounded by implements necessary for waging war: chariots, horses, and the bow of battle (9:10). The great expense to the Persians to fortify the port cities and wage war against Egypt also meant a drain on the resources of the Jews residing in the Levant.

The opening oracle of this section addresses this sense of anxiety and fatigue. Some of this prophecy employs images and language one would expect of words assuring the Jews dwelling in an unstable and depleted Levant. YHWH will strike Tyre so that it burns (9:4) and remove kings from Gaza and Ashkelon (9:5), effectively removing the threat presented by traditional enemies of Israel. Closer to home, YHWH will serve as a garrison for Jerusalem, protecting the city that houses the sanctuary of YHWH (9:8) in the same way that Sihon brought the armies of the Amorites to Jehaz to defend their land against the perceived threat of Israel in the days of the Judges (Judg 11:19–20). While mustering an army for the defense of a city was certainly expected in times of war, sometimes officials failed in this duty, as Marduk-mushallim accuses his fellow Babylonian official, Marduk-lamassashu, of in the seventh century BCE. Marduk-mushallim writes to King Ammi-Saduqa to inform the king that the governors have neglected the king's orders to muster armies to defend against marauders and that the troops remain in their local villages busy with other things.[2] In the case of Zechariah 9, the prophet promises that YHWH will not fail in YHWH's duty to defend the city of Jerusalem.

---

[2] Charlie Trimm, *Fighting for the King and the Gods: A Survey of Warfare in the Ancient Near East* (SBLRBS 88; Atlanta, GA: SBL Press, 2017), 176–177.

However, YHWH will not simply act in ways that the people might expect. The text also envisions less violent, though no less transformative, actions taken by YHWH. The opening of this oracle makes the astonishing claim that YHWH will reside in the land of Hadrach and Damascus (9:1). The word "to reside" (*mənūḥâ*) communicates finding a place to settle or rest, as when David wanted to find a place for the Ark of the Covenant "to rest" (rather than wander about with the Tabernacle). Hadrach refers to the old Assyrian province of Khatarikka, which is part of northern Syria.[3] Damascus, in southern Syria, likely served as the seat of the governor of the Trans-Euphrates who exercised authority over the district of Yehud.[4] Trevor Bryce speculates that Damascus would, then, have been the headquarters for the Persian forces in Syria.[5] If this is so, then the claim that YHWH will come to find rest, that is, reside in the region of Syria, signals a transformation on par with the promises in Isaiah 19, which envision an altar for sacrifice to YHWH in the land of Egypt (Isa 19:19–22). Instead of Damascus and Hadrach as symbols of localized imperial threat, they will become places where YHWH has residence, much like the kings of Persia had residences in several cities throughout the empire.

Likewise, even though YHWH will bring down the pride of Philistia, YHWH will also, rather amazingly, cleanse the bloodstained teeth of Israel's traditional enemy (Zech 9:7). The image of blood between Philistia's teeth would have been striking to the

---

[3] James B. Pritchard, ed., *HarperCollins Atlas of the Bible* (rev. ed.; London: HarperCollins, 1989), 114.
[4] Pierre Briant, *From Cyrus to Alexander: A History of the Persian Empire*, trans. Peter T. Daniels (Winona Lake, IN: Eisenbrauns, 2002), 585.
[5] Trevor Bryce, *Ancient Syria: A Three Thousand Year History* (New York: Oxford University Press, 2014), 149.

audience of the Book of Zechariah as it evokes eating flesh with blood in it, a practice forbidden to Israel, with the consequence that those who did so would be cut off from the people of God (Lev 7:26–27; 17:10–11). The promise in this oracle is that YHWH will cleanse the Philistines after bringing down their pride so that those who remain become a "remnant" to YHWH, just like the "remnant" of the Jews who returned to Yehud (Zech 8:6, 11, 12). Philistia would become a clan of Judah, rather than part of the Persian defense on the coast. The inhabitants of Ekron, another major city of the Philistines, would become like the Jebusites (9:7), who originally lived in Jerusalem and were absorbed into Israel during the reign of David.

The oracle implies that YHWH's effort to change the relationship with the surrounding nations who threaten the Jews arises from God's awareness that "the eye of humankind and the tribes of Israel [are] toward YHWH" (9:1). The claim sounds a lot like one made in Psalm 145, which declares that it is not only Israel who depends upon YHWH: "the eyes of all look unto you [YHWH] to give them food to eat in its time" (Ps 145:15). The ideology of the Great King of Persia was that the king fed his subject people, including even displaced communities within the empire, as when Darius I provided rations to Ionian women.[6] As the Great King of the nations, YHWH calls nations to account for their misdeeds. But YHWH is also responsible to provide for the peoples of these same nations even though they pose a threat to the returned exiles of Israel.

The claim that YHWH Sabaoth is the one who provides for the peoples in major cities of the surrounding nations is a "hidden secret" that this prophecy reveals to the book's audience. This

---

[6] Briant, *From Cyrus to Alexander*, 315, 506.

would also have been news to the provinces and city-states listed in 9:1–8 and, even more so, the Persians, if they paid any attention to the prophets in the small district of Yehud. In Persian imperial propaganda, the nations within the empire depended upon the king but also upon the god Ahuramazda, who blesses the king. As we have noted before, Xerxes I recorded all the nations he ruled by the favor of Ahuramazda and, at the end of one inscription, exhorted the people to worship Ahuramazda properly so that they might be "happy in life and blessed in death."[7]

Zechariah 9:1–8 proclaims that it is not Ahuramazda who makes the nations "happy in life and blessed in death," but YHWH Sabaoth. Perhaps the audience of the book would also think that, when the oracle claims "the eye of humankind ... [is] toward YHWH," this would include their Persian overlords, including the king. Thus, Zech 9:1–8 presents a paradox. All humankind looks to YHWH, which means that YHWH exercises the right to call even the Persians and their king to account for their aggressions that trouble the Jews in the Levant. And, all of humankind looks to YHWH, which means YHWH, not Ahuramazda, serves as the source of happiness, even for Artaxerxes I and the rest of Persia.

This oracle confirms that, in an important way, the intentions of YHWH did not change across generations. While the surrounding nations feel threatening to the Jews in Yehud and the lands to the north, YHWH still intends to surround and protect Jerusalem (2:5) and to include surrounding nations as God's own people (8:20–23). Nevertheless, one of the changes introduced in this oracle is the vision of YHWH residing among the nations

---

[7] See the translation of XPh in Amelie Kuhrt, *The Persian Empire* (London: Routledge, 2010), 304–305.

rather than the nations coming to Jerusalem. Another new element introduced in this oracle is the promise that YHWH will encamp at Jerusalem "because now I have seen with my own eyes" (9:8c).

Zechariah 1–8 promises on multiple occasions that YHWH will dwell in the midst of the people. But the narratives often indicate some distance between YHWH and the people, for example, by the fact that angels report to YHWH about the status of the earth (1:10–11) rather than YHWH having direct knowledge of the same, or the fact that winged women remove Wickedness from Yehud (5:9–10), not YHWH, or that messengers of the four winds search the earth and discover the spirits of the north at rest (6:1–8). When Zechariah 9:8c reports that *"now [ʿattâ] I have seen with my own eyes,"* this change in circumstance presents a theological problem. Was YHWH not paying attention before now, not perhaps since the last reported words of Zechariah? While the oracle in 9:1–8 does not indicate how long YHWH may have been turned away from the Jews in the Persian Levant, "I have seen with *my own eyes*" certainly represents a positive development. The fact that YHWH sees with his own eyes echoes the story in the Book of Exodus where God heard the groaning of Israel enslaved in Egypt, saw Israel, and knew their troubles (Exod 2:24–25). In the current time of distress, YHWH again sees the Jews subject to an imperial power, knows their troubles, and comes to aid them.

As much as the oracle affirms YHWH's rule over the nations, Zech 9:1–8 ultimately intends to persuade the Jews in Yehud and Jerusalem and lands to the north to obey the command in 9:9:

> Rejoice greatly, daughter of Zion, shout in triumph daughter of Jerusalem.

> Behold, your king is coming to you, just and saving,
> humble and riding upon a donkey, even the foal of a female donkey.

The promise of a king riding into Jerusalem comes as a bit of a surprise in the flow of the book. Zechariah would likely have imagined the possibility of Zerubbabel as king of Jerusalem, given his vision that Zerubbabel would finish building the Temple, a role often taken on by kings in the ancient Near East.[8] Yet, while Zechariah was apparently reticent to make such a claim during the reign of Darius I, this prophecy shows no such hesitation. Perhaps the prophetic community behind this oracle felt emboldened by the fact that the Egyptians executed a successful rebellion against Artaxerxes I. In the context of open rebellion just south of Yehud, the prophecy offers a word that the people long to hear, one that promises a king who comes "just and saving," offering justice to the Jews exploited in the mechanisms of Persia's wars and saving the Jews from their violence.

The contrast between the king coming to Jerusalem and the promise to end kingship in Gaza (9:5), indirectly affirms YHWH's unique relationship to Jerusalem, Yehud, and the remnant. Moreover, the humble nature of the promised king of Jerusalem contrasts with Philistia's pride, which the oracle derides. The pride of the Philistine cities, like the wealth of Tyre, apparently stems from Persia building up their fortifications and constructing great navy ships in those cities. The king who will come to Jerusalem will not build up the city to prepare for war but will eliminate the bow of battle from the land and speak peace to the nations (9:10).

---

[8] See the essays in Richard S. Ellis, Mark J. Boda, and Jamie R. Novotny, eds., *From the Foundations to the Crenellations : Essays on Temple Building in the Ancient Near East and Hebrew Bible* (Münster: Ugarit-Verlag, 2010).

The image of the king riding on a donkey reaffirms the idea that the king eliminates implements of war as the horse was used for battle but the donkey for simple transportation.[9]

Asserting that the king of Zion offers peace to the nations makes an implicit challenge to a key element of the ideology of the *Pax persica*. Darius I, for example, asserted that under his rule many nations that were once at war no longer fought each other and under his law the strong no longer preyed upon the weak.[10] The experience reflected in Zech 9:1–8 contradicts this imperial ideology. The Egyptians rising up in rebellion against their imperial overlords makes a sham of this ideology as the implements of war – horses, chariots, bows (and ships) – stand ready to put down the rebellion. But in Zech 9:9–10, YHWH asserts that the future king of Zion will make wars cease and establish peace among the nations, in marked contrast to the arrogance of the nations and the violence such arrogance perpetuates. The king of Zion will come with justice and salvation that makes for peace both within the traditional lands of Israel and also within every nation that has reason to fear the violence of empire.

That the oracle in Zechariah 9 envelopes the nations around Yehud in peace is stunning. Perhaps as noteworthy to the book's audience is the fact that this prophecy embraces the tribes of Northern Israel from the very beginning (9:1). The narrative material ascribed to Zechariah in the days of Darius I mentions North Israel only two times. Meanwhile, 9:1–10:12 refers to the former territory of Northern Israel five times (9:1, 10, 13; 10:6, 7),

---

[9] Philip J. King and Lawrence E. Stager, *Life in Biblical Israel* (LAI; Louisville, KY: Westminster John Knox Press, 2001), 114–116.
[10] See the clay tablets of Darius from Susa; DSe (Kuhrt, *Persian Empire*, 491).

including the promise that YHWH will cut off chariots of war, not only in Jerusalem but also in Ephraim (9:10).

The theological implication is that the promises in Zechariah 1–8 were not enough because they did not extend to the returnees descended from the tribes of Northern Israel. Knowing this may help explain the line in 9:11: "Also *you*, by the blood of your covenant, I have freed your prisoners from the pit with no water in it."[11] The logical antecedent to the feminine singular in 9:11 is the Daughter of Zion/Jerusalem directly addressed in 9:9. The "blood of the covenant" appears just one other time in the Old Testament, in Exodus 24, after Moses receives the first laws given by YHWH at Sinai. There Moses reads the laws, which the people promise to obey, and then sprinkles them with the "blood of the covenant which YHWH makes with you in accordance with all these words" (Exod 24:8). In Zechariah 9, the oracle claims that the covenant that YHWH made with Israel at Sinai is the covenant between the city of Jerusalem and YHWH. When Moses established the covenant at Sinai, he also built twelve pillars to represent the *twelve tribes of Israel* (Exod 24:4). Consequently, when Zech 9:11 affirms to Jerusalem that YHWH has freed its prisoners from the pit by the blood of the covenant, this furthers the vision of God's care for all Israel as the twelve tribes together committed to the covenant at Sinai. YHWH did not simply deliver the remnant of Judah and return them to the land. YHWH freed all the captives of Israel who made a covenant of blood in the days of Moses, a community whose center is in Jerusalem, where YHWH reigns.

---

[11] I have italicized *you* to indicate that presence of the second-person-singular feminine pronoun *'att* in the Hebrew text, which seems to me to indicate an emphatic address.

These former prisoners are then transformed into renowned warriors as YHWH uses Judah and Ephraim to do what the Persians have found nearly impossible: defeat the Greeks. The oracle's image of YHWH drawing the string of Judah taut on the bow of Ephraim to shoot arrows at the children of Javan (Greece) is particularly striking. Following tradition in the ancient Near East, the seals of the Persian kings often employed the image of the king riding into battle with bow drawn, firing at the enemy.[12] Thus, Zech 9:13 undermines the ideology of the Persian kings, who portrayed themselves as agile and fervent warriors but, at least since the defeat of the armies of Xerxes at the Battle of Mycale, struggled to gain the upper hand in their relations with Greece.[13] YHWH's future king will come to Jerusalem in humility and establish peace with the nations. But that peace, apparently, will emerge because YHWH drives out the enemies of Yehud with the combined forces of Judah and Northern Israel. YHWH the Great King will do this, not with an army of trained warriors but with former prisoners in exile, with a humble king at their head.

As the oracle draws to a close it offers one final claim that undermines the Persian kings' self-importance and discloses YHWH's care for the remnant of Judah and Northern Israel. YHWH will save them from their enemies, like a shepherd saving his sheep, and they will be like crown jewels shining out from the dust (9:16). The odd combination of images offers a unique

---

[12] See, for example, the variety of seals of this image in Deniz Kaptan, *The Daskyleion Bullae: Seal Images from the Western Achaemenid Empire* Vols. 1–2 (Leiden: Nederlands Instituut voor het Nabije Oosten/Netherlands Inst. for NE, 2003). See also Ryan P. Bonfiglio, "Archer Imagery in Zechariah 9:11–17 in Light of Achaemenid Iconography," *JBL* **131** (2012): 507–527.

[13] Matt Waters, *Ancient Persia: A Concise History of the Achaemenid Empire, 550–330 BCE* (New York: Cambridge University Press, 2014), 129–131.

perspective of the future of Judah and Ephraim. The first image draws on the shepherd imagery in the Books of Jeremiah and Ezekiel, where the failure of the shepherds – the kings of Judah – led YHWH to promise to intervene and shepherd the people so that they would no longer suffer under incompetent rulers (Jer 23; Ezek 34). Of course, kings in the ancient Near East often envisaged themselves as shepherds and the Book of Isaiah famously refers to Cyrus as the shepherd of YHWH who will fulfill YHWH's plans to rebuild Jerusalem and the Temple of YHWH (Isa 44:28).[14] Zechariah 9:16a implies that the kings after Cyrus, or at least Artaxerxes I, have failed the city of Jerusalem, so that they struggle amidst the violence of the nations. And so YHWH promises to come as the shepherd who cares for the sheep.

The second image portrays the people like crown jewels lying in the dust.[15] The people of Judah and Ephraim may seem like

[14] Jack W. Vancil, "Sheep, Shepherd," in *ABD* 5:1187–1190.
[15] This last part of this verse presents two problems. First, the root of the verb could be either *nws* in the Hithpael or *nss* in the Hithpolel. But, either root word makes it difficult to determine the exact meaning of the phrase, which could either be "crown jewels *fleeing* upon the land" or "crown jewels *displayed* as a banner over the land" (on the latter translation, see the argument in Mark J. Boda, *The Book of Zechariah* [NICOT; Grand Rapids, MI: Eerdmans, 2016], 592). The term *nāsas* is so rare that it seems best to follow Wilhelm Rudolph (*Haggai; Sacharja 1–8; Sacharja 9–14* [KAT 13/4; Gütersloh: Gütersloh Verlag, 1976], 185) and accept that the word is *nws* but with the meaning "to shine" (I found this proposal originally in Carol L. Meyers and Eric M. Meyers, *Haggai, Zechariah 1–8* [AB 25B; Garden City, NY: Doubleday, 1987], 159). I accept Rudolph's proposal to translate *nws* as "to shine," additionally, because of its relationship to the following *kî* clause in 9:17, "For what is his [YHWH's] goodness and what is his beauty? Grain that makes young men flourish and wine that makes young women bear fruit" (following Marvin A. Sweeney, *The Twelve Prophets*, vol. 2 [Berit Olam; Collegeville, MN: The Liturgical Press, 2000], 668). Essentially, the crown jewels shining in the dust are the young men and women who flourish and represent the beauty of YHWH. The fact that *nws* then appears in the

nothing to the kings of Persia, of no account except as the king needs a staging ground for war. But, to YHWH, these people are crown jewels that shine in the dust, precious stones of great worth to YHWH, though easily discarded by their Persian overlords. The kings of Persia prided themselves on their ostentatious wealth and jewelry, which they gained at the cost of their subject peoples but gave to the administrators who won their favor.[16] But to YHWH these former prisoners and their descendants are crown jewels. The fact that the people are imaged as "crown jewels" allies the people with their Great King YHWH, as the Great King was distinguished in court ceremonies in part by his dress, including his headdress.[17] Thus the former exiles have a special relationship to YHWH and should not be despised any more than one should despise the king's crown jewels. YHWH will not let the people be exploited but will cause them to flourish by giving them the grain and the new wine that have for too long gone to the tables of the kings and their imperial administrators.[18]

Zechariah 9 seeks to motivate the book's audience to return to YHWH by convincing them that, though the future glory promised by Zechariah may have been delayed, YHWH offers an even more glorious future. Yes, YHWH will come and do what the

---

Hithpael introduces further problems if the Hithpael must convey reflexive/reciprocal meaning (so Bill T. Arnold and John H. Choi, *A Guide to Biblical Hebrew Syntax* [Cambridge: Cambridge University Press, 2003], 47–48). It seems best to take the verb here as denominative, indicating "a derived verbal idea related to the noun or substantive" (ibid., 48), that is, the crown jewels (noun) shone (verb) in the dust.

[16] See the discussion on robes and jewelry as "archetypal gifts" from the Persian kings in Briant, *From Cyrus to Alexander*, 304–307.

[17] Lloyd Llewellyn-Jones, *King and Court in Ancient Persia 559 to 331 BCE* (Edinburgh: Edinburgh University Press, 2013), 43, 60–61. See the texts and images in Kuhrt, *The Persian Empire*, 531–540.

[18] Briant, *From Cyrus to Alexander*, 314–315.

people expect in some ways, for example, serving as a trustworthy, protective garrison for Jerusalem. But Zechariah 9 claims that YHWH will go beyond expectations and come to rest in the lands of Hadrach and Damascus and purify the Philistines of their uncleanness. The oracle intimates that the audience should see these nations from YHWH's perspective, that is, people who also need YHWH's care, and not just as prospective or real enemies. The prophecy also envisions YHWH drawing near to Jews living in lands associated with the former Northern kingdom of Israel, seeing their struggles, and offering both them and Yehud a humble king who eliminates war in the land. Eliminating war does not mean that the people will not engage in war but that they will defeat the Greeks, which will lead to peace. Again, this victory will come to the remnant of Judah and the remnant of Northern Israel as YHWH protects them like a shepherd and values them all like crown jewels. In all these ways, the Great King offers assurance to an anxious people, gives them reason to rejoice and shout, while undermining the ideology of the Persian kings and their god.

ASK YHWH

In the second argument in this fourth section of the Book of Zechariah (10:1–12) the prophecy identifies a second problem for the people, one that the prophets saw as more of a problem than did the people. The people need rains, the late spring rains that foster the growth of the wheat and barley harvests (10:1).[19] Needing rain does not necessarily signal a season of drought,

---

[19] On *malqôš* referring to the late spring rains, see King and Stager, *Life in Biblical Israel*, 86–87.

Victory for Judah, Salvation for Joseph   137

especially given the lack of other language to indicate a long-term lack of rain (see Hag 1:6, 9–11). Rather, the people are more likely simply seeking divine assistance in the appropriate season. The problem, as far as this oracle is concerned, is that the people use illicit sources of divination (Zech 10:2). YHWH lays this problem at the feet of the shepherds of Yehud (10:3).

The Book of Zechariah does not have a clear, structural marker between 9:17 and 10:1. So, when the prophecy in 10:1 begins with the imperative "Ask for rain from YHWH in the time of the late spring rains," the audience of the book would naturally have in mind the immediately preceding material. On its face, it makes good sense to ask YHWH for rain when the previous oracle shows YHWH as the God who stands as a garrison to protect Jerusalem, transforms their enemies into fellow devotees of YHWH, defeats the Greeks, and holds the descendants of Judah and Northern Israel as crown jewels of the Great King. But, it might be that the Jews see YHWH as a warrior God and so seek aid for rain via other divine or heavenly beings.

Whether the people simply refuse to seek YHWH for aid or whether they see YHWH as authoritative within a restricted domain (war), the prophecy exhorts the people to turn away from various forms of false divination (10:2). This divinization can involve non-specialized forms, that is, asking for assurance for the spring rains from one's household gods (*tərāpîm*) or more specialized varieties, like soliciting augurs or "dreamers."[20] The problem is not that the people seek divination, but that they do not use the correct form, which in the biblical world is nearly

---

[20] King and Stager note the obscure nature of *tĕrāpîm* but consider them to be cult objects within the household (ibid., 9–10).

exclusively the prophet.²¹ Since YHWH is the God who gives rain, if the people want rain at the right time, they should inquire of YHWH through the channels that YHWH approves.

But YHWH does not blame the people for their failure to seek YHWH for seasonal rains. YHWH blames the shepherds of the people (10:3), much in the same way an owner of sheep would not blame the sheep for wandering off but the appointed shepherd for letting them do so. The incompetence of the shepherds is so bad that the prophecy claims that the people basically have no shepherd (10:2c).

The previous oracle ended with a vision of YHWH intervening on behalf of the people like a shepherd rescuing their sheep from danger (9:16). In that earlier instance, it seems that the prophecy implicitly challenged the ideology of the Persian kings. Here, however, the shepherd seems much closer to home, shall we say, as the shepherd should have already turned the people of Judah/Yehud (10:3) away from illicit sources of divination and toward YHWH. In the Old Testament, the term "shepherd" can refer to a variety of authority figures in Israel including God (Ps 29:1), Joshua (Num 21:17), judges (2 Sam 7:7), kings (2 Kgs 22: 17), and perhaps the king and his officials (Jer 23:1). Given that the term predominantly points to the leading political figure in the community, it seems to me that "shepherd" here – and in Zech 11:4–17 and 13:7–9 – refers to the succession of governors in Yehud.²²

One of the problems that the Book of Nehemiah identifies with the governors previous to Nehemiah is that they facilitated the

---

[21] Nissinen, *Ancient Prophecy*, 335.
[22] For a full discussion of the shepherds in 11:4–17, see Robert L. Foster, "Shepherds, Sticks, and Social Destabilization: A Fresh Look at Zechariah 11:4–17," *JBL* **126** (2007): 736–741. I believe the argument there also applies similarly to the identification of the shepherds in 10:2–3.

people's neglect of the Torah. In fact, Nehemiah's renewal efforts include having Ezra read the Torah to the people gathered in Jerusalem, followed by a time of repentance and prayer for forgiveness because of their neglect (Neh 7–8). While certainly not referring to the same problem, the Books of Nehemiah and Zechariah both witness to a problem in Yehud during the middle of the Persian period as the people who should practice devotion to YHWH seem to know little to nothing about Torah and lack knowledge or conviction to seek YHWH for the needs of their land.

Zechariah 10's first argument for why the people should obey the command to ask YHWH for rain confidently appeals to the future action of YHWH: "and YHWH will give to them, *to each person*, rains and grain in the fields" (10:1).[23] The appeal sounds like a modern political campaign attempting to convince people that YHWH is not simply concerned about the welfare of the collective but of each individual in Judah and Ephraim. YHWH observes each person and the fields they till, promising to answer each person as they cry out.

Behind the explicit exhortation to ask YHWH for late spring rains and the condemnation of failed leadership lies the implicit theological assumption that YHWH appoints leaders and relies on them to perform their duties so the people and land may flourish. YHWH wants to answer each individual's prayer. But the failure of a key leader, the governor (shepherd), puts the people at risk. So, YHWH sends other people who mediate relationship to YHWH – prophets – in order to put both the people and their rulers back on track with God.

---

[23] Taking *lāhem lĕ 'îš* as a focalization or specification.

Thus, YHWH's anger at the shepherds stems from his care for the people of Yehud. According to this oracle, YHWH does not want the people to continue an existence that constantly approximates the life of sheep without a shepherd. Rather, YHWH promises to make the people of Yehud "like a majestic horse in battle" (10:3c). Just as the prophecy in chapter 9 promises to take former prisoners and make them like implements of war in the hands of YHWH (9:11–13), chapter 10 promises to take sheep and to make them war horses. And, just as the previous prophecy expanded its vision beyond Judah to include Ephraim (9:13), this oracle proclaims YHWH's aid in battle for Judah and Joseph (10:6). YHWH will give the House of Judah victory, just as YHWH granted Israel victory over the Amalekites when Israel came out of Egypt, and save the House of Joseph. The Jews in Judah and Joseph will no longer need to fear the might of the Persian army or their surrounding enemies. The Houses of Judah and Joseph will be the ones to fear, like one would fear a majestic horse in the heat of battle.

As YHWH transforms the people, YHWH will also transform the people's leadership. And, just as the oracle shifts the metaphor for the people from sheep to a majestic horse, the passage shifts the metaphor for the leaders from shepherd to various, other images: "From them-a cornerstone. From them – a tent peg. From them – a bow of battle. From them will arise all leaders" (10:4).[24] "Cornerstone" apparently signifies foundational leaders, solid leaders, which is similar to the image of the tent peg that anchors

---

[24] Meyers and Meyers argue that *kol nôgēś* ("those leading") should be read positively, making this is a rare instance of a positive use of a term that often conveys the idea of oppression (Exod 5:6, 10, 13, 14). I find compelling their idea that this use of *nōgēś* provides an ironic twist on the notion of oppression found in 9:8 (*Zechariah 9–14*, 203).

the tent to the ground.²⁵ All the leaders that YHWH will cause to arise from the people will be solid and able to lead the people into battle (10:5a).

YHWH's presence gives the people courage to fight, transforming them and their leadership: "And they will fight because YHWH is with them" (10:5b). Again, YHWH is not distant from the people but will fight alongside them like the armor bearer of Jonathan who encouraged Jonathan to do whatever was in his heart when he went to fight the Philistines, pledging to Jonathan, "I am with you" (1 Sam 14:7). With YHWH fighting alongside them, the House of Judah and the House of Joseph will put their enemies' horses and chariots to shame.

The victory of Joseph and salvation of Judah stem from what may seem like an unlikely source: the motherly compassion (*rḥm*) of YHWH (Zech 10:6). YHWH's motherly compassion is not so much the driving force behind the battles themselves but the virtue that compels YHWH to bring people home from exile (the Hiphil form of the verb *šwb*; see similarly Isa 49:5, 6). YHWH sees people imprisoned in a pit with no water (Zech 9:11) and reacts like a mother who sees her child in danger. And so YHWH will redeem (*pdh*) the people from death (10:8). The metaphor of redemption to which this prophecy refers is not the act of purchasing a family member out of debt slavery but the redemption of the firstborn commanded in the Exodus narrative. YHWH makes a claim on every firstborn of Israel but commands the nation to redeem the firstborn among their children through the sacrifice of an animal (Exod 13:11–15). YHWH, as a compassionate mother, does not want to see the death of her firstborn child,

---

25 For the "cornerstone" leaders, see Judg 20:2; Isa 19:13.

Israel, in the pit of a foreign land, and so redeems Israel from death.

This second oracle in the fourth section of the Book of Zechariah, then, expands the vision of the inclusion of the people of Israel caught up in the redemptive, salvific work of YHWH. The people whom YHWH returns to the land now explicitly includes the descendants of Northern Israel originally exiled to Assyria (10:10). It is not enough for YHWH to restore the descendants of those families whose genealogy is rooted in Judah. No, some eighty years after Cyrus sent the exiles home from Babylon, YHWH is moved by motherly compassion for those languishing in exile in the land of Assyria: YHWH has compassion for *all* Israel.

And there are others of course. Other Jews dwell in the land of Egypt, likely descendants of those who fled to Egypt after the demise of Jerusalem in the days of Jeremiah (Jer 43:1–7). Perhaps these Jews feel particularly at risk as they reside in a land in open rebellion against the Persians, fearing that they will be collateral damage in the imperial reprisal. The theological implication of Zechariah 10 is that YHWH answers YHWH's people wherever they reside, not only in Yehud or, more broadly, in the former territories of Southern Judah and Northern Israel. No, YHWH answers, redeems, and transforms all Israel affected by the wars of Persia.

The underlying narrative of the Jews suffering in exile in Assyria and Egypt, whom YHWH will hear, redeem, and transform, introduces a deeply ironic, possible third reason that at least some of the Jews do not seek YHWH for late spring rains. Besides perhaps simply not knowing to seek YHWH or thinking of YHWH as a God of war and not rain, these exiles may simply believe that YHWH will not answer them because YHWH has cast them off. The oracle acknowledges as much when it asserts that YHWH will redeem these others from exile in motherly compassion so that "it will be just like I had never cast them out" (10:6b). "Cast them out" (*znḥ*) puts things in rather stark terms, a word used in 2 Chronicles to describe the way Jeroboam "cast out" the Levites from Northern Israel (11:14) and Ahaz "cast out" some of the vessels used in service of YHWH in the Jerusalem Temple (29:19). Maybe these people need direction from their shepherds because they have reasonable doubts about YHWH's beneficence toward them. After all, YHWH cast them out of the Promised Land. Since the shepherds of the people are not offering such assurances, and apparently not even ensuring that the people hear and respond to the Torah, YHWH assures the people through the prophetic word: YHWH *does* grant victory, *does* save, *does* feel motherly compassion, and, indeed, *does* answer the people when they cry out.

One can readily see that the use of "Joseph" as a metonymy for Israel might derive from the fact that the oracle focuses in part on Jews exiled in Egypt, much as Joseph languished in prison and servitude in Egypt long before, where he was threatened with death more than once. But the memory of Joseph possesses still more visceral power over the imagination of the audience as it recalls the story of one who endured unjust suffering because his own brothers sold him into slavery, which turned out to be a reprieve from the murderous intent of those same brothers. Yet, Joseph did not die in slavery in Egypt. Rather, as Joseph tells his story, what the brothers intended for harm, God turned to the good, raising Joseph to second-in-command in Egypt, not only for Joseph's benefit but also for the benefit of his brothers who had betrayed him. The God of Joseph now addresses Joseph's descendants to assure them that, not only will they not die in prison in a foreign land, YHWH will actually make them great, mighty warriors and leaders, while "the pride of Assyria will be brought low and the staff of Egypt will fall" (10:11b).

We know from Persian inscriptions that the kings of Persia, especially Darius I and Xerxes I, offered thanks to Ahuramazda for victories in battle. In truth, we do not know how the average Persian related to Ahuramazda. Nevertheless, we may imagine that at least the elite of the land also offered thanks to Ahuramazda for the king's victories and the various benefits the elite accrued because of them. By comparison, Zechariah 10 offers us a glimpse into the complicated relationship between YHWH and the descendants of Judah and Joseph, whether in Yehud, the former lands of Northern Israel, or still in exile in Assyria and Egypt. Though YHWH wants their exclusive loyalty, many of them either do not know to seek YHWH or they find it difficult to believe that the God who once rejected them will now answer their prayers. To make matters worse, the shepherds who rule over them, their local governors, do not point the people to YHWH but, as we will see in the discussion of Zech 11:4–17, use the people for their self-aggrandizement. So, the prophetic tradition associated with Zechariah offers a new word to this generation, a word that moves outside of the circle of Yehud and the city of Jerusalem.

All of this leads to the final transformation signaled in this chapter: "and in his [i.e., YHWH] name they will walk, declares YHWH" (10:12b). At some level, this final claim seems to answer the imperative at the beginning of this oracle. The people have not, metaphorically, walked in the name of YHWH, not lived the day-to-day journey of their lives in singular, devoted relationship to YHWH.[26] Still, given that the latter half of this oracle claims that YHWH will "bring back" those YHWH once "cast out" (10:6, 10), and "gather" those exiles back in (10:8, 10), perhaps we should imagine the people "walking" on their way home from exile in Assyria and Egypt, confident that it is YHWH that summons them home after generations of rejection. Whatever the case, the prophecy offers these people instruction in the name of YHWH, their God, who promises *all* Israel a brighter future that should inspire them to ask what they need of YHWH, the one who will answer them (10:1, 6).

WAIL, CYPRESS AND OAKS OF BASHAN

The prophecies in Zechariah 9 and 10 account for the return of additional exiles from Egypt and Assyria in fairly straightforward, geographical terms. If YHWH fulfills the promise to return the Jews in ever-increasing numbers (10:8), the little district of Yehud will not be able to hold all of them. The prophetic oracle is cognizant of this problem and promises that not only will the nation of Israel expand to resettle the ancient lands east of the Jordan (Gilead and Bashan), they will also expand northward into territories not traditionally under the dominion of the united or divided monarchies. Jews will now also settle in lands currently belonging to the Phoenicians, identified in Zechariah 10 as "Lebanon" (10:10).

---

[26] For a discussion of how "to walk" (*hlk*) functions as part of the metaphorical concept of the journey, symbolizing the people's relationship to YHWH, see Michael J. Seufert, "A Walk They Remembered: Covenant Relationship as Journey in the Deuteronomistic History," *BibInt* **25** (2017): 149–171.

The unfortunate reality described in Zech 9:1–11:3 is that, for the people of Israel to flourish, other peoples must suffer subjugation or displacement, including the impoverishment of Tyre (9:4), the downfall of Philistia's pride (9:6), the defeat of the Greeks (9:13), and the downfall of the pride of Assyria and the scepter of Egypt (10:11). Now, in the closing oracle of this section, the Book of Zechariah envisions the devastation of the lands of Gilead, Bashan, and Lebanon for the sake of the people of Israel. A "fire that consumes" the cedars of Lebanon draws on familiar images of the way that armies utterly destroy areas when they wage war.[27] The devastation of one of the most precious resources of Phoenicia – cedars – should strike fear in the personified trees in other territories, like the oaks of Bashan, where the devastating might of YHWH is about to be displayed.

The actual aim of the prophetic warning of oncoming devastation is not directed at trees, however. Rather, YHWH addresses the leaders of these neighboring lands, warning that the "shepherds" will wail at the destruction of their riches (11:3). "Riches" (*'adderet*) is actually quite a specific term, often used in the Old Testament to refer to garments, like the rich mantle that tempted Achan, listed among the materials he stole from the spoils of Jericho (Josh 7:21, 24). The use of "riches" in 11:3 seems to symbolize the way that the leaders in Lebanon, Gilead, and Bashan enrich themselves, just as the governors of Yehud enriched themselves with the wealth furnished by the imperial system that simultaneously despoiled the people of the land (Neh 5). In fact,

---

[27] See the imagery in Amos 1:3–2:5 and examples from the archaeological record at Lachish (David Ussishkin, "Answers at Lachish," in 5 *BAR* [1979]: 19–34) and Ashkelon (Lawrence E. Stager, "The Fury of Babylon: Ashkelon and the Archaeology of Destruction," *BAR* 22 [1996]: 56–69, 76–77).

rich robes are one of the more frequently attested royal gifts distributed to high officials who earned the favor of the Persian kings.[28] The fire will not just consume major resources of local economies but will impact the people most benefitting from the economics of empire.

Zechariah 11:1–3 creates several rhetorical layers in its indictment of failed leadership by means of two other metaphors. The various trees mentioned in these verses – cedars, cypress, oaks, and thickets – not only exemplify the economic resources of each region but also appear in the preexilic prophets to describe the power and arrogance of rulers whom YHWH is about to topple (Isa 2:6–21; 10:5–34; 14:2–23; Jer 21:11–14; 22:1–22; Ezek 17; 31).[29] In consonance with the former prophets, Zech 11:1–3 warns the elite that YHWH intends to bring these failed leaders down from their heights. The second metaphor speaks of lions who roar as the fire rages. The governors of these other regions have not cared for the people of their lands like a shepherd cares for their sheep. Rather, they have devoured their people, with the lion metaphor evoking feelings of fear by its violent imagery.[30] Certainly, lambs do not feel safe walking among lions, just as the people of the surrounding nations do not feel safe under the leadership of their local governors.

Perhaps, then, this final oracle with its commands for Lebanon to open its doors to consuming fire (11:1) and for Gilead and Bashan to wail (11:2), should be read in light of the opening of

---

[28] Briant, *From Cyrus to Alexander*, 304–307.
[29] This list comes from Sweeney, *Twelve Prophets*, 676.
[30] On the lion imagery representing the violence of one's enemies see, e.g., Pss 7:2, 10:9; 17:12; 22:13, 21; Isa 5:29; Amos 3:12; also Brent A. Strawn, *What Is Stronger than a Lion? Leonine Image and Metaphor in the Hebrew Bible and the Ancient Near East* (OBO 212; Fribourg: Academic Press, 2005).

this section, where YHWH acts in judgment but also promises to come to rest in Syria (9:1) and cleanse the remnant of Philistia so that they become like the descendants of the Jebusites incorporated into the community in Jerusalem (9:8). In this case, YHWH attacks the power and riches of the minority elite, which will not only benefit the Jews returning from Assyria and Egypt but also the poor among Israel's neighbors.

This final oracle in 9:1–11:3 invites the audience of the Book of Zechariah to obey YHWH (cf. 1:1–6), to enact justice for the needy among the Jews (cf. chs. 7–8) by arguing that YHWH will clear space for them in lands to the north and east of Yehud and the traditional lands of Northern Israel. The implication for those who have suffered for so long in exile is that YHWH will act, not just for their sake, but for all who suffer violence and exploitation at the hands of their governors. That means that Yehud's governors should take to heart YHWH's judgment against the governors of their neighbors lest they, too, meet a similar, untimely and violent demise.

BIBLICAL THEOLOGY AND THEOLOGICAL ETHICS

Divine Motivation

This collection of oracles only mentions one virtue ascribed to YHWH: motherly compassion. The text defines this virtue in terms of its antithesis: abandonment. So, at some level the ethical witness of this text is that the ideal of God's interaction with people is to feel what a mother feels toward her own children and to refuse to abandon them in times of trouble. One could also see motherly compassion as a virtue that resonates throughout the text as YHWH sees the people in the prison of exile and delivers them, or on their way to death and redeems them. Motherly compassion moves YHWH to act for the people because she cannot stand to see her children suffering.

If this passage is lacking in theological virtues, it makes up for it in terms of divine action. YHWH claims to have (finally) seen with her own eyes the sufferings of the people and pledges to answer the people in their time of need. The poor leadership that the people suffer under angers YHWH and moves God to action. YHWH will save them from raging wars and redeem them from death in exile. When YHWH returns the people to the land, YHWH will dwell with the people and guard them like a garrison and protect them like a shepherd. God will not leave them in a weakened position but will strengthen them, making former prisoners into warriors and sheep into war horses. YHWH will provide rains and grain and feed the people, not just as a collective, but as specific individuals, as each calls out to YHWH. Perhaps the most striking transformation will come as God cleanses the Philistines who have eaten flesh with blood in it and makes those living in Ekron like the Jebusites that were included in the city of Jerusalem after David took the city. Finally, not only will YHWH, the Great King, reside among the people but he will also establish another royal residence, a place of rest, in the land of Syria, in the city of Damascus.

Doubts

If we find motherly compassion and the various actions of YHWH listed above as worthy of imitation, there is still the problem of the various images of God's violence against the nations, striking Tyre's forces at sea, shooting arrows and slinging stones at the Greeks, and devouring the wealth of Lebanon and Bashan with fire. While my own commitments lead me to side with people like Martin Luther King, Jr. and to practice pacifism,

I think it is worth considering these images of violence and whether, in certain cases, violence is justifiable. I recall a number of years ago a discussion about race among black and white Christians about whether shooting someone was a justifiable response to violence done against the African American community. Are Christians duty-bound to die at the hands of the oppressor or is this simply a trope of the oppressor class? On the question of whether any form of violence is permissible in Christianity, one may think not only of Dietrich Bonhoeffer's alleged collusion in the attempt to assassinate Hitler but also his writing in his posthumously published *Ethics*. Bonhoeffer writes there about the person who takes on guilt for the sake of others in imitation of Christ, which seems to be the approach he took when he joined the plot against Hitler.[31] All of this means that, though I myself do not find divine violence something that I can imitate, I can understand why some of my African American Christian friends said they would use violence to defend themselves. And I understand why Bonhoeffer took on sin by setting aside his pacifism when the opportunity to kill Hitler arose. One of the concerns that remains, however, is whether anyone who chooses violence does so for self-aggrandizement or other motivations that would call into question the possibility of a "virtuous violence."

Divine Command

None of the three imperatives in this section is ethical per se: rejoice, ask, cry out. But each could help readers imagine various motivations for ethics. Take for example, the command to *rejoice* as one sees the defeat of enemies and the coming, humble king

---

[31] Dietrich Bonhoeffer, *Ethics*, trans. Neville Horton Smith (New York: MacMillan Publishing Company, 1955), 236–238.

who saves, ensures justice, and establishes peace. Joy could easily serve as a foil to thinking that our lives are self-generated and might function to call us back to the conviction that God provides for humans in every way. Likewise, the command to *ask* seems to emphasize dependence upon YHWH and may serve as a prophylactic against pride in our own achievements, which too easily leads to treating others as "less than." Finally, to *cry out* may sometimes be the only responsible thing to do in the face of injustice, especially when, among other examples, we think about the history of white churches in the violence done to black bodies or the way the trope of "pagan religion" enabled seizure of Native American lands or the way government officials use Rom 13:1–7 to justify lack of sufficient care for undocumented immigrants.

The ideals in this text come from two models of leadership. On the one hand, there is the future king who will come to Jerusalem to do justice, to save, and to make peace with the nations. We know that the shepherds of the land *are not doing justice*, and Zechariah 7–8 indicates that this justice concerns the poor, widow, alien, and orphan. *To save* means that the coming king will defeat the enemies who assault "Fair Zion." And *making peace* with the nations means that the implements of war will disappear from the land. On the other hand, the passage also envisions officials who, despite being somewhat lower in status, nevertheless have a significant role to play for the people, including as a cornerstone, providing a secure place for the people, and a tent peg, helping anchor the people and their life in the land.

Prophetic Witness

As I think about this material from Zechariah 9:1–11:3, it seems to me that one important part of the prophetic witness of communities of faith is to speak out against corrupt and greedy leadership. Christians who understand the call to justice and the need to live gratefully in the world should also have the courage to confront greed and corruption as less than the ideal that God holds for all leaders, whether within or outside of the church. This means that another important part of the witness of communities of faith is to live lives of humility, thanksgiving, prayer, and sorrow. We cannot accuse others of greed and corruption if our own lives are prideful, greedy, self-reliant, and unaffected by our past and present sins. As a white, middle-class American I must continually evaluate whether I am pursuing simplicity, generosity, dependence, and godly sorrow in order to witness to the justice that God requires in the United States and beyond.

For this life of humility, gratitude, dependence, and godly sorrow to emerge requires developing motherly compassion and indulging anger at injustice. We cannot harden our hearts to the suffering and exploitation of other human beings. The church should be a primary place where we, frequently enough, look squarely at the suffering of the world and are affected by it. Certainly one of those affections should be anger, anger that injustice spans across generations, that leaders keep failing their people, that violence is done against other human beings generation-to-generation. The church's life is one of constant paradox: full of thanksgiving to God for provision and sorrow for the suffering of the world, full of humility before God on whom we depend, and full of anger at the injustices of the world.

This leads to a final point and a final paradox. What we see in Zechariah 9:1–11:3 is both that YHWH exercises special care for the suffering people of Jerusalem and Yehud and Jews in the lands formerly given to Northern Israel and also that YHWH makes provision for all peoples and purifies them, incorporating them into God's people. Perhaps one of the most important aspects of the prophetic witness of communities of faith in our time is to practice a preferential option for the poor, for the suffering of the world in its many forms and many bodies, *and* also to live into the hope of transformation, where enemies become part of the people of God and wars end while peace endures.

CHAPTER 7

Woe to the Worthless Shepherd

What Zechariah 9:1–11:3 only briefly remarks upon – the failure of the governors of Yehud that, for the disciples of Zechariah, would prove to postpone the glorious promises of Zechariah into the ill-defined future – comes to massive scale in 11:4–17. As becomes apparent in the narrative of Zech 11:4–17, the governors of Yehud too readily share characteristics of the governors of their Levantine neighbors, including the concern to increase their wealth with its concomitant lack of concern for suffering people.

 The problem, of course, is that the book's audience already has an idea of what YHWH will do to the governors of Yehud and the lands formerly belonging to Judah and Northern Israel: destroy both land and shepherd (11:1–3). The Book of Zechariah intimated from the start that stubborn refusal to respond to the prophet's exhortation could effect something like exile and that the postexilic community would do well to learn the lessons of the exilic era. If the governors appointed over Yehud, like their regional counterparts, value increasing their wealth more so than the concern for the justice demanded by YHWH, there does not seem to be much hope for the future of Yehud and the ever-increasing population of repatriates.

Woe to the Worthless Shepherd

Zechariah 11:4–17 narrates two dramatic acts carried out by one of the prophets who adhered to the tradition of Zechariah.[1] The narrative presents the unnamed prophet initiating an "encounter" with an event that lies in the future, seemingly on the near horizon.[2] The dramatic acts intend to help the people see, feel, and hear the outcome of generations of failed leadership before it actually happens. Perhaps the scribes of the book wanted the audience to see that this break and the delay of the glorious promises of Zechariah were not inevitable. However, if the dramatic acts failed to persuade the governors, elites, and people to change, the audience still might see the negative outcomes as predictable given the nature of YHWH and the recalcitrance of the governors.

MERCHANTS OF HUMANITY

The narrative begins by invoking common ground with the audience, utilizing a metaphorical concept of the sheepherding economy with owners and shepherds, merchants and buyers.[3] The setting for the dramatic acts introduces these elements rather succinctly:

> This is what YHWH my God said, "Shepherd the flock set aside for slaughter. Those who are buying them are killing them and do not feel guilty. Those who are selling them are saying,

---

[1] I am utilizing the terminology of David Stacey, in his *Prophetic Drama in the Old Testament* (London: Epworth, 1990).

[2] Stacey asserts that the dramatic action can as easily facilitate an encounter with a future event as it may an event from the past (ibid., 55).

[3] For a good, brief introduction to common ground in a communicative act, see Herbert H. Clark, *Using Language* (Cambridge: Cambridge University Press, 1996), 92–121.

'Blessed be YHWH' and 'I am rich.' And those who are shepherding them do not have pity on them." (Zech 11:4-5)

None of these mundane realities should disturb the audience who would clearly understand the sheepherding economy. Though people raised sheep primarily for their wool, some sheep provided meat and hides.[4] There was no reason for those who purchased sheep for the express purpose of slaughtering them to feel guilty. For a pious owner to offer blessings to YHWH for granting them wealth seems like an appropriate way to honor YHWH for YHWH's beneficence. And, though the shepherd was the sole provider and protector of the sheep,[5] a shepherd pitying the sheep set aside for slaughter and attempting to spare them from death would strike the observer as at least abnormal.[6]

Of course, the rub is that this narrative is not about literal sheep and shepherds, sheep buyers and sellers. No, this language symbolizes human beings and their rulers and people who buy and sell other humans. As I have argued elsewhere, the mercantile language of buying and selling used in 11:4-17 is often used in the Old Testament in contexts dealing with debt-slavery.[7] Moreover, the Book of Nehemiah contains a narrative that describes just this

---

[4] Philip J. King and Lawrence E. Stager, *Life in Biblical Israel* (LAI; Louisville, KY: Westminster John Knox Press, 2001), 113-114.
[5] Ibid., 114.
[6] "To pity" (ḥml) often implies the corresponding action of sparing a life, as in Saul "sparing" the best of the sheep after defeating the Amalekites (1 Sam 15:3, 15) or when David spared Saul's life when he could have killed him (2 Sam 23:21). In an earlier article on this passage, I translated this word as "to have compassion" but, to my mind, "pity" has a stronger association with the corresponding intervention in order to "spare" a life. See Robert L. Foster, "Shepherds, Sticks, and Social Destabilization: A Fresh Look at Zechariah 11:4-17," *JBL* **126** (2007): 735.
[7] Ibid., 744-745.

sort of situation in the time period reflected in Zechariah 11. Nehemiah 5 reports that those who immediately preceded Nehemiah as governor (shepherd) in Yehud failed to show proper pity for the people (sheep), who lived in subsistence while the governors filled their tables with food and drink from tax collections (Neh 5:14–19). The fact that many people lived in poverty meant that they were going into debt simply to buy grain and pay the king's taxes, with the additional offense that the nobles and officials (sellers) of the land charged interest on their loans to the impoverished masses (5:3, 4, 7). The sizable debts that the families, who often worked tenant farms, owed to their creditors led to many people selling their sons and daughters (sheep) into temporary, debt-slavery rather than suffer the worse fate of the loss of their rights to farmland (5:2, 5).[8] According to the Book of Nehemiah, Nehemiah was so offended by both the practices of debt-slavery and the enrichment of the governors table via receipt of the king's food allowance that he immediately put an end to both (5:10–12, 18).

Zechariah 11:4–5 offers a metaphorical and theological commentary on the situation described in Nehemiah 5. When earlier prophets condemned the shepherds (kings) of Judah, the prophets focused their accusation around the "simple" failure of the shepherd to exercise care for the sheep (Jer 23:1–2; Ezek 34:1–5). The prophetic condemnation expands in Zech 11:4–5 with a broader use of the metaphor of sheepherding. The economic system that lies behind the sheepherding metaphorical concept is inhumane and leads to a chasm between the elites of the land

---

[8] Samuel L. Adams, *Social and Economic Life in Second Temple Judea* (Louisville, KY: Westminster John Knox, 2014), 77–79, provides a good summary of the situation reflected in Neh 5:1–13.

and the majority populace. The shepherds/governors of Yehud should have had pity on the populace and spared them from such suffering, just as Nehemiah did in Nehemiah 5. But the governors failed in their duty to protect the people because they benefitted from the system.

The theological blow that stems from this sin against humanity lands in the final line of the opening of the narrative and serves as the conflict that drives it. In Zech 11:6 YHWH states, "For I will not have pity again upon those dwelling in the land," declares YHWH. "And behold, I will be delivering each person into the hand of their shepherd and into the hand of their king, and they will utterly desolate the land but I will not deliver [the people] from their hands."

To "not have pity" echoes language that occurs mainly in Jeremiah and Ezekiel with reference to God, who does not pity the people of Judah and Jerusalem and so sends them into exile (Jer 13:14; Ezek 5:11; 7:4, 8; 8:18; 9:10). The narrative in Ezekiel 9 goes so far as to state that the reason that YHWH will not pity Israel and Judah is that the land is full of blood and Jerusalem is full of injustice (Ezek 9:9). God's lack of pity and a people who practice injustice go hand in hand.

A lack of pity, an unwillingness to spare peoples' lives, in such contexts reflects the anger (ʾp; Ezek 7:3, 8:17) and fury (ḥmh; Ezek 7:8, 8:10, 9:8) of YHWH. Similarly, the fact that YHWH refuses to deliver (nṣl; Zech 11:6) the people from their shepherd and king may indicate YHWH's wrath (ʿbrh; see, e.g., Ezek 7:19). Perhaps Zech 11:6 intends to evoke the image of the Great King, who exercises just judgment. Part of what made the Persian king just, according to Herodotus, is that Persian law did not allow the king "to slay someone for a single guilty deed" Rather, on balance, if "more and greater are the wrongs" than a person's acts of service, then "he [the king] may inflict his anger."⁹ YHWH has found that the governors fail to render even the basic service of pointing the people to YHWH in prayer (Zech 10:1–3) and their offenses, their injustices, accumulate over the years so that YHWH justifiably inflicts anger on the leadership, land, and people.

The strong language that echoes the threat of exile found in Jeremiah and Ezekiel makes this narrative a cataclysmic turning point in the Book of Zechariah. The audience recognizes that YHWH has completely lost patience with the governors and elite of Yehud, and so the threats that overtook the people in the time of the exile (Zech 1:1–6) now threaten to overtake postexilic Yehud. The dramatic irony that Zech 11:4–17 introduces is that the prophetic tradition that grew out of the preaching of Zechariah apparently came to a place of agreement with Jeremiah and Ezekiel, who considered exile *better* than letting injustices continue unabated. The Book of Jeremiah especially emphasizes the benefit of the exile, both for those in exile whom YHWH will cause to flourish (Jer 29:1–9) and also for the poor of the land who received vineyards and fields after the elite were exiled (Jer 39:10). Though Zech 11:4–17 does not state this directly, perhaps the prophet performing these dramatic actions hoped that a similar benefit could accrue for the poor in Yehud.

A BROKEN COVENANT WITH THE NATIONS

In order to carry out the two dramatic acts at the heart of this narrative, the prophet finds gainful employment as a shepherd. The next two units (11:7–11, 12–14) drive home the harsh outcomes of YHWH's refusal to pity the people any longer, such that they

---

⁹ Herodotus, *The Persian Wars* I.137.

will not be delivered from the devastating violence feared in Zechariah 9–10.

When the merchants hire the prophet to shepherd the flock for slaughter, the prophet takes two staves and gives them symbolic names: "Favor" and "Ties" (11:7). And, while the prophet runs off three other shepherds in just one month's time, the prophet also claims that the sheep could not stand him, nor he them (11:8). So, the shepherd leaves the flock to fend for themselves, which can only end badly (11:9), and he breaks the staff "Favor," "to break the covenant made with the peoples" (11:10). According to the prophet, the covenant was broken that day and the merchants understood that the drama act was a word from YHWH (11:11).

The metaphorical concept of sheepherding comes to life and adds dimension and further dramatic tension to the speech in 11:4–6. The former shepherds that the prophet chases off continue to symbolize the governors of the land who exploited the people. The prophet, however, apparently plays the role of YHWH as shepherd, which should not surprise the audience given numerous references to YHWH shepherding Israel in the Old Testament (e.g. Pss 23:1; 29:1; Ezek 34:11–16). The fact that the prophet portrays YHWH in their role as shepherd means that the prophetic drama claims that YHWH got rid of all the previous, bad shepherds in Jerusalem and Yehud.[10]

But the fact that YHWH rid the land of bad leaders did not endear the people to YHWH. Instead, YHWH lost patience with the people and they grew impatient with YHWH, leading to a vision of violence and anarchy (Zech 11:8b–9). While the narrative does not indicate what caused YHWH's impatience with the

---

[10] For the number "three" as representative of "wholeness" or "totality" see Foster, "Shepherds, Sticks, and Social Destabilization," 745 n. 46.

people, the trajectory of the Book of Zechariah indicates that injustice continued to prevail (see chs. 7–8) and the people continued to fail in seeking YHWH (10:1–2). Perhaps the people's frustration with YHWH stemmed from the fact that the prophets continued to prophesy, confronting the elites and the people, so that the people grew impatient with this manifestation of the divine word.

All of the above leads to the dramatic action when the prophet breaks the staff "Favor" (Zech 11:10a). In dramatic action, it is not the visible or, in this case, the imagined mundane act and object that were key, but rather the relationship of the action and mundane object to an unseen event or reality, usually one of large scale.[11] In Zechariah 11, the significance of breaking the staff "Favor" lies in the fact that it symbolizes breaking "my covenant which I made with the peoples" (Zech 11:10b). The language of "covenant with the peoples" ties this passage directly to similar phrases in the so-called Servant Songs of Isaiah 42 and 49. In those oracles, YHWH promises to give the Servant as a covenant to the peoples, which means that YHWH will bring the exiles back to the land of Israel (Isa 42:7, 16; 49:6, 8, 9–11).[12] The dramatic action in Zech 11:7–11 places YHWH's lack of pity on a historical and empire-wide scale. The promising days of Cyrus and Darius I have come to an end and the exiles will no longer return to their homeland as they did previously.

The editors of the Book of Zechariah insert this narrative here as a way of reminding the audience that the prophetic word was not powerful enough on its own.[13] This dramatic action within the

---

[11] Stacey, *Prophetic Drama in the Old Testament*, 260.
[12] Foster, "Shepherds, Sticks, and Social Destabilization," 748–749.
[13] See Stacey, *Prophetic Drama in the Old Testament*, 267.

book encompasses prophecies of many generations: the prophets before the exile (Zech 1:1–6), the various promises and demands of the prophet Zechariah (1:7–8:23), the prophecies from the Zechariah tradition in 9:1–11:3, and even the prophecies of the Isaiah tradition recorded in Isaiah 42 and 49. YHWH wanted to bless the people but stipulated that, in returning to them, YHWH expected them to return to him by, especially, enacting justice for the marginal. But neither the fulfillment of the warnings of the prophets before the exile nor the visions and proclamations of Zechariah, nor the prophets who developed the Zechariah tradition, nor the prophets who extended the Isaiah tradition, could convince the governors and the elite of the land to do justice; meanwhile the people seem to have lost patience with the whole lot of YHWH's prophets. And so the editors insert this story to confront the audience with the fact that an era of promise has now come to an end, with the covenant broken, because the people refused to return to YHWH, in spite of *all the words* YHWH had spoken through the prophets.

In the opening of this narrative, the editors make it clear that the prophet acted at the behest of YHWH.[14] The theological claim here is not simply that YHWH responds as the Great King in anger because generation-after-generation of leaders refused to do justice. The dramatic action intends to drive home to the book's audience that YHWH controls history, reinforcing this "hidden secret."[15] Zechariah 9–10 reflected the fears of the people and offered YHWH's assurances to protect those who had returned

---

[14] Ibid., 61.
[15] Stacey claims, broadly, "The work of the prophet is primarily related to [YHWH] and his historical activity, not to [the prophet's] audience and their response" (ibid., 281).

from exile and to transform their enemies into compatriots. But, apparently the people who received these oracles did not take to heart the implications of YHWH's control, not only over Jerusalem and Yehud, but also of Philistia, Syria, Lebanon, and the Transjordan, any more than the previous generation listened to Zechariah. So, now, the Book of Zechariah claims that the people will experience YHWH's control of history to their detriment rather than to their benefit.

THE BROKEN FAMILY BOND

As dramatic as the outcome of breaking the staff "Favor" was, when the prophet gained employment as a shepherd he also took a second staff, "Ties," which leads to an expectation for the other shoe to drop. And, while the first dramatic action functions as the climactic moment in 11:4–17, the fallout for Israel and Judah feels just as devastating for the hopes of the book's audience.

This narration of the second dramatic action (11:12–14) picks up right after the prophet quit his job and broke the staff "Favor." The prophet reasonably asks for wages for his labors, though he acknowledge that the merchants of the flock have every right to deny him payment (11:12a). The prophet receives the "princely" sum of 30 silver pieces (11:12b–13a) but then, at YHWH's request, throws the silver pieces to the "molder," the metal worker in the temple who melted down metals donated to the temple.[16] Then the prophet breaks the second staff "Ties," symbolizing the fracture in the family bond (brotherhood) between Judah and Israel (11:14).

---

[16] On the person in question as a "metalworker" see Foster, "Shepherds, Sticks, and Social Destabilization," 749–751.

When the prophet quits their job as shepherd, they simultaneously quit representing YHWH ridding the land of the previous pernicious governors. In this story of the second dramatic act, the prophet comes to represent those sold into debt-slavery as indicated by the fact that the merchants pay him 30 pieces of silver, the exact amount the Torah prescribes as compensation for someone whose slave was gored by an ox (Exod 21:32).[17] The merchants continue to stand in for the elite and nobles of the land who profit from this inhumane system. YHWH is symbolized in the text by the metalworker (*yôṣēr*) in the Temple, a term that is used on numerous occasions to refer to YHWH as an artisan who shapes creation (e.g. Gen 2:7–8; Job 10:8–12; Amos 4:3; Isa 45:18; Jer 33:2).[18]

This reference to YHWH the artisan further links Zech 11:4–17 to texts associated with the disciples of Isaiah who lived in the days immediately after the return from Babylon. Isaiah 44:21–28 envisions Israel as a people "formed" by YHWH (44:21, 24), whom YHWH redeemed from exile (44:22, 23, 24), with benefits for Judah and Jerusalem (44:26) under Cyrus, whom the text claims will commission the rebuilding of Jerusalem and refounding of the Temple (44:28).[19] As Zech 11:12–14 repurposes these images, the scribes want the audience to see that the metalworker symbolizes, not YHWH the artisan who creates the world, but YHWH the artisan who created the union between Judah and Northern Israel.

This episode, like the previous one, reinforces to the audience the reversal of the visions recorded in Isaiah. In this case, the

---

[17] Ibid., 745.
[18] Othmar Keel and Silvia Schroer, *Creation: Biblical Theologies in the Context of the Ancient Near East*, trans. Peter T. Daniels (Winona Lake, IN: Eisenbrauns, 2015), 96–97.
[19] See Foster, "Shepherds, Sticks, and Social Destabilization," 751–752.

dramatic action of breaking the staff "Ties" breaks the family bond (brotherhood) between Israel and Judah (Zech 11:14). Envisioning Israel and Judah as brothers draws on the metaphorical concept of the "house of the father," the *bêt 'āb*. The *bêt 'āb* is the basic household structure of a man, woman, and two or three surviving children, with a larger household structure including a married son and wife with a couple of children, and perhaps a servant or two.[20] Breaking the staff "Ties," then, does not simply disrupt the relationship between Judah and Israel but signifies a disruption in the household of YHWH. The implications are even broader than the dissolution of the household of YHWH, as the household was also the basic economic structure of ancient Israel's economy, the "domestic mode of production" in agriculture and/or animal husbandry.[21] Breaking the family bond between Judah and Israel, then, also implies a threat to production and to land possession, calling to mind stories like the division between Isaac and Ishmael and the threat to Ishmael and Hagar after being thrust out of Abraham and Sarah's household (Gen 21:8–20) or the threat to Jacob fleeing Esau after Jacob stole the blessing of the firstborn (Gen 27).

This representation of a prophetic drama introduces a second story demonstrating the editors' belief that the audience needed to

---

[20] Adams, *Social and Economic Life in Second Temple Judaism*, 10–15; John J. Collins, "Marriage, Divorce, and Family in Second Temple Judaism," in Leo G. Perdue et al., *Families in Ancient Israel* (Louisville, KY: Westminster John Knox Press, 1997), 105–106; William G. Dever, *The Lives of Ordinary People in Israel: Where Archaeology and the Bible Intersect* (Grand Rapids: Eerdmans, 2012), 151.

[21] Adams, *Social and Economic Life*, 19; Joseph Blenkinsopp, "The Family in First Temple Israel," in Perdue et al., *Families in Ancient Israel* 53–57; Dever, *The Lives of Ordinary People*, 156–178, 237.

hear something more than a prophetic word. The power of the drama again includes overturning the words of earlier prophets, both of the immediately previous oracles in the Book of Zechariah (chs. 9–10) and also the oracles from the disciples of Isaiah (44:21–28). This drama's allusion to Isaiah 44, however, highlights both the call of YHWH for the people to return (Isa 44:22; see Zech 1:1–6) and also the long-standing promise to rebuild Jerusalem and the Temple since the time of Cyrus (Isa 44:28). The prophetic drama proclaims a truth that the editors believe needs expression.[22] YHWH exercises the power of the father in the *bêt 'āb*, just as Abraham did when he sent Hagar and Ishmael away and just as Isaac did in blessing Jacob and claiming to be unable to offer that same blessing to Esau. Thus, the narrative reminds the audience that the descendants of Northern Israel and Judah have acted like recalcitrant children, constantly refusing to honor the instructions of their father YHWH through the prophets for a long time. So, YHWH exercises the right of the father and disrupts the familial bond, placing both the descendants of Northern Israel and Judah at economic risk, an ironic outcome in an economy already clearly divided between haves and have nots.

A WOEFUL END

As the editors bring this narrative to a close, they add one last, brief story in which they refuse the audience any of the hope that was sounded throughout the previous ten chapters. The moment reflected in 11:4–17 is for the editors a point of *no return* after generations of prophetic calls *to return*, accompanied by promises of future glory, were steadfastly refused.

---

[22] Stacey, *Prophetic Drama in the Old Testament*, 277.

In the narrative, YHWH addresses the prophet one last time, telling him to take up the implements of a worthless shepherd (11:15). What likely surprised the audience was the explanation that YHWH intended to raise up a worthless shepherd over the people (11:16), whereas previous prophets declared YHWH's intent to rescue the people from such scoundrels (Jer 23:1–4; Ezek 34:1–10). The description of the shepherd's worthlessness is nearly farcical, except that it portends more suffering for the people: "those being destroyed he will not care for; the young he will not seek; the ones being broken he will not heal; those being set apart he will not feed; and the fatty flesh he will eat and their hooves rip off." This future shepherd basically violates every standard expectation an owner might have of a sheepherder.[23]

As the editors of the Book of Zechariah see it, the people's generational refusal to listen to YHWH's prophets leads YHWH to this fatal choice to facilitate the demise of Yehud, however temporary. If the people could not see that YHWH removed poor shepherds for their good and, instead, they became frustrated with the continued presence of YHWH's prophets calling for justice, then they reap the consequences of their own refusals. Maybe this final narrative tells the audience that it is better to get this over with than to allow the inhumane system to go on for another generation. And so YHWH cries out,

> Woe to the worthless shepherd forsaking the flock!
> A sword upon his arm and upon his right eye.

---

[23] See the list and discussion of protocols for owners and herders based on documents from Larsa and Nuzi in Victor H. Matthews and Don C. Benjamin, *Social World of Ancient Israel 1250–587 BCE* (Peabody, MA: Hendrickson Publishers, 1993), 55–58.

> May his arm be completely withered and his right eye
> completely dimmed. (Zech 11:17)

The prophet's cry of "woe" expresses both a warning to the final, worthless shepherd and YHWH's grief as things have finally come to this.[24] YHWH simply cannot find a shepherd who will lead the people to YHWH but only those who seek their own gain (10:1-3; 11:4-5). In spite of all that God wills, and all the prophets' exhortations across generations, the land still lacks a shepherd who cares for the people as God desires. And so YHWH cries "woe" for Israel, but also "woe is God," who is forced to choose this dark path.

Nevertheless, YHWH still exercises some control, not only by appointing a worthless shepherd to end this miserable era but also by inflicting punishment upon this shepherd. Though YHWH appoints this final governor for this purpose, YHWH holds them accountable for their actions. The pain and harm that the shepherd causes others, both by failing to care for hurt sheep and by actively harming them, YHWH will now inflict on the body of the shepherd (i.e., governor).[25] The woe of YHWH indicates that YHWH truly wishes that he could find a good shepherd to set things right in Yehud. But just because YHWH could make no other choice does not mean that the shepherd will go unpunished. After all, YHWH is still the Great King and though the governor

---

[24] For the idea that "woe" expresses both judgment and grief see Waldemar Janzen, *Mourning Cry and Woe Oracle* (BZAW 125; Walter de Gruyter, 1972); Terence E. Fretheim, *The Suffering of God: An Old Testament Perspective* (OBT; Philadelphia: Fortress Press, 1984), 135-136.

[25] See Robert L. Foster, "An Exegesis of the Sign-Act Narrative of Zechariah 11:4-17 and Its Theological and Pastoral Implications" (MA thesis, Abilene Christian University, 2000), 59-60.

will predictably fail, YHWH will not fail to punish the governor for falling well short of the justice demanded by the Great King.

BIBLICAL THEOLOGY AND THEOLOGICAL ETHICS

This section of the book does not provide us much in the way of positive examples of YHWH's virtue or action and lays out no commands or ideals for the people. Nevertheless, we can take the negations in the text and easily infer a positive ethic.

Divine Motivation

One "positive" insight we might take away from this text is the grief that YHWH expresses over the failure of leadership in Yehud that leads to the appointment of a final, worthless shepherd that guarantees more suffering for the people. The final woe expresses a deep sorrow, knowing that God acted across generations to make things better, only to see God's will rejected across those generations. Additionally, the text implies that the Great King enacts just judgment against shepherds who fail to do what pleases God. This judgment on the shepherds, including the final shepherd, the elite, and the people who reject God's prophets does not come after one failure but because of continuous failure. If God continued to let the community persist in economic inequality and allowed the leaders to continue to exploit the poor, this would constitute a failure on God's part who, as the Great King, must exercise justice and just judgment.

The staffs themselves also exemplify a positive ethic of action on God's part. On the one hand, God shows "favor" to the people by negotiating a covenant with the nations so that the exiles may return to their homeland. God knows the sufferings the people experienced in exile and decides to show them favor and bring their time of punishment to an end. On the other hand, God is a Great Artisan who creates "ties" between Judah and Northern Israel. This unity is also exemplified in the idea of God procreating this unity, giving birth to two children who dwell in the *bêt 'āb*, with the intention that they share together in the blessing of their father.

Divine Command

In Zech 11:4–17, the examples of human action are totally negative, though their positive restatement provides a clear and better ethic. The basic failure of the shepherds across the generations is their lack of pity for the sheep. What God desires is for governors who are moved by the people's suffering and so spare the people from hardships like debt-slavery. The fact that some people sell their fellow Yehudites into debt-slavery and others buy them offends God. God desires, instead, that the people treat one another as humans, not as commodities. The final woe-oracle enumerates a variety of things that the governors ought to do for the people: attend to the lost, seek those who stray, heal the broken, and feed those who are exhausted.[26] The shepherds/governors ought to do what one normally expects of any hired shepherd: to help the sheep get well when they come to harm of any kind.

Prophetic Witness

One potential way this text helps communities of faith is to encourage the dramatic presentation of injustice. When African Americans in the Civil Rights Movement sat in at lunch counters and walked arm-in-arm in cities across the southern United States, they

---

[26] On one possible meaning of *nṣb* as "those who are miserable, exhausted," see *HALOT* 1:715.

sought to dramatize their experience of a broken system and to reveal their humanity to white people. The dramatic actions at that time, which differed from those done by Jeremiah and Ezekiel and the prophet in the Zechariah tradition, encourage communities of faith to continue to find new and striking ways to dramatize long-standing injustices when words seem to fail.

Following God's example, it would also be a powerful witness to the world if communities of faith were known as "artisans of community." The world continues to experience division while faith communities are called into the ministry of reconciliation. As we think of reconciliation in light the Book of Zechariah's trajectory, we recognize that seeking reconciliation without seeking justice will never do. If we want to see right relations in divided communities, then the church will have to work to ensure things are set right when communities have been harmed.

Finally, an important part of the church's witness is to publicly grieve over the brokenness of the world that persists across generations: the harm to black bodies from slavery to police shootings, the persistence of sexism and violence against women since what appears to be the beginning of human relationships, the exploitation of lands by imperialists that has fostered an inordinate amount of poverty in these same countries hundreds of years later, and so on. If anyone should be able to look out over a broken world and grieve, certainly it should be the people who see that God grieves over this same brokenness and that admits, as Miguel De La Torre has reminded us, that even our best efforts often will not fix generational brokenness.[27]

---

[27] Miguel A. De La Torre, *Embracing Hopelessness* (Minneapolis: Fortress Press, 2017).

CHAPTER 8

On That Day

As the narrative in Zech 11:4–17 ends, YHWH hands the people and land over to a worthless shepherd, and the book turns toward the future. The phrase "in that day" (*bayyôm hahû'*) occurs only five times in Zechariah 1–11 but seventeen times in Zechariah 12–14. In the overall argument of the book, the promises and visions of 1:1–11:3 seemed always just on the horizon, if only the people would return to YHWH. But the governors, elites, and the peoples consistently refused to obey the prophet's call across generations. So the final oracles look toward "that day," in the future, when YHWH will act decisively to finally renew Yehud and Jerusalem as YHWH intended all along.

But the break that occurs in 11:4–17 leads, in the short term, to a series of oracles about a diminished future. While this section names Israel as it begins (12:1), the rest of the section defines Israel solely in terms of Yehud and Jerusalem. The relationship between Northern Israel and Judah is broken and the Father, YHWH, elected one son and apparently sent the other away. Meanwhile, as the oracles unfold concerning "that day," Yehud and Jerusalem will face the struggles that chapters 9 and 10 said the people feared. Nations war against Yehud and Jerusalem and, though there are initial promises of salvation (12:6–9), this will not end war. Instead the people will experience defeat and suffering like nothing since the Babylonians overthrew Judah and Jerusalem (13:6). Only after purification – and more war – will Jerusalem finally dwell securely (14:11).

So the book introduces one last "burden" (*maśśā*'; 12:1), words that weigh down the prophet and the people with images of war, violence, and weeping. But someday, in *that* day, YHWH will relieve the people's burdens. There is no command to return to YHWH, to do justice, to hope in YHWH. It is as if the editors of the Book of Zechariah simply wanted to make one more declaration on YHWH's behalf, telling the people what YHWH intends to do in the future, with or without the people's cooperation.

YHWH CREATES

Apparently the scribes who produced the Book of Zechariah wanted the audience to take this final collection of oracles with utmost seriousness. They signal this by the piling up of introductory formulae: "A burden, a word of YHWH against Israel, a declaration of YHWH" (12:1a). While the *maśśā*' marks the burden that the implied prophet carries, the "word of YHWH unto . . ." likely marks the prophet as the messenger of the Great King whose authoritative message should not be taken lightly.[1] The addition of "a declaration of YHWH" (*nə'um yhwh*) marks what follows as direct speech, quoting YHWH.[2] Whatever the audience thought of the previous material, the editors want them

---

[1] Samuel A. Meier, *Speaking of Speaking: Marking Direct Discourse in the Hebrew Bible* (VTSup 46; Leiden: E.J. Brill, 1992), 315, 318.
[2] Ibid., 305. This is the only time in the Book of Zechariah that "a declaration of YHWH" functions as part of an opening formula.

to understand that the following words truly come from YHWH's mouth, a burden carried faithfully by the messenger.

Perhaps the editors placed such emphasis on the following words truly coming from YHWH because much of what they contain speaks *against* Israel. The formula "the word of YHWH against [ʿal] Israel" deviates from the regular formula "the word of YHWH unto [ʾel] . . ."[3] Zechariah 1–10 calls the audience to repent of injustice and to seek YHWH's beneficence in the cult, basing their demands on visions of YHWH fighting for Yehud (and Northern Israel) and YHWH's promises to protect them from war. But 11:4–17 offered a dramatic turn in the book so that now the audience understands that, though YHWH will fight on Jerusalem and Judah's behalf "in that day," that day also includes times when YHWH fights *against* them (13:8; 14:2). YHWH will purify the House of David and Jerusalem (13:1), refining them so that those who emerge from the fire are truly devoted to YHWH (13:2, 9) and so the city is truly "Holy to YHWH" (14:20–21). The scribes seek to persuade the people that these visions of violent purification are also the word of YHWH, in fact, direct quotation from the divine.

The scribes add another descriptor of God before finally reporting the actual "declaration of YHWH," which starts in 12:2. It is a description and declaration of YHWH who is "Stretching out the heavens and founding the earth and forming the spirit of humans in their inward parts" (12:1b). This short line presents diverse images of creation in a compact space. YHWH stretches

---

[3] "Unto . . .," with ʾel, is the expected formula; see ibid., 314; also Martti Nissinen, *Ancient Prophecy: Near Eastern, Biblical, and Greek Perspectives* (Oxford: Oxford University Press, 2017), 28n105.

out the heavens like a tent that covers the earth.[4] YHWH founds the earth as if building a great fortress in which animals and humans dwell.[5] And YHWH forms the spirit of human beings like a sculptor forms a sculpture.[6] The God speaking through the prophet is none other than YHWH, who performs basic acts of creation that make YHWH worthy of hearing.

This theological assertion that YHWH is worthy of attention as the God of creation is not framed in terms of YHWH's past creation but in terms of God presently creating, as each verb is a present participle. YHWH is stretching out the heavens and founding the earth and forming the breath of humans in their inward parts. A theological tension emerges here as YHWH speaks "against" Israel and yet is creating, in the present, the heavens and the earth and the life of human beings. Perhaps the scribes who framed the declaration of YHWH in this way wanted to give the book's audience a note of hope after so many words of devastation in 11:4–17[7] and the prophecies that follow 12:1. The era that began under Cyrus has ended but the audience should not despair. The God who addresses them is also *creating* and, if the audience responds faithfully to the call to return (1:1–6), they may participate in the community purged by fire, who take YHWH as

---

[4] For *nṭh* as "stretching out, pitching" a tent see, e.g., Gen. 12:8; 26:25; 33:19; 35:21. In one of the more complex images of the world in the ancient Near East, the Egyptian goddess Nut bends protectively over the earth with her body bearing the tent of the stars and sun disk and its rise, zenith, and setting; see Othmar Keel and Silvia Schroer, *Creation: Biblical Theologies in the Context of the Ancient Near East*, trans. Peter T. Daniels (Winona Lake, IN: Eisenbrauns, 2015), 80.
[5] See the image from Mesopotamia and discussion in ibid., 81–82, fig. 84.
[6] Ibid., 94–96.
[7] See the list in Robert L. Foster, "Shepherds, Sticks, and Social Destabilization: A Fresh Look at Zechariah 11:4–17," *JBL* **126** (2007): 752.

their God (13:8) and so experience a New Creation in that day, *their* day.

SALVATION AND PURIFICATIONS

The actual "declaration of YHWH" comes in the form of two collections of prophecies, each marked by an introductory *hinnēh*, "Behold" (12:1, 14:1). The first collection contains four units – 12:1–9; 12:10–14; 13:1–6; 13:7–9 – developing several themes, even as the editors present them as a single "word" from YHWH.

Much like 9:1–11:3, this "burden" begins well enough. Though enemies come against Jerusalem and Judah, YHWH promises to save (12:7). The rhetoric of the series of declarations reinforces the claim that this is direct discourse from YHWH as YHWH initiates the action: "*I* will place Jerusalem as a bowl of reeling" (12:2). "*I* will place Jerusalem as a burdensome stone" (12:3). "*I* will strike every horse and charioteer" (12:4). "*I* will place the clans of Judah as a fiery brazier and as a fiery torch" (12:6). "*I* will seek to destroy all the nations that come against Jerusalem" (12:9). The actions of YHWH save and shield Judah and Jerusalem but also have baleful effects upon the nations that attack them (12:7–8). Nations will reel as if drunk with wine, a symbol of the shame the nations will experience in their defeat (12:2).[8] The nations will injure themselves on the burdensome stone of Judah (12:3). Horses and charioteers will panic (12:4) and the people besieging Jerusalem will be devoured as when someone lights a field with a torch (12:6).

---

[8] Philip King and Lawrence Stager, *Life in Biblical Israel* (Louisville, KY: Westminster John Knox Press, 2001), 102, remark on the fact that drunkenness was considered disgraceful in the Bible.

And, as noted already, YHWH intends to destroy all the nations that come against Jerusalem (12:9).

The overall claim of 12:1–9 is that YHWH promises to act violently, destructively against the nations that attack Jerusalem. In a way, the opening of this section reverses all the promises YHWH made to act violently and destructively against the people of Yehud and their final, worthless governor in 11:4–17. Perhaps we should not see the promises in 12:1–9 as a change of mind on YHWH's part but, rather, as YHWH acting in a future time – "on that day" – to punish the nations who have harmed Jerusalem and Yehud, as YHWH promised to do in 1:18–21. YHWH ends an era begun in the days of Cyrus but will not prolong the people's suffering. Instead, YHWH will save and shield them. Still, in terms of the way the theological discourse propels the rhetorical argument, it may be that the editors of the book found it necessary to open with this positive vision of YHWH fighting on behalf of Jerusalem and Yehud in order to draw the audience past the distressing visions of 11:4–17, in an effort to move the audience to fulfill the call to return to YHWH.

According to 12:5, YHWH's actions on behalf of Jerusalem will finally lead the people to return to YHWH because in that day, "the leaders of Judah will say in their hearts, 'Those dwelling in Jerusalem are a strength to me by YHWH Sabaoth their God.'" Admittedly, this line's meaning is not totally clear but it seems that the verse promises that the inhabitants of Jerusalem will clearly claim YHWH as their God (see also 13:2, 8). Thus, the future will reverse the failure to seek YHWH reported in 10:1–3. This in turn will cause the leaders in the rest of Yehud to find strength in the way the inhabitants of Jerusalem trust in YHWH so that "Judah" will catch fire and come to the city's defense (12:6). YHWH's actions will finally transform Jerusalem and Yehud, producing unmistakable devotion to YHWH.

Yet YHWH will grant victory in battle in a certain order, with YHWH saving the tents of Judah first, ensuring that the House of David and those dwelling in Jerusalem are not too greatly honored (12:7). Also for the first time in the Book of Zechariah the audience encounters the name of David, though the description is not of a future David but the future of the house of David. If the genealogy in Matthew 1 is trustworthy, then we know – and presumably the original audience of the Book of Zechariah also knew – that the book introduced an eminent Davidide once before in Zerubbabel son of Shealtiel. But the book never discusses Zerubbabel as David's descendant, perhaps because Zerubbabel never carried out a messianic mission, in spite of the fact that the prophet referred to Zerubbabel as "the Branch." Zerubbabel was apparently as unsuccessful in getting the people to obey YHWH's call to do justice and to seek YHWH as any subsequent governor. But, 12:7–9 promises that "in that day," YHWH will cause the House of David to rise again. And, even though this passage claims that YHWH does not want the House of David to receive honor too much greater than the tents of Judah, in the end YHWH promises that the House of David will be so great that the descendants of David will seem like gods,[9] like the angels of YHWH. The fact that the oracle sees the House of David as angels intimates that they will serve a reliable source for understanding the will of YHWH, just like the angels.

---

[9] Or "like God" (so NRSV); Hebrew *ʾĕlōhîm*.

A Spirit of Favor

Even though YHWH will grant salvation to Judah and Jerusalem over all the nations that besiege the city, the narrative does not go on to talk about the city or people rejoicing in their victory. Instead, YHWH makes a declaration that would likely stun the original audience. YHWH will pour out upon the House of David and those dwelling in Jerusalem "a spirit of favor and supplications" so that they mourn to YHWH about those they have pierced, lamenting and grieving over them like they would the loss of their only son or their firstborn (12:10).

Noticeably absent from 12:1–9 is any language labelling the nations as enemies or evil or wicked, though the people would understandably see them as such. Perhaps this opening section lacks enemy language because YHWH does not want the people to view these nations as enemies but as an only son or their firstborn. YHWH, who forms the spirit (*rûaḥ*) within human beings (12:1), will pour out upon the people a spirit (*rûaḥ*) of favor and supplications so that the people mourn over the nations. Favor here refers to the way that people find approval in the eyes of someone with whom there is, or is the potential for, tension, like Jacob seeking the favor of Esau (Gen 35:10) or Ruth finding favor in the eyes of Boaz (Ruth 2:2, 10) or Esther finding favor in the sight of the king (Esth 5:2). And the supplications that the people will raise echo the way Solomon imagined that people would supplicate YHWH at the Temple (1 Chr 6:21) and the way Daniel offered supplications with fasting, sackcloth, and ashes in a spirit of repentance for the wickedness of the people of Israel (Dan 9:3, 17, 18). The people's mourning and lamenting as if for their firstborn or only child conjures up images of Jacob weeping over the presumed death of Joseph (Gen 37:34–35) or

David fasting and weeping for his firstborn son, appealing to YHWH to save the baby from death (2 Sam 12:15–23).

The people weeping over their fallen enemy echoes the idea in the wisdom literature that one should not celebrate the fall of one's enemy because this would displease God (Prov 24:17; Job 31:29). In Zech 12:10–14, YHWH intervenes and ensures the people will not gloat in their victory but seek YHWH for those who came against Jerusalem. After all, YHWH is a God who continues to create life (12:1). YHWH pours out this spirit of favor and supplications upon the House of David and inhabitants of Judah for them to share in God's perspective as creator and ruler of all nations and who mourns the death of all peoples. This spirit will pervade all the peoples associated with Jerusalem: the houses of David and Nathan and Levi and Shem, man and woman, each and every clan, as each laments the harm inflicted on the nations (12:12–14).

This vision for the way YHWH draws the people into YHWH's care for the nations resonates with visions earlier in the book where YHWH facilitates nations joining themselves to YHWH and the people of YHWH (Zech 2:15; 9:7). This vision of former enemies joining themselves to YHWH and worshiping will emerge one more time in chapter 14. For now the editors of the book turn to the further transformative work that YHWH, who continues to create, intends to do.

Opening a Fountain

Zechariah 13:1–6 begins with an image of a fountain that opens to the House of David and the people of Jerusalem for their sins and impurities (13:1). The particular sins and impurities that the text narrates are idolatry and false prophecy (13:2), though prophecy receives the most attention in this passage. The opposition of a fountain and idolatry occurs in one other passage in the Old Testament, in Jeremiah 2, where YHWH accuses the people of Judah and Jerusalem of abandoning YHWH, "the fountain of living water," for broken cisterns, that is, idols (Jer 2:11–13). The contrast in the Book of Jeremiah between a living, constantly flowing source of water and the failure of cisterns, which stored water to help communities make it through the long, dry season in Israel, helps us understand the implications of the metaphor in Zech 13:1. Rather than the fountain cleansing the people of sins and impurities, the metaphor implies that sins and impurities leave the people in a life-threatening situation, like people without water in a parched land.[10] YHWH promises that in the future a fountain will open for the people, a fountain that will help them live or, as stated at the end of this chapter, help the people respond to YHWH's declaration "You are my people" with the affirmation "YHWH is our God" (13:9).

The first thing that will happen when the fountain opens is that YHWH will cut off the names of the "idols" (*ăṣabbîm*) from the land and they will not be remembered again (13:2). The word *ăṣabbîm* refers to images associated with particular gods, like the statues of the Ashtaroth in her temple in Philistia (1 Sam 31:10). As will become apparent momentarily, the fact that the text does not explicitly refer to other gods, combined with the lack of statues of other gods in the lands of Judah and Samaria in the archaeological record of the Persian period, cautions us against assuming that the images and names YHWH will make the people forget are the

---

[10] See Ferdinand E. Deist, *The Material Culture of the Bible: An Introduction* (ed. Robert P. Carroll; BS 70; Sheffield: Sheffield Academic Press, 2000), 127, on the way that fountains provide an important source of water in the dry season or seasons of drought.

names of foreign gods. Rather, it may be that YHWH wants families and communities to rid themselves of statues devoted to YHWH with local names and devote themselves solely to "YHWH Sabaoth" (13:2), the name of their God who brought the hosts of Israel out of Egypt.[11]

The possibility that this prophecy is concerned with worship of YHWH under other names, likely within households and not at the Temple, finds some support in the second outcome of a metaphorical fountain opening for the House of David and those dwelling in Judah. YHWH promises to drive out prophets and "the spirit of this uncleanness" from the land (13:2b), just as Asa drove out the male "consecrated workers"[12] and associated images that his ancestors had made (1 Kgs 15:12). Even though the parents of anyone who prophesies in the future will accuse them of prophesying "falsehood" (Zech 13:3), this accusation is rather non-descript.[13] The passage's more concrete descriptions of these prophets – their hairy mantles and their bodies' wounds – indicate a rather extreme form of prophetic divination.[14] The response

---

[11] See the discussion on the way gods could be known by different names based on the location of their shrines, in addition to the way devotees might call deities by a particular epithet to appeal to a particular characteristic of the god, in Michael B. Hundley, *Gods in Dwellings: Temples and Divine Presence in the Ancient Near East* (SBLWAW 3; Atlanta, GA: Society of Biblical Literature, 2013), 368–369.

[12] This translation follows CEB. Scholars often connect qədēšîm with cult prostitutes but nothing in the text indicates that this is the concern. Rather, it seems best to simply take these as people set apart for the deity; see Volkmar Fritz, *1 & 2 Kings: A Continental Commentary*, trans. Anselm Hagerdorn (CC; Minneapolis, MN: Fortress Press, 2003), 161.

[13] Martti Nissinen, "The Dubious Image of Prophecy," in *Prophecy, Prophets, and Prophetic Texts in Second Temple Judaism* (ed. Michael Floyd and Robert D. Haak; LHBOTS 427; New York: T&T Clark, 2006), 36.

[14] Ibid., 37–38.

in the text by the mothers and fathers of those who dare to prophesy in that day is also extreme: they will pierce (*dqr*) their own children, just as enemies of Jerusalem were pierced in battle (13:3; see 12:10).

The opening of this utterance affirmed that YHWH is forming the "spirit" (*rûaḥ*) of humans inside of them (12:1). But YHWH also intends to rid the land of the spirit (*rûaḥ*) of "this uncleanness" (13:2). "This uncleanness" does not seem to refer to false prophecy but rather, simply, prophecy itself as represented in these extreme forms of divination.[15] The problem seems to be that this standard form of divination yielded truth in terms of judgment; the people of YHWH often suffered the kinds of afflictions the prophets predicted. However, the positive predictions of a good future in returning to the land, like those offered in Zechariah 1:7–6:15 or Isaiah 40–55 (or Jer 29–33) often turned out to be "falsehoods," which the Book of Zechariah is at pains to make clear is not YHWH's fault. This oracle, then, signals a new time moving forward that relies more on the interpretation of earlier prophetic materials (Zech 1:1–6; 7:7–14) and not on the word of ecstatic prophets. The theological vision here is that the fountain that YHWH opens for the people will be the scribal traditions that faithfully interpret the prophets because the ecstatic prophets' "falsehoods" and "spirit of uncleanness" leave the people at risk in a land suffering metaphorical drought.[16]

This faithful interpretation of the earlier prophets will also nurture the tradition of honoring YHWH as YHWH Sabaoth.

---

[15] Ibid., 41.

[16] In my judgment, the consistent failure of the prophecies of weal in Isaiah, Jeremiah, Ezekiel, Haggai, Zechariah, et al. to come to pass is what contributed to the development of apocalyptic literature in Second Temple Judaism.

It is noteworthy that 30 percent of the references to YHWH Sabaoth appear in the prophetic books that end the Old Testament (Haggai, Zechariah, Malachi), while another 52 percent appear in the Books of Isaiah and Jeremiah. Meanwhile, Ezekiel has no references to YHWH Sabaoth. As a potential corollary, the Book of Haggai never uses ’ĕlōhîm to refer to YHWH; the Book of Zechariah uses it only one time; while Malachi uses ’ĕlōhîm on five occasions as a designation of YHWH. The point is that, just as YHWH Sabaoth opens a fountain to nourish the people via scribal interpretation of earlier prophets, it appears that the scribes of the Book of Zechariah see this interpretation emphasizing the identity of their God as "YHWH Sabaoth," YHWH who led the "hosts" of Israel out of Egypt. Other names associated with images of YHWH (or ’ĕlōhîm) will be forgotten as the scribes draw on the tradition emphasized in Isaiah and Jeremiah and not so much the tradition of Ezekiel.

A People Refined

Zechariah 13:7–9 draws the opening portion of this final word/declaration of YHWH to a close by bringing the audience back to YHWH's judgment against the shepherds/governors of Yehud. The book's editors remind the audience that, though "in that day" the people will gain victory over their enemies (12:1–9) and mourn them (12:10–14), and that YHWH will open a fountain that nourishes the life of the people (13:1–6), this all comes later, after YHWH executes judgment against the final shepherd of Israel (11:15–17). The fact that the editors do not utilize the phrase "in that day" in this final section signals to the audience that the horizon of this final oracle is the present, not the future.

The return to the sheep/shepherd metaphorical concept reminds the people that the path to salvation, where YHWH shields Jerusalem from their enemies, passes through a valley of trouble. If someone comes and kills the shepherd, the sheep scatter (13:7). When YHWH turns against the "leading man" in Yehud, YHWH will also turn against the "least persons" in the land.[17] This will have devastating effects as two-thirds of the people will die, while one-third remains (13:8). The language of "thirds" echoes Ezekiel 5 where the prophet warns that one-third of the inhabitants of Jerusalem will die by famine and pestilence, one-third by the sword, and one-third will be scattered (Ezek 5:2, 12). Thus, Zech 13:7–8 evokes an exilic image with sheep scattering and two-thirds dying with only a third remaining. The reversal of fortune from the visions in Zech 1:7–6:15 is nearly complete. The people's failure to return to YHWH will lead to a time horrifyingly reminiscent of the Babylonian exile.

What little hope this prophecy introduces is signaled in the final phrase of 13:8 "and one-third will remain in it," that is, in the city of Jerusalem. But even those that remain in Jerusalem YHWH will refine like silver and test like gold (13:9a). In the refining process in the ancient Near East the smelter put metals into a melting pot, placing the pot into a furnace, and removing the liquid dross that rose to the top as it melted. High-quality metals required the repetition of the process several times.[18] Gold and silver, the most precious metals in the ancient Levant, would

---

[17] Hebrew *geber* can simply refer to an older man, someone who is fully mature (see 1 Chr 23:3). 1 Chronicles refers on a couple occasions to the *ro'šê haggəbārîm*, "the chief men" among the priestly descendants (24:4) and gatekeepers (26:12). In Zech 13:7, the anarthrous "man" paralleling "shepherd," in contrast to the "sheep" – that is, the "least" or "smallest" (*haṣṣō'ărîm*) – leads me to see *geber* there as designating the shepherd's position as the "leading man" (governor) in Yehud.

[18] Deist, *Material Culture of the Bible*, 211.

undergo this kind of repetitive refinement as people used these metals to make precious items.[19] YHWH wants a purified people, a people who will respond to YHWH's claim "This is my people" by saying "YHWH, our God" (13:9b).

As the scribes who wrote the Book of Zechariah see it, even after YHWH deposed of several worthless shepherds/governors (11:4–6), the people still did not respond to the message of YHWH through the prophets (11:8), and did not seek YHWH as the source of their life (10:1–2; 13:9). YHWH who creates the human spirit within them will create a spirit within YHWH Sabaoth's own people, though shaping the people as a Great Artisan will take a particular form, as a metallurgist who refines the precious metals to make them malleable to form, in this case, into the people of YHWH.

This, then, is the great "burden" of the prophet: to proclaim to the people that this is truly a word of YHWH, a declaration that comes from YHWH's mouth (12:1). Even though YHWH is, in the end, for the people, the declaration recorded in 13:1–9 still speaks against a narrowly defined Israel, portending both potential death for would-be prophets at the hands of their own parents for giving the people false hopes and a much greater violence that will decimate the population of Jerusalem and Yehud. The theological problem of the Book of Zechariah is that YHWH wanted the people to return (1:1–6) and gave the people a variety of promises to motivate them to return (1:7–6:15; 9:1–11:3). But not only did the leadership fail them, the people grew impatient with the prophets (11:4–7). And so, YHWH must work to bring a people back in

---

[19] For a discussion of the valuation of gold and silver, see King and Stager, *Life in Biblical Israel*, 169–176.

order for them to honor YHWH as YHWH Sabaoth, and become people who heed the faithful interpretation of the former prophets to do justice in the land and call on YHWH as their God. Tragically, to make this happen requires that YHWH refine the people in fire. The editors of the Book of Zechariah work to make it clear that this is the way it *had* to be, not the way it was *supposed* to be.

YHWH SABAOTH, GREAT KING OVER ALL THE EARTH

Prophets speak as intermediaries. This simple fact reminds us that the editors who shaped the Book of Zechariah, like the scribal groups editing other prophetic books, considered YHWH as the major subject in their book. What the editors were doing in the Book of Zechariah was presenting the words of the prophet in order to persuade their audience not only to return to YHWH Sabaoth but also to convince them that the whole presentation was, in the end, "the word of YHWH, a declaration of YHWH" (12:1).

The corollary to the belief that YHWH wants to address the people in Jerusalem and Yehud during the Persian period is that YHWH is an agent in history. The editors of the book mark this idea of YHWH-as-agent in a fairly unique way as they open the final series of messages from YHWH to the people: "Behold, a day is coming for YHWH and your spoil shall be divided in your midst" (Zech 14:1).

As already mentioned, the Book of Zechariah makes a turn in chapter 11, dramatically demonstrating that the days of hope for rebuilding Jerusalem and peaceful relations with Yehud's neighbors, inaugurated in the days of Cyrus, have ended. But as the editors draw the book to a close, the final oracle tells the audience that the end of an era does not mean that YHWH quits acting in history for Israel. A day is coming "for" (lə-) YHWH, temporally,[20] which will result in the citizens of Jerusalem dividing their spoils in their midst. Things have changed for now but a day will come when YHWH will act in history for Jerusalem (and Yehud), giving them victory over their enemies as they divide the victor's spoils amongst themselves, much as Joshua encouraged the half-tribe of Manasseh to return home and divide the spoils of victory (Josh 22:8) and David shared the spoils of his victory over the Philistines with the cities who supported him and his men (1 Sam 30:26–31).

But the editors remind the audience that a war that will devastate the city must first take place (Zech 14:2; see 13:7–9). The words from YHWH that follow are disturbing: "*I* will gather unto Jerusalem all the nations for war" who will capture the city, plunder their homes, rape women, and take part of the city into exile (14:2a–b). Yet, as promised in 13:9, there will be others who remain in the city and these people (14:2c) who express their devotion to YHWH will experience the power of YHWH on their behalf.

On the day that is coming for YHWH, YHWH will go out and wage war against those nations as one does when a day of battle draws nigh (14:3). The editors again depict YHWH as the Great King who leads the army into battle, perhaps in contrast to some of the kings of Persia like Xerxes I, who had a reputation of cowardice among his adversaries and who, famously, never took

---

[20] For temporal use of the preposition lə-, see Bill T. Arnold and John H. Choi, *A Guide to Biblical Hebrew Syntax* (Cambridge: Cambridge University Press, 2003), 111.

part in combat in Persia's wars against the Greeks.[21] The reason that YHWH delays in fighting on behalf of Jerusalem is in order to purify the people (13:7-9), not because YHWH is afraid or unable to wage war.

On that day, when the battle draws nigh, YHWH will stand with his feet on the Mount of Olives, which will then split east and west, creating a great gorge (14:3). This theophanic image shows YHWH taking a position to do battle, similar to ancient Near Eastern images that show divine warriors planting their feet on the mountains.[22] The image signifies YHWH's greatness, reminiscent of Egyptian imagery of the king in battle, which presents the king's absolute superiority with the concomitant insignificance of the army.[23] This first image of YHWH standing ready on the day of battle contrasts strikingly with Xerxes in the middle of his armies in order to protect his life or Artaxerxes retiring to a nearby hill in the battle of Cunaxa.[24] Perhaps the image of YHWH's feet on the Mount of Olives, which splits in two, intends to evoke the image of the king ready to strike his opponents, as often seen in ancient Near Eastern iconography,[25] since that is what YHWH will soon do (14:12). Still, YHWH will bring an army of "holy ones,"

---

[21] Pierre Briant, *From Cyrus to Alexander: A History of the Persian Empire*, trans. Peter T. Daniels (Winona Lake, IN: Eisenbrauns, 2002), 227.

[22] Carol L. Meyers and Eric M. Meyers, *Zechariah 9–14* (AB 25C; New York: Doubleday, 1993), 419; Eric Nels Ortlund, *Theology and Chaoskampf: The Interpretation of Theophanic Imagery in the Baal Epic, Isaiah, and the Twelve* (GUS 5; Piscataway, NJ: Gorgias, 2010), 237.

[23] Othmar Keel, *Symbolism of the Biblical World: Ancient Near Eastern Iconography and the Book of Psalms*, trans. Timothy J. Hallet (Winona Lake, IN: Eisenbrauns, 1997), 291.

[24] Briant, *From Cyrus to Alexander*, 227.

[25] See the various images in Keel, *Symbolism of the Biblical World*, 293–296.

angelic armies, to be "with you," with those dwelling in Jerusalem, to fight on their behalf (14:5).[26]

This theophany contains dimensions of YHWH's goodness and reign that extend beyond the divine warrior. YHWH will also provide light so that there is no need for sunlight or moonlight because there is one continuous day (14:6–7). Light is often a way of communicating life in opposition to death.[27] Thus, this image of continuous day "which will be made known by YHWH" connotes to the audience that YHWH comes to give the residents of Jerusalem continuous life (see also 14:11).[28] Alongside the image of continuous light the oracle refers to fresh water flowing in Jerusalem, summer and winter, while all the surrounding countryside becomes like a desert (14:8, 10a). Here the editors invoke another image of the Great King as the Good Gardener, so that Jerusalem becomes a paradise fed by living waters, even in the face of unfavorable natural conditions.[29]

It is little wonder that "in that day" (14:4, 6, 8) YHWH will be acknowledged as king (14:9a). YHWH does what the Great King

---

[26] For "holy ones" as heavenly beings, see Ps 89:6, 8; Dan 8:13. I take the phrase 'immāk as locative, following Meyers and Meyers who link the feminine suffix with the feminine suffixes referencing Jerusalem in 14:1 (*Zechariah 9–14*, 431; see similarly Mark J. Boda, *The Book of Zechariah* [NICOT; Grand Rapids, MI: Eerdmans, 2016], 759–760; Marvin A. Sweeney, *The Twelve Prophets: Volume Two* [Berit Olam; Collegeville, MN: The Liturgical Press, 2000], 700). Cf. Petersen who follows the Greek, Syriac, and other Hebrew versions against the MT to read 'immô, "with him [i.e., YHWH]" (David L. Petersen, *Zechariah 9–14 and Malachi: A Commentary* [OTL; Louisville, KY: Westminster John Knox Press, 1995], 134, 136).

[27] Keel, *Symbolism of the Biblical World*, 186–188.

[28] I take the Niphal of yd' as stative and the preposition $lə$- as denoting in this case the agent by whom the knowledge of this continuous day is made known. See Arnold and Choi, *Guide to Biblical Hebrew Syntax*, 41 and 114.

[29] On the Great King as Good Gardener see Briant, *From Cyrus to Alexander*, 232–234.

should do: go out into battle, stand in absolute superiority above the fray, and provide life for the residents for Jerusalem, making their city a paradise. As the people of the whole earth come to recognize YHWH as the Great King, they will know YHWH to be one and YHWH's name to be one (14:9b). In light of 12:1–13:9, the one name by which the nations will know YHWH's name must refer to YHWH Sabaoth.[30] YHWH Sabaoth is the Great King over all the earth, who defeats nations in battle so that they will never again put Jerusalem to the ban (14:11).

Gary Knoppers has observed that invasion and dislocation were facts of life in the Southern Levant for at least 250 years: under the Assyrians with Tiglath-pileser III and then Shalmaneser V and Sargon II and, finally, Sennacherib. Under the Babylonians, the people of the Levant suffered further dislocation at the direction of Necho II and then Nebuchadnezzar in the exile in 586 BCE, followed by flight to Egypt just a few years later after a failed rebellion against the Babylonians.[31] The reports in Zech 9:1–8 point to a renewed fear of dislocation at the hands of the Persians or maybe the Egyptians or, possibly, Yehud's neighbors who find strength from Persian investment. But in that future day, when YHWH asserts himself on the Mount of Olives and establishes the one name of YHWH Sabaoth in the city (14:4, 11), "never again" will the names of the idols be remembered in the city of Jerusalem (13:2) and "never again" will destruction come upon the city.

YHWH will finally move against the nations that surround Jerusalem, promising to smite them with a plague (14:12), much

---

[30] See 14:16–17, where the nations come to the Temple to bow down before YHWH Sabaoth; see also the preceding discussion of Zech 13:1–6.
[31] Gary N. Knoppers, "Exile, Return, and Diaspora," in *Texts, Contexts, and Readings in Post-Exilic Literature* (Tübingen: Mohr Siebeck, 2011), 30–35.

like the story of YHWH promising via Elijah to strike Jehoram and his family with a plague, one that the Chronicler claimed had the gruesome effect of Jehoram's bowels spilling out of him (2 Chr 21:11–20). This last section of the Book of Zechariah promises a similarly gruesome effect on the nations that war against Jerusalem. The contrast in this final oracle is of YHWH, standing with his feet on the Mount of Olives, unassailable and ready for battle, and the peoples who surround Jerusalem standing on their feet but with bodies falling into decay, flesh rotting away, eyes falling out of their sockets, and their tongues dissolving in their mouths.[32]

Alongside this grisly image, the next line promises that the prodigious figure of YHWH will cause the people to panic and to kill one another (Zech 14:13). Again the text images YHWH in a way reminiscent of an Egyptian king, whose powerful presence causes people to panic and lie down before the king or flee in horror.[33]

Plagues and panic lead to plunder. Gold and silver and clothing in great abundance will be gathered to Jerusalem (14:14). Thus the plunder mentioned in 14:1 becomes more specific in 14:14. The God who continues to create will not only renew life in the city of Jerusalem but will also cause the city's enemies to devolve. The people and their war camps will fade away while Jerusalem becomes a paradise full of the wealth of the nations. Meanwhile,

---

[32] In all three of these examples of the people's flesh being corrupted or consumed, the verb is the same, *mqq*. I have chosen to translate the verb differently in this case to indicate both that the form differs (e.g., the first instance is in the Hiphil and the second in the Niphal) and to convey what kind of corruption/consumption it seems the editors wanted their audience to envisage.

[33] Keel, *Symbolism in the Biblical World*, 297–298, fig. 405 and discussion.

the remnant refined like gold and silver (13:9) will have gold and silver in abundance.

Though YHWH smites the nations with plague and causes them to turn against one another in panic, YHWH will not destroy them all. After the defeat of the nations, people from those nations will go up to Jerusalem to bow down before YHWH Sabaoth during the Festival of Booths (14:16). At last, the nations will acknowledge the "hidden secret" of YHWH as the Great King as they bow down to the King in Jerusalem. The combination of nations coming to Jerusalem, with their wealth, and bowing down before YHWH evokes the image of dignitaries bringing tribute to Darius and Xerxes in the Apadana reliefs at Persepolis.[34] The idea that those who come to Jerusalem come "from *all* the nations that came against Jerusalem" may convey the unbounded nature of YHWH's authority over populations and territories, similar to the inscriptions and reliefs that Darius I and Xerxes I produced.[35]

At the same time, the Festival of Booths is a festival of first fruits, which means that the gifts coming into Jerusalem will bring sustenance for the city's residents. The Festival of Booths originally marks a celebration of YHWH giving the people the Promised Land after they lived for years in tents in the wilderness. The focus on Egypt as one of the key peoples subject to YHWH (14:18–19), then, may serve two purposes. First, the Egyptians' presence hearkens back to Israel's slavery in Egypt, when YHWH originally

---

[34] See images and discussion in Donald N. Wilber, *Persepolis: The Archaeology of Parsa, the Seat of the Persian Kings* (rev. ed.; Princeton, NJ: The Darwin Press, Inc., 1989), 73–84; also Brent A. Strawn, "'A World under Control': Isaiah 60 and the Apadana Reliefs from Persepolis," in *Approaching Yehud: New Approaches to the Study of the Persian Period* (ed. Jon L. Berquist; Semeia Studies 50; Atlanta, GA: Scholars Press, 2007), 85–116.

[35] Briant, *From Cyrus to Alexander*, 177.

asserted authority among the nations by overcoming Pharaoh and his armies. Second, the promise that the Egyptians will bring tribute and bow before YHWH assures the book's audience that Yehud will no longer serve as the "middle territory" between Egypt and aggressors to the north. The wars between Persia and Egypt will cease and Jerusalem will finally serve as the center of world.

This leads ultimately to the transformation of the Temple. Even bells on horses and metal pots within the city will be inscribed "Holy to YHWH" (14:20). This phrase describes a variety of sacred items and persons in the Torah: engravings on the priestly implements (Exod 28:36; 39:30), the altar of incense (Exod 30:10), sacrifices (Lev 22:15; 23:20; 27:9), tithes (Lev 27:30, 32), and Nazirites (Num 6:5, 8). But as the people come to Jerusalem to the one YHWH whose one name is associated with this house, the House of YHWH Sabaoth (Zech 14:20, 21), even common things will be set apart especially to YHWH. This is the vision that the editors want the audience of the Book of Zechariah to embrace. They are to become a people who have returned to YHWH Sabaoth, the Great King of the hosts of Israel and all nations. Then, not only will these lesser things like horses and metal pots be devoted to YHWH Sabaoth, but the people of Yehud and the city of Jerusalem will be ready to respond to YHWH who calls them to return by saying, "YHWH is our God."

BIBLICAL THEOLOGY AND THEOLOGICAL ETHICS

Divine Motivation

Zechariah 12–14 contains only one virtue ascribed to God, and that only indirectly. YHWH shows courage in heading the heavenly and earthly armies to fight against the nations surrounding

Jerusalem. God has the inner fortitude requisite not to shrink back on the day of battle.

What predominates this final collection of oracles are God's actions. The vision of 12:1 seems intended to provide a lens by which to read the rest of the words of God. God is creating, not just heaven and earth, but also shaping like an artisan the spirit of humans within them. This crafting of the human spirit takes a variety of forms in this passage. God will craft the spirit of the residents of Jerusalem and people of Yehud so that they mourn and lament over those whom they kill. God will form the spirit of the people so that prophets stop leading people astray. The remnant after the days of war will have their spirits refined so that they respond to God's by saying, "YHWH is our God." And the spirits of the nations will be formed so that they come year by year for the Festival of Booths to worship God.

Meanwhile God will do a variety of things we expect by providing benefactions for Jerusalem and the district of Yehud. God will save them from their enemies in the day of battle and shield them from further assault. This will, in turn, enrich the city with spoils of war and the tribute of the nations. God will open a fountain of scribal leadership that will interpret the prophetic traditions to guide the people on the right path. In turn, God will eliminate poor leadership from Jerusalem. When victory comes because God stands on the Mount of Olives, God will also make Jerusalem a paradise, like the great gardens of the kings of Persia.

Doubts

The predominating image in Zechariah 12–14 is of war. We may feel somewhat encouraged by the idea that God will create the people of Jerusalem and Yehud in such a way that they do not gloat in their victory, but the horrific visions of the least persons in society caught up in war, the rape of women by armies that *God* assembled against Jerusalem, two-thirds of the population of Jerusalem decimated, all give one pause about this presentation of God. While I address this topic at greater length in the next chapter, it is important here to recognize the tension that exists in the Book of Zechariah. At the beginning, the angels challenged God about the way that the Jews remained suffering in exile, with God both expressing regret over the people's suffering because of God's anger (1:13) and calling nations to account who inflicted harm on Northern Israel and Southern Judah (2:1–4). In this light, it seems wise to doubt that, in our own ethic, we could determine the appropriate levels of violence that would somehow rectify wrongs. Surely the atom bomb contributed toward the end of World War II just as surely as the images of the annihilation of Hiroshima and the threat of nuclear holocaust haunt us these many years later. If we add our desire to use God to sanction our own human violence, surely the theological justification is as much a temptation as it is a possible motivation to see the end of oppression. It seems to me that we must always doubt such use because we must always wonder who will be harmed in our attempts to do good by means of violence.

Divine Command

God does not give any commands in these final chapters. However, two ideal images arise in this section, both stemming from the action of God toward the people. On the one hand, God will give the people such favor toward their enemies that they will pray, mourn, and lament for those they struck as if for their firstborn or only child. On the other hand, at the end of the wars against Jerusalem, even bells on cows' necks and pots in Jerusalem will be engraved "Holy to the LORD." God's refinement of Israel will be so complete that bells and pots will be found "Holy to the LORD."

Prophetic Witness

The prophetic witness of communities of faith seems to rely in no small measure on the virtue of courage. Given the doubts just raised about the violent imagery in Zechariah 12–14, I do not have in mind not courage to fight or go to war. Rather, communities of faith need fortitude and willingness to risk themselves in a variety of ways. This includes having the courage to risk speaking out to confront corrupt power and to offer a word of hope to people often suffering in, among other things, generational poverty. Courage also means developing a healthy sense of risk-taking to stand in solidarity with the marginalized that might lead to getting arrested, losing a job, even losing one's life.

As I think about God giving the people of Jerusalem and Yehud a spirit of "favor" toward those who fought against Jerusalem so that they mourned their deaths, I wonder about the continuing role of lament in the church. What is our practice of lament – do we lament? How often are we lamenting the violences we see in the world? It seems that we turn callously from so much violence in order to protect ourselves, much like our neighbors. But, what would happen if the church in a local community became known for its public invitations to lament death and suffering that have occurred to us as human beings, even if only indirectly? Is this not part of the church's role in society to awaken us more fully to the fact that things are not the way they are supposed to be?

Finally, prophetic witness includes interpreting the prophets within Scripture for the sake of the church and world. We must resist those who would call us to "unhitch" ourselves from the Old Testament and especially its sometimes problematic ethics.³⁶ Rather, we must continue to wrestle with the text, knowing that as much as we may doubt some of its perspectives, so different from our own, we also know these prophets will continue to confront us and our culture with demands for motherly compassion, justice, zeal, lament, and so much more. In the imitation of the prophets this interpretation will necessarily be a public exercise. The prophets confronted their own people but sometimes also called heaven and earth as witnesses, opposed surrounding nations, and even condemned great empires. The prophetic witness of a community of faith is a public witness because it stems from a belief that the God of Israel is also God of all the nations.

---

³⁶ See, e.g., Andy Stanley, *Irresistible: Reclaiming the New that Jesus Unleashed for the World* (Grand Rapids: Zondervan, 2018).

CHAPTER 9

The Theology of the Books of Haggai and Zechariah within the Old Testament

THE THEOLOGY OF THE BOOKS OF HAGGAI AND ZECHARIAH

No two prophets within the canon of the Old Testament are as closely linked as Haggai and Zechariah. Other prophetic books indicate that two prophets delivered their oracles during the reigns of the same kings (e.g., Isaiah and Micah or Jeremiah and Ezekiel). But only the Books of Haggai and Zechariah explicitly indicate that the messages of these two prophets overlapped at one point during the same year in the same location: the second year of the reign of Darius I in the city of Jerusalem. Moreover, only Haggai and Zechariah are named together in a third book purporting to tell the history of their time period, the Book of Ezra. And, of course, they appear next to each other in the Hebrew canon of Scripture, like Jeremiah and Ezekiel, but unlike Isaiah and Micah.

The strong ties between these two books implies that the audience who receives the Books of Haggai and Zechariah within the canon should see their messages as complementary to one another. The Book of Haggai's vision of the future is rooted squarely in the Book of Exodus, exhorting the people of Jerusalem and Yehud to see that their historical moment is not as bleak as it appears but is, instead, the time of the New Exodus. The Book of Zechariah ties the present and future of the people to the preexilic prophets, drawing on the tradition of the great "writing prophets" as sources of hope for its audience. The combination of these theological foundations makes for a particularly robust vision of hope by rooting that hope in more than one tradition.

These two books together also offer a more complete picture of YHWH's demands upon the people in Jerusalem and Yehud. The Book of Haggai asserts that honoring YHWH requires that the people build a sanctuary worthy of their God, that making sacrifices to YHWH at a basically barren site dishonors God. The Book of Zechariah introduces a different dimension by reiterating the demands of the preexilic prophets that the people practice true justice in the courts and protect the rights of the poor, widow, alien, and orphan. The two books combine to instruct the audience that seeking divine benevolence requires exhibiting faithfulness both to the cult and to the ethics of the Torah and prophets.

A third way in which these books enrich one another is in their overlapping understandings of divine benevolence. Both books promise that YHWH will establish peace in Yehud and Jerusalem in a way that the *Pax persica* could not. Both books promise that the political future lies in the figure of Zerubbabel, as an engraving in the Book of Haggai and the Branch in the Book of Zechariah. Both books imagine a day in the near future when the nations will bring tribute to the house of YHWH that seems meant to exceed the tribute carried to Persepolis. And both books see that the exaltation of Jerusalem will bring many nations also to seek YHWH's benefactions at the Temple in Jerusalem, just like representatives of the nations sought the beneficence of the Great King in Persepolis (or another of Persia's capital cities).

Each of these prophetic visions emphasizes fulsome commitment to YHWH, whether honoring YHWH wholly by finishing the construction of the Temple, in addition to offering the required sacrifices, or by wholly listening to the voice of YHWH, who reminds the people of the basic moral vision that reflects God's character. Ironically, though both books call for complete commitment to YHWH, neither book's instructions on how to please YHWH is complete without the other. Honoring YHWH demands sacrifice and justice, rebuilding the Temple and the pursuit of truth in the gate. The people of Yehud are wholly the people of YHWH when their identity flows from the one God worshipped in the Temple and whose Torah is adjudicated in the Temple and by the ruler of the people.

The addition of the material preserved and edited by the scribes in the latter portion of the Book of Zechariah (chs. 9–14) emphasizes that returning to YHWH must involve a holistic experience. YHWH wants people who seek YHWH in expected, ritual practices like asking for beneficence from YHWH, while eschewing other forms of divination. Alongside of this, and more pronounced in the latter portion of the Book of Zechariah, the scribes continued to signal the importance of pursuing justice, so much so that the book claims that failure to do so brought the end of an era begun in the days of Cyrus. The final chapters in the Book of Zechariah both undo the future promised by the prophets Haggai and Zechariah and domesticate their words and visions to the scribal community interpreting the prophets. Thus, faithfulness to YHWH going forward means turning to the Former Prophets for guidance and rejecting ecstatic prophecy because ecstatic prophets too easily speak falsehoods. In fact, it is not so much the words of the prophets but the theological interpretation of the prophets by the scribal community that carries the most authority.

THE THEOLOGY OF THE BOOKS OF HAGGAI, ZECHARIAH, AND MALACHI

The Book of Malachi opens in a way similar to the Book of Zechariah, with YHWH asserting that God has loved the people but the people doubt YHWH's love and ask just how God has loved them. And so YHWH offers an illustration, reminding the people that YHWH elected Jacob but rejected Esau, which YHWH proves by acting "beyond the borders of Israel" to punish Edom's wickedness (Mal 1:1–5).[1] One of the interesting theological implications of the opening sections of Zechariah and Malachi is that YHWH does not refuse to address the people's doubts about whether YHWH has returned to them or loves them. The Books of Haggai, Zechariah, and Malachi all point to the struggles that the postexilic community faced in different ways that gave legitimate reasons to doubt God's concern for the people. The presence of these books together, then, constitutes a significant part of the canon's argument that YHWH hears, cares, and will answer the people's doubts, even if, in the end, they remain unpersuaded. We might even see this collection of books as a witness to the faithfulness of YHWH to pursue people within and beyond their doubts.

Meanwhile, the Books of Haggai and Malachi share parallel concerns about the way that the people of Yehud neglect the honor of YHWH. In the Book of Malachi, the prophet sees that

---

[1] The biblical vision is that the Edomites were descended from Esau. See Gen 36:1.

the people come to God with unacceptable offerings, animals that are blind, lame, and sick, and profane the name of YHWH by offering what they have stolen from others (Mal 1:4-14). The Book of Malachi also shares the Book of Zechariah's concern that the people refuse to return (*šwb*) to YHWH, though Malachi focuses on the way the people "rob"[2] YHWH by neglecting to give the tithes commanded in Torah, which Malachi defines as "returning" (*šwb*) to YHWH and claims will cause YHWH to return (*šwb*) to the people. The Old Testament witness, and particularly the combined witness of Haggai and Malachi, will not allow the commandments of God to be reduced to the so-called moral law, as important as this is to the Book of Zechariah. Ritual and place play crucial roles in forming identity and honoring YHWH. In neglecting these formative acts and places the people betray their relationship with God in a way that wounds YHWH who has sustained the children of Jacob through time (Mal 3:6).

Meanwhile, the combined witness of Zechariah 7–8 and Mal 3:1–5 will not allow the people to seek YHWH without also seeking justice, with Malachi 3 arguing that the people of Jacob must not swear falsely, withhold the wages of the laborers, widows, and orphans, and turn away the stranger – all of which are proof that the people do not fear YHWH (3:5d–g). The Book

---

[2] See the brief discussion in *HALOT* 2:1062 for the rare word *qbʿ*. Sweeney translates this as "to rob" (Marvin A. Sweeney, *The Twelve Prophets: Volume Two* [Berit Olam; Collegeville, MN: The Liturgical Press, 2000], 742–743), while Petersen follows the LXX, reading the verb as *ʿqb*, "to deceive," which plays on the name of Jacob used in Mal 3:6 (David L. Petersen, *Zechariah 9–14 and Malachi: A Commentary* [OTL; Louisville, KY: Westminster John Knox Press, 1995], 212, 214–215).

of Malachi adds further layers to the concerns in Zech 7:8–10 and 8:16–17 by also condemning sorcery and adultery (Mal 3:5b–c). Be that as it may, caring for the orphan, widow, and alien serves as the foundational theological ethics for these prophets, reiterating what the Torah and the Former Prophets state: faithfulness to YHWH means acting faithfully toward the people under God's care, especially those most at risk in the community.

Nevertheless, the pressing issue for the people in the Book of Malachi is whether "It is useless to serve God," and the urgent question "what have we gained by keeping God's charge and thus walking in awe of YHWH Sabaoth?" (Mal 3:14). The tension evident in the combination of Zechariah 9–14 and Mal 3:13–24 is palpable as the promises of YHWH's care do not emerge immediately but are postponed into an ill-defined future. As much as the Books of Haggai, Zechariah, and Malachi call the people of Israel to account for their faithfulness, or lack thereof, to YHWH, these books also mark the resounding struggle of the postexilic community with the faithfulness of YHWH. The Book of Malachi does not resolve this problem but rather promises that YHWH will send the prophet Elijah to reconcile parents and children, "lest I strike the land with destruction" (ḥērem, Mal 3:24), ending on a foreboding note. YHWH promised at the end of the Book of Zechariah to make Jerusalem secure so that it would "never again" suffer such destruction (ḥērem, Zech 14:11). But as the Book of Malachi ends, the whole land has reason to fear, and those who have read both the Books of Zechariah and Malachi have a reasonable concern, that the promise of YHWH to work reconciliation among the people will not come to fruition and the land will suffer destruction once again. That means the people still have reason to doubt the love and faithfulness of YHWH.

HAGGAI AND ZECHARIAH AND THE BOOK OF THE TWELVE

Reading the Book of the Twelve as a unit leads the reader through the prophetic interpretation of the troublesome history of Israel's relationship to YHWH, from the days of Uzziah in Judah and Jeroboam in Northern Israel (Hosea 1:1) to the time after the exile, in the days of Darius I (Hag 1:1; Zech 1:1) to at least the time of Artaxerxes I. Perhaps most striking element in reading the prophetic interpretation of Israel's history in the Book of the Twelve is the weight of the negative evaluations of the people of God, particularly in Hosea, Joel, Amos, Micah, Habakkuk, and Zephaniah. The theological reading of Israel's history in these prophets is that YHWH was greatly displeased with Israel, who refused God's call to a special relationship with them via covenants, Torah, cult, kings, sages, and, last but not least, prophets.[3] The Books of Haggai and Zechariah offer two emphatic responses to the former prophets. First, they offer the prophetic confirmation that exile occurred. Of course, the original readers of these two books would already know this based on the witness of their parents or grandparents or more general cultural memory. The significance of the claim in Haggai and Zechariah is that exile was *an act of YHWH*: YHWH acted in Assyria and Babylon to remove the people from their land. For a time, YHWH chose not to interfere any longer in the life of Israel as God shut the door on prophecy and enacted the exile(s) (Amos 8:11–12).[4] The Books of Haggai and Zechariah then make their claim that the future of the people descended from Israel lies not

---

[3] See the brief summary of the theological explanation of the prophetic books in Donald E. Gowan, *Theology of the Prophetic Books: The Death and Resurrection of Israel* (Louisville, KY: Westminster John Knox, 1998), 9.

[4] See Abraham Heschel, *The Prophets* (New York: Harper & Row, 1962), 193–194.

in making peace with nations nor in making offerings to Ahuramazda at the right time but in returning to YHWH in the way these later prophets commanded, which echoes the demands made through the former prophets.

Second, and just as importantly, Haggai and Zechariah witness within the Book of the Twelve to the fact that YHWH offered the postexilic generations a word of resurrection.[5] The consistent testimony in these two books is that YHWH both confronted the failures of the postexilic community and also offered mercy, motherly compassion, and strength to achieve the directives YHWH gave to the people. If those who returned from exile failed to experience the heights these books envisioned, the prophetic message asserts that the fault lies with the people, not YHWH Sabaoth. YHWH returned to the people, bringing the people back to the land and helping them complete the new Temple, the site from which they might receive YHWH's beneficence. Far too often, however, YHWH had said, "You are my people" but the people failed to reply with "YHWH is our God."

Marvin Sweeney considers the Book of Twelve as, at least in part, a sequence of books that emphasize the divine purpose in relation to the fate of Jerusalem.[6] This theme falls out unevenly across the minor prophets; Sweeney notes that even the Book of Hosea, which focuses on Northern Israel, still looks forward to the reunification of Israel and Judah under a Davidic monarch (Hos 3:5), which certainly alludes to Jerusalem, the City of David.[7] Other books have a more intense focus on Jerusalem, like the

---

[5] Borrowing Gowan's descriptor of the postexilic prophets (*Theology of the Prophetic Books*, 143–187).

[6] Marvin A. Sweeney, *Tanak: A Theological and Critical Introduction to the Jewish Bible* (Minneapolis, MN: Fortress Press, 2012), 343.

[7] Ibid.

Book of Joel's depiction of YHWH's intention to defend Jerusalem on the Day of YHWH and the Book of Zephaniah's call for a purge of Jerusalem.[8] The Books of Haggai and Zechariah proclaim YHWH's renewed involvement with Jerusalem's fate, envisioning a future elevation of the city as the center of the known world with the nations coming to the city to honor YHWH Sabaoth. But the final chapter in the Book of Zechariah agrees with the Book of Zephaniah by claiming that the postexilic city also needs to be purged in order to be the city of YHWH Sabaoth.

One of the theological themes that finds special emphasis within the Book of the Twelve is "the Day of YHWH."[9] The perspective on the "Day of the LORD" varies within the Book of the Twelve, even within the Book of Joel, which makes it a major theme. At first, "the Day of YHWH" befalls Israel (Joel 1–2) while, at the end, the coming Day brings divine judgement against Israel's enemies (Joel 3 [Hebrew chap. 4]).[10] What the Book of Twelve agrees upon regarding the Day of YHWH is that this "day" (or moment in history) will greatly change the present state of political realities in Syro-Palestine.[11] The Book of Zechariah uses different phrasing: not "the Day of YHWH" that "draws near" – the usual verb associated with the Day of the LORD – but rather the day that will "come to YHWH" (*lə-yhwh*; Zech 14:1–2). The different language seems to indicate that the

---

[8] Ibid., 343–344.
[9] Rolf Rendtorff, "How to Read the Book of the Twelve as a Theological Unity," in *Reading and Hearing the Book of the Twelve* (ed. James D. Nogalski and Marvin A. Sweeney; SBLSymS 15; Atlanta: Society of Biblical Literature, 2000), 75–87.
[10] Ibid., 78.
[11] John Barton, *The Theology of the Book of Amos* (OTT; Cambridge: Cambridge University Press, 2012), 65.

"Day of the LORD" normally represents YHWH bringing a particular time to its end by divine fiat. Zechariah 14:1-2 suggests something else – namely, that YHWH watches history unfold, sees a time period come to an end, and then chooses to act. But even in this latter case, the vision still promises to transform political reality as Jerusalem moves from the periphery of political reality to the center.

Though the Book of Zechariah reinforces the theme of impending judgment often associated with the Day of YHWH, the book also joins with the Book of Jonah in confirming that words of judgment against the nations are not final. Obadiah imagines the downfall of Edom for their betrayal of their brother "Jacob." Nahum promises that YHWH will overthrow the violence of Assyria. Habakkuk envisions a day when YHWH will take vengeance on Babylon for their devastating acts against Judah and their plundering of the nations. And though the Book of Zechariah certainly sees a future judgment for the enemies of Yehud, the prophecies gathered in the book consistently affirm that the enemies of YHWH will become those who seek YHWH and even become part of God's people (see Zech 2:15; 8:20-23; 9:7; 14:16). The Book of the Twelve affirms that YHWH judged nations and that, indeed, nations fell by God's judgment. Yet the Book of Zechariah suggests that God's anger does not obscure God's redeeming love, even for enemy nations because they will, in the end, come to YHWH.[12]

---

[12] Heschel, *The Prophets*, 194, in a chapter entitled "Chastisement," nicely articulates this grand vision of not allowing God's anger to obscure God's redeeming love, though Heschel is more concerned with the word to Israel than to the nations.

HAGGAI AND ZECHARIAH AND THE BOOKS OF ISAIAH, JEREMIAH, AND EZEKIEL

As noted in Chapter 3, the Book of Zechariah's vision of the breath of YHWH enabling the people to finish building the Temple echoes the language in Ezekiel 37 of YHWH breathing life back into the bones of the whole house of Israel. Additionally, Zechariah's proclamation that the people finishing the Temple will signal the surety of the prophet's speaking for YHWH (Zech 4:8–9) and Haggai's exhortation to the people to devote themselves completely to YHWH by finishing the Temple echo Ezekiel's vision that the future of the people of God lies in the rebuilding of the Temple (Ezek 40–48). By implication, the Books of Haggai and Zechariah aver that YHWH intends to fulfill the words spoken through Ezekiel and Ezekiel's disciples, not only about the Temple but also about the restoration of the priesthood and the reunification of Northern Israel and Judah. The witness – albeit oblique – of Zechariah 11 is that the people did not complete the Temple rebuilding and, in this way, a significant piece of the future promised in Ezekiel 40–48 went unfulfilled. At the same time, the Books of Haggai and Zechariah struggle with the fact that the vision of divine–human synergism envisioned in Ezekiel 40–48, with its accompanying vision of Edenic-like flourishing, did not emerge.[13] The Edenic future in Ezekiel 40–48 is based on a vision of a community that remedies past abuses of power and establishes a more just society.[14] The Book of Zechariah echoes this demand for justice in the land that leads to human

---

[13] Jon Levenson, *Theology of the Program of Restoration of Ezekiel 40–48* (HSM 10; Cambridge, MA: Scholars Press for the Harvard Semitic Museum, 1976), 162.
[14] Ibid., 124.

flourishing. And so Zechariah 14 and Ezekiel 40–48 agree that the vision of Zion and the Temple as a new Eden, with a river-nourishing paradise, requires an act of YHWH.[15] The major theological regret of Zechariah 14 is that this vision of Zion as the new Eden has had to be pushed even further into the postexilic future because of the failure of justice in Jerusalem and Yehud.

Meanwhile, we might view the Book of Haggai as an important canonical response to the way some Christians read and respond to the message of Jeremiah 7, which condemns those who see the Temple as a guarantor of Jerusalem's safety despite egregious injustice (Jer 7:1–5). The conversation on Jeremiah 7 in the context of the extreme Protestant polemics of the past posited that this passage opposed the cult, though many modern scholars see Jeremiah's polemic as addressing the abuse of the cult.[16] The Book of Haggai does more than affirm that "stylized practice of symbolization is indispensable for the sustenance of intentional ethical practice," as important as this idea is.[17] Rather the Temple is a place that honors the greatness of YHWH and divine beneficence requires that people truly honor YHWH, not just in ethical praxis but also in ritual praxis. The sacraments themselves are a participation in the life of God and so must be done in ways that reflect the honor due to God.

Still, the fact that Zech 11:4–17 draws on the tradition about shepherds in Jeremiah and Ezekiel confirms that YHWH entrusts certain leaders to ensure justice for those in the community who

---

[15] Ibid., 32.
[16] Walter Brueggemann, *Theology of the Old Testament: Testimony, Dispute, Advocacy* (Minneapolis, MN: Fortress Press, 1997), 678.
[17] Ibid.

most need protection. Jeremiah 23:1-2 and Ezek 34:1-6 show the prophets attributing the destruction of 587 BCE to the failure of monarchy, asserting that political power cannot guarantee security if that power is not based in YHWH's requirement to do justice.[18] Zechariah 11:4-17 confirms that YHWH does not change and so true administration of justice is the only right exercise of power. When power exploits the poor then exile-like outcomes result and promises of a rich future are postponed until YHWH sets things aright.

Space prevents me from pursuing any number of connections between the Books of Haggai and Zechariah and the Book of Isaiah. Still, the resonance and direct links to Isaiah 40-55 deserve some attention. Isaiah 40's vision that YHWH's judgment against Jerusalem's sin has come to an end and its imperative to comfort Jerusalem connects well with Zechariah 1:7-2:17, as well as the implicit theological claim in the Book of Haggai that YHWH returned the people to Jerusalem. The Books of Haggai and Isaiah 40-55 both draw upon the Exodus and wilderness traditions to affirm that YHWH will (Isaiah 40-55) or has (Haggai) redeemed Israel from Babylon in a New Exodus.[19] Both Isaiah 40-55 and Zechariah present strong arguments to convince their audiences that YHWH is returning to them and intends to bless them (Isa 41:8-10; 43:25; 44:22; 54:7-8; Zech 1:7-6:8).[20] The renewed care of YHWH should summon forth shouts of joy (Isa 40:3-11; Zech 2:14-17). But the collective witness of these prophetic texts indicates that the restoration of the people to YHWH and Jerusalem

---

[18] Ibid., 614-615.   [19] See the discussion in Sweeney, *Tanak*, 284-288.
[20] See Gowan, *Theology of the Prophetic Books*, 149-151 on the rhetoric of Isaiah 40-55 to convince the people that YHWH has forgiven them and is ready and able to deliver them from their captivity.

proved complicated, to understate things considerably. Haggai raises concerns about the devotion of the people to YHWH in light of their neglect of the House of YHWH. Zechariah 7–8 raises concerns about the people's devotion to YHWH in light of their neglect of the justice demanded in Torah and the Former Prophets. And, if Abraham Heschel's statement, "No word is God's last word,"[21] is correct, then Zech 11:4–17 shows the unfortunate side of that reality because the prophet's dramatic actions overturn the promises in Isaiah 40–55 regarding peaceful relations with the nations and the reunification of Judah and Northern Israel. In overturning those promises, the Book of Zechariah raises the question of whether the prophet of Isaiah 40–55 was a false prophet,[22] or at least whether or not YHWH would any longer utilize ecstatic prophets or would, instead, rely on scribal communities to correctly interpret the prophetic traditions (Zech 13:1–6). Then again: "No word is God's last word."

HAGGAI AND ZECHARIAH AND THE BOOKS OF DANIEL AND ESTHER

The Books of Haggai and Zechariah communicate clearly the struggles that the postexilic community faced in Jerusalem, Yehud, and the lands formerly belonging to Northern Israel.

---

[21] Heschel, *The Prophets*, 193–194.
[22] So R. Norman Whybray, *Second Isaiah* (T&T Clark Study Guides; Sheffield: Sheffield Academic Press, 1983), 80. I owe this reference to Gowan, *Theology of the Prophetic Books*, 161, who comments further, "We should not let the beauty and the power of the poetry blind us to these problems, for they were real ones for the post-exilic community" (161–162). This is particularly true for the prophetic traditions associated with Haggai and Zechariah, which is the basis of Whybray's query.

Haggai and Zechariah within the Old Testament 213

The message of these books affirms that, though the community struggles, YHWH has not abandoned them but works to restore them while still demanding that the people respond faithfully to YHWH so as to experience YHWH's beneficence. The Books of Esther and Daniel work in combination with the Books of Haggai and Zechariah to fill out the picture of the struggle of Jews in the postexilic period. Together they declare that YHWH works to aid the Jews subject to the varieties of imperial violence, whether in Yehud or in the lands to which the previous generations were exiled.

One of the major differences between the Book of Esther and the Books of Haggai and Zechariah is the fact that Esther never mentions God. This does not mean that God is absent from Esther, however. The number of "coincidences" in Esther that lead to the Jews' deliverance from the threat of Haman, the idea that someone or something would raise up another deliverer if Esther refused to help her people (Esth 4:13–14), and the perception by Gentiles in the story that the arc of history is bending toward justice for the Jews (Esth 6:13; 8:17; 9:2–3) collectively allude to God working behind the scenes on behalf of the Jews.[23] The Books of Haggai and Zechariah also affirm that YHWH works behind the scenes, whether in the natural order (Hag 1) or in the heavenly realms (Zech 1:7–6:8). The obvious difference lies in the fact that the Books of Haggai and Zechariah reveal YHWH's work that has, heretofore, remained hidden.

The demand in the Books of Haggai and Zechariah to respond to the acts and words of YHWH points to another key difference

---

[23] The preceding discussion summarizes the insights of Jon D. Levenson, *Esther: A Commentary* (OTL; Louisville, KY: Westminster John Knox Press, 1997), 18–21.

between these prophetic texts and the Book of Esther, as well as the Book of Daniel. The people for whom God intervenes in the Books of Esther and Daniel are all innocent so that their deliverance is YHWH's administration of just judgment. What the Books of Haggai and Zechariah add to this testimony is that YHWH also works on behalf of the unjust and those who have rejected the overtures of God, though not without difficulty. The Books of Daniel and Esther show that those who intervene – Daniel, Shadrach, Meshach, Abednego, Esther, Mordecai, and the other Jews in the Book of Esther who fast on her behalf – enjoy some success. Each person faces peril at the hands of an imperial power and each one receives salvation from God, explicitly (Daniel) or implicitly (Esther). In this way, the Books of Esther and Daniel support the testimony of the Books of Haggai and Zechariah that people must honor God in order for God's promises to come to fruition.

Nevertheless, the visions in the second half of the Book of Daniel (chs. 7–12) interact with the emphasis in Zechariah 9–14 that the completion of YHWH's salvific work lies in the future. If the people in Yehud experienced anxiety about YHWH's sovereignty in the wars between Persia and Egypt in the days of Artaxerxes I, how much more those who suffered the violence of Antiochus Epiphanes IV?[24] Zechariah 9–14 invites both resistance to Persian rule, especially as manifest in Persian representatives, the governors/shepherds (10:1–5; 11:4–17; 13:7–9), and seeks to resolve the tension between the affirmation of YHWH

---

[24] Amy C. Merrill-Willis argues that the driving problem of the visions of Daniel 7–12 is God's sovereignty, not the problem of evil (*Dissonance and the Drama of Divine Sovereignty in the Book of Daniel* [LHBOTS 520; New York: T&T Clark, 2010], 181).

Sabaoth's rule and the troubles faced by the community of Yehud and Jerusalem. This corresponds well with the similar function of the Danielic visions, which symbolically demonstrate how YHWH's will tries to "adjudicate the contradictions surrounding the experience and perception of divine sovereignty in the historical realm."[25]

HAGGAI AND ZECHARIAH AND THE BOOKS OF EZRA AND NEHEMIAH

The Book of Ezra adds an important dimension to the theology of return and the rebuilding of the Temple in Jerusalem. Ezra 1:1–4 makes the strong claim that YHWH spoke directly to Cyrus to send the descendants of Israel back to their land, to rebuild the Temple, and to make sacrifices. The Book of Ezra wants its audience to see that YHWH works in human hearts, especially in the heart of the most powerful individual the Jews know.[26] Thus, the Book of Ezra takes the perspective of the Books of Haggai and Zechariah a step further by beginning with a story of how Cyrus recognized the work of YHWH on his behalf and responded obediently to YHWH's command to send the exiles home. By contrast, the references to Darius I in the Books of Haggai and Zechariah simply serve to mark the time of the prophecies with no sense that Darius works for the Jews, much less at the impetus of YHWH's command. One might say that YHWH's sovereignty exercised in the course of human events is

---

[25] Ibid., 189.
[26] Christopher J. H. Wright, "Reading Ezra-Nehemiah Canonically," in *Ezra and Nehemiah*, David J. Shepherd and Christopher J. H. Wright (THOTC; Grand Rapids, MI: Eerdmans, 2018), 115.

more explicit in the Book of Ezra, which sees the "hand of God" moving kings, providing for a successful journey with no trouble from bandits, and helping Ezra gather Levites and temple servants (Ezra 7:6, 8–9, 27–28; 8:18–20, 22, 31–32).[27] In the Book of Haggai the prophet must show the people YHWH's work in nature, though YHWH does stir up the spirits of Zerubbabel, Joshua, and the people. The Book of Zechariah reveals YHWH working in the heavens and often points to the future activity of YHWH.

As I argued in the first chapter of this book, it appears that scribes finished writing the Book of Zechariah some time before Nehemiah came to Yehud and became its governor. The Book of Nehemiah within the biblical canon, in a way, answers the struggles of the Book of Zechariah that blamed the governors of Yehud for the continued delay of YHWH's promises of a grand future. At the most basic level, Nehemiah prays to YHWH, seeking the aid of YHWH (Neh 1:11; 2:4), while the Book of Zechariah criticizes the governors for failing to point the people to authorized forms of divination (Zech 10:1–5).[28] Moreover, when Nehemiah seeks the favor of YHWH he confesses Israel's sins while invoking the memory of YHWH's promise through Moses to restore the people "if you return [*šûb*] to me" (Neh 1:6–9). The Book of Zechariah begins by telling the people that YHWH has already returned to them as the theological motivation for the people to return to YHWH, but the overall testimony of the book is that the people never returned to YHWH.

According to the Book of Nehemiah, what distinguishes the career of Nehemiah from previous governors is that he "feared

---

[27] Ibid.
[28] On the charismatic leadership of Nehemiah grounded in prayer, see David J. Shepherd, "Leadership and Ezra-Nehemiah," in ibid., 205.

God" (Neh 5:15), which is the criterion Nehemiah uses to select other leaders, like his brother Hanani (7:2).[29] So, Nehemiah not only exercised needed, charismatic leadership by enacting justice in his position as governor (ch. 5), he also sought to routinize just leadership in the appointment of Hanani.[30] Nehemiah proves to be the person that YHWH and the prophets in the Zechariah tradition longed for after Zerubbabel faded quietly from the scene. The canonical witness offers a response to the tragedy of failed leadership by noting that YHWH did in fact find the person needed to lead the people faithfully to their God, to exercise justice, and to routinize just leadership in Jerusalem and Yehud.

HAGGAI AND ZECHARIAH AND THE BOOK OF THE PSALMS

The central book of the Psalter, Psalms 73–89, is the one that burns the hottest, with the psalmists lamenting the anger of YHWH that has been poured out on the people (e.g., Pss 74:1; 76:4, 11; 77:10; 78:62–63; 79:5). The psalmist in Psalm 79 asks the question, "How long, YHWH, will you be angry forever? / Will your jealousy burn like fire?" (79:5). The Books of Haggai and Zechariah function within the canon as a partial answer to questions like these. The psalmist wants YHWH's motherly compassion to come swiftly to the people (79:8) and to let the groan of the prisoners, a fitting metaphor for the temporary but oppressive experience of exile, reach God, who should then defeat the enemies of the people and lead them like a flock (79:11–13).[31]

---

[29] Ibid., 208.   [30] Ibid.
[31] See the discussion of Psalm 79 in Robert L. Foster, *We Have Heard, O LORD: An Introduction to the Theology of the Psalter* (Lanham, MD: Lexington Books/Fortress Academic, 2019), 94–96.

The Books of Haggai and Zechariah attest to the fact that YHWH did hear the prayers of the exiles and returned them to the land and worked for their flourishing, with the Book of Zechariah especially affirming the motherly compassion of YHWH. Simultaneously, these books attest to the idea that any ongoing struggles the people experience stem from the fact that they have not committed themselves wholly to the commandments of YHWH.

Psalm 1 opens the Book of Psalms by commending the person who does not keep company with sinners but devotes themselves to Torah.[32] Such people practice justice, which means that YHWH will watch over them, while the way of the wicked will perish. The Book of Zechariah confirms this perspective as it calls the people to walk in paths of justice, eschewing false testimony and exploitation of the poor, widow, and orphan, while pursuing justice, compassion, and faithful love. But, because the people of Yehud and Jerusalem refuse to pursue the just requirements of YHWH, their way will perish, especially the shepherds who lead the people astray and do not care for the needs of the flock (Zech 11:17; 13:7).

For its part, the Book of Haggai affirms the view of psalmists like the one in Psalm 84, who longs for the courts of YHWH, who sees the beauty of God's temple, and who wishes to find a nesting place near the altar of YHWH (84:1–5). Haggai would approve of the psalmist who prays for Jerusalem because the house of YHWH resides there and who rejoices anytime someone invites them to go up to Jerusalem (Ps 122). Rebuilding the Temple honors YHWH's name but it also provides a place for the people to delight in the presence of YHWH. The Temple is the place for

---

[32] For the argument that the term *'ašrê* should be translated as "commendable" or "admirable," see C. L. Seow, "An Exquisitely Poetic Introduction to the Psalter," *JBL* **132** (2013): 277.

all the tribes of Israel to journey on their pilgrimage feasts and be reminded together that all the tribes of Israel belong to YHWH (Ps 122:3). Wholly committing to YHWH will bring wholeness to the people who belong to God.

HAGGAI AND ZECHARIAH AND THE BOOKS OF THE TORAH

One of the key passages for many interpreters of the Book of Genesis is Gen 12:1–3, where God promises to make Abram a great nation so that he will be a blessing and "in you all the families of the earth will be blessed" (Gen 12:3b). Christian interpreters especially understand this passage in line with Paul (Gal 3:6–9), believing that this promise that the families of the earth will be blessed in Abraham finds its fulfillment in the preaching of the Christian gospel.[33] R. W. L. Moberly suggests that such interpretations miss the real aim of the text in which the final phrase reproduces a general blessing (and cursing) idiom. The actual promise, according to him, is that, because YHWH will bless Abram in a foreign land, nations will see this and "pronounce blessings upon one another" with Abram as the model of the life they desire.[34] Zechariah 8:13 employs this blessing idiom in imagining the future of Yehud as the nations see YHWH blessing the "House of Israel" and the "House of Judah." The nations will then quit invoking curses over one another with the struggles of Israel and Judah exemplifying the harm they wish on others and,

---

[33] See the good summary of this passage in prior scholarship in R. W. L. Moberly, *The Theology of the Book of Genesis* (OTT; Cambridge: Cambridge University Press, 2009), 141–148.

[34] Ibid., 148–155.

instead, pronounce blessings on themselves, holding up Israel and Judah as models of the blessings they desire. Whether the scribes of the Book of Zechariah intended to evoke Gen 12:1–3 is debatable. But certainly Zech 8:13 and Gen 12:1–3 share the same worldview that the God of Abraham (and his descendants) will bless them so greatly that the nations will invoke them as the model of the life they desire.

Samuel Balentine astutely observes that wherever the Temple becomes the subject of major concern in literature from the Persian Period, the Temple imagery comes from traditions canonized in the Pentateuch and, specifically, from the Priestly account of the Tabernacle.[35] This is certainly true of the Book of Haggai, which sees the return of the people to the land of their ancestors to rebuild the Temple as a New Exodus. This evocation of the Tabernacle narrative comes to light particularly in YHWH's promise to "fill this house with glory" (Hag 2:7), on the heels of the assurance that "my spirit stands in your midst" (Hag 2:5). The term "glory" conveys something of the special presence of YHWH in the midst of the people, and the Exodus narrative seems to transfer the "glorious" presence of YHWH on Mount Sinai (Exod 24:16–17) into the midst of the people (Exod 29:42b–46; 40:34–35).[36] What the Book of Haggai confirms in conjunction with the narrative of Exodus is that, though covenant partnership with God involves commandments (Exod 20–23), it also includes the consecration of the Tabernacle, which mediates the special presence of YHWH in the midst of the people (Exod

---

[35] Samuel E. Balentine, *The Torah's Vision of Worship* (OBT; Minneapolis, MN: Fortress Press, 1999), 57.
[36] Donald E. Gowan, *Theology in Exodus: Biblical Theology in the Form of a Commentary* (Louisville, KY: Westminster John Knox Press, 1994), 184–186.

25–31; 35–40).³⁷ The Book of Haggai reminds the audience of the Book of the Twelve, who see the Books of Haggai and Zechariah as a pair, that the call to obey the commandments is an incomplete vision of covenant partnership without the accompanying sanctuary filled with the glorious presence of God.

Even so, the Book of Zechariah's continues to affirm that obeying the commandments is an essential part of covenant partnership with YHWH. After all, the people of Yehud experience that land as temptation, with the elite of the land coveting what belongs to others and coercively appropriating what they desire.³⁸ The people most easily coerced for gain, according to the Book of Deuteronomy, are the poor (Deut 15:7–11), alien (Deut 10:19), widow, and orphan (Deut 24:19–22),³⁹ the same peoples for whom the Book of Zechariah seeks justice (Zech 7:9–10). The Book of Zechariah also agrees with the Book of Deuteronomy in asserting that the key to justice in the community is ensuring justice in the courts (Deut 1:9–18; Zech 5:1–4; 8:16–17). Likewise, Zechariah affirms Deuteronomy's assertion that fair treatment of debt-slaves will make or break the people in the land (Deut 15:1–6; Zech 11:4–17). Deuteronomy specifies that, if the people want to experience freedom from the domination of other nations, they must set those debt-slaves free every seventh year (Deut 15:1, 9, 12). Zechariah 11:4–6 alludes to the fact that the governors and elite in Yehud gave in to the temptations of the land and became crass merchants of humanity, rather than remembering that they, too,

---

³⁷ Balentine, *Torah's Vision of Worship*, 137.
³⁸ According to Walter Brueggemann, this is one of two basic temptations in the land; with the other being to devote oneself to other gods besides YHWH. See his *The Land: Place as Gift, Promise, and Challenge in Biblical Faith* (2nd ed.; OBT; Minneapolis, MN: Fortress Press, 2002), 55.
³⁹ Ibid., 61. Note that Brueggemann's list also includes the Levites.

were once slaves in Egypt (cf. Deut 15:15) – and Babylon! And so the Book of Zechariah warns the people that they will experience a new exile (Zech 13:7–8; 14:2a-b), just as the Book of Deuteronomy forewarned (Deut 28:64–68).

BIBLICAL THEOLOGY AND THEOLOGICAL ETHICS

Divine Motivation

As we consider theological ethics that we may derive from the Books of Haggai and Zechariah in conversation with the rest of the Old Testament, one key divine virtue is faithfulness, though the specific word for "faithfulness" does not describe God in either book and the term for "loyalty" occurs only once in the Book of Zechariah. However, if we consider the manifestations of God's loyalty (*ḥesed*) that Katherine Doob Sakenfeld has found in the Psalms – deliverance, protection, and forgiveness – we readily see that Haggai and Zechariah imply God's loyalty to those who returned from the exile to Yehud.[40] One important aspect emphasized in these two books and reflected elsewhere in the Old Testament is the surprising nature of God's faithfulness, a commitment beyond what the people deserve.[41] Thus, not only does God deliver people from exile without any evidence of their having "earned" deliverance but Zechariah 14 also foresees a future for the people where they flourish in spite of generations of failed leadership and injustice.

Likewise, both books witness to God's just nature that is so pervasive across Scripture. Haggai and Zechariah affirm that this

---

[40] See Katherine Doob Sakenfeld, *Faithfulness in Action: Loyalty in Biblical Perspective* (OBT; Philadelphia: Fortress Press, 1985), 83–100.
[41] Ibid., 51, 75, 84.

characteristic of the ideal leader that manifests itself in equitable judicial decisions is, ultimately, a character trait of God.[42] Somewhat ironically, the equitability of God's judgment manifests itself in God judging the people of Yehud. God's justice means impartial judgment while, paradoxically, showing special care to the oppressed as their champion.[43] Still, perhaps we should view God's willingness to champion the poor, not as partiality, but God's impartial care for those who suffer because of society's partiality toward the elite.

Finally, though only mentioned once in these two books, God's motherly compassion deeply impacts God's interactions with the people of Yehud. The image of God as mother in the Old Testament implies an inclination toward Israel connoting selfless participation in the life of the people that seeks their wholeness and well-being in the way a mother would.[44] This virtue is meant to assure God's children (Israel) that God will not forsake them but will continue to care for them, especially when they find themselves in desperate circumstances.[45]

One major tension running throughout the Book of Zechariah, and much of the Old Testament, is the fact that the God who

---

[42] Hilary Marlow, "Justice for Whom? Social and Environmental Ethics and the Hebrew Prophets," in *Ethical and Unethical in the Old Testament: God and Humans in Dialogue* (ed. Katharine J. Dell; LHBOTS 528; New York: T&T Clark, 2010), 105–106. Marlow discusses Psalm 72 and the king who exercises ideal leadership because God gives the king justice. Given the fact that many Old Testament texts image God in terms of the Great King, there is a symbiosis between God's justice and the expectations of royal justice.

[43] See J. David Pleins, *The Social Visions of the Hebrew Bible: A Theological Introduction* (Louisville, KY: Westminster John Knox Press, 2001), 395, in reference to the Book of Zephaniah.

[44] Phyllis Trible, *God and the Rhetoric of Sexuality* (OBT; Philadelphia: Fortress Press, 1978), 33.

[45] Brueggemann, *Theology of the Old Testament*, 288.

saves, also judges – and vice versa. This undoubtedly has something to do with the fact that much of the Old Testament's presentation of God is monotheistic, though plenty of texts manifest a henotheistic perspective, the idea that God is the greatest of all gods (e.g., Ps 95:3). From a more restricted monotheistic perspective, God is a God who both kills and brings to life (1 Sam 2:6) because no other "god of death" exists to whom to ascribe killing. At the same time, the overall impression of God in the Old Testament is that God does not use God's power to torment the human race but to promote human good. When God oversteps the bounds in using divine power, several passages in the Old Testament indicate that someone holds God accountable, as the angel does in Zech 1:8–12, with a variety of actions resulting for the good of the people.[46] One way to consider God's judgment in the Old Testament is to see it as God enforcing the Torah, which God gave to promote life.[47] From this perspective, God's salvation is not that distant from judgment, if we see salvation as seeking the people's good through deliverance from enemies. Salvation can also mean restoration after punishment, knowing that judgment is not annihilation (Gen 9:15) but a temporary act meant to elicit a course correction back to the good life. And, if God's judgment breaks the bounds so that it produces more harm than is warranted, then someone, angelic or human,

---

[46] This discussion of God, judgment, and working for the good of the human race relies on John Barton, "The Dark Side of God in the Old Testament," in *Ethical and Unethical in the Old Testament*, 127–128. Barton is summarizing the work of Walter Dietrich and Christian Link, *Die dunklen Seiten Gottes* (2 vols.; 2nd ed.; Neukirchen–Vluyn: Neukirchener Verlag, 1997), which Barton seems to appreciate but also critiques at some points.

[47] Reinhard Felmeier and Hermann Spieckermann, *God of the Living: A Biblical Theology*, trans. Mark E. Biddle (Waco, TX: Baylor University Press, 2011), 470–471.

may call God to account, with God repenting and working again for life through salvation.

In order for God to save, though, God must return to Israel in the postexile, as affirmed in Zech 1:1–6. Returning to the people after rejecting them creates a sense of wonderment because, often enough, the text does not say why YHWH returns, though the Book of Zechariah implies God's return stems from both repentance over unchecked anger and for the nations overstepping their mandate to punish Israel.[48] What we do know from the Books of Haggai and Zechariah, as well as from Isaiah 40–55 and the promises of a future in the Books of Jeremiah and Ezekiel, is that God's return means a renewal of God's benefactions: protecting Jerusalem and Yehud and sustaining their rains and crops. For the Jews to have a future, God must return to them and give them life, whether in returning to the Promised Land or in the diaspora (Esther, Daniel).

God's salvation does not belong only to Israel, however. God rules over all the nations that God made and so promotes their good as well. Thus, we must modify Richard Feldmeier and Hermann Spieckermann's claim that Zechariah 12–14 "interweaves destruction of the nations and the salvation of Jerusalem."[49] That claim is incomplete because, after God defeats the nations who war with Jerusalem, the texts envision the nations participating in the life of God's people and their pilgrim festivals. This more positive future for the nations echoes images earlier in the Book of Zechariah and across the Old Testament, whether that is the vision of Israel as a royal priesthood, which implies mediating a relationship between God and the nations (Exod

---

[48] Brueggemann, *Theology of the Old Testament*, 440.
[49] Felmeier and Spieckermann, *God of the Living*, 474.

19:5–6);⁵⁰ God's care for all those whom God made, which leads God to wish to save them from death (Ps 33:13–19); or Isaiah's vision of the future when the people in Egypt cry out to God and God delivers them (Isa 19:19–21). In line with Zechariah 8, the witness of the Old Testament includes the idea that, when the nations see the way God blesses Israel, they will want that blessing for themselves, with no indication that God would withhold such blessings, but, rather, that God would share them – just as for Israel.⁵¹

Doubts

One of the major concerns that emerges from pursuing a theological ethics from the Books of Haggai and Zechariah, and across the Old Testament, relates to the portrait of God's violence, whether in all-out war or in lesser forms such as by starving people. At some level we may acknowledge that trying to interpret God in relationship to humanity means the biblical writers inevitably used familiar language and that, because they related to God in history, this almost required them to think of God in terms of violence and war, given the prevalence of each in the ancient world.⁵² One of the concerns I share with others is not the truly violent images from the ancient past, but how Christians have enacted their own violence across history into the present.⁵³ Given the prevalence of violence and ongoing religious violence, we simply cannot ignore the Bible's violent imagery but should use

---

⁵⁰ On Israel mediating a relationship between the nations and God, see William H. C. Propp, *Exodus 19–40* (AB 2A; New York: Doubleday, 2006), 159.

⁵¹ See Brueggemann's discussion of Psalm 126 in *Theology of the Old Testament*, 500.

⁵² Peter C. Craigie, *The Problem of War in the Old Testament* (Grand Rapids: Eerdmans, 1978), 94–97.

⁵³ Ibid., 103.

violent texts as an invitation to raise our own consciousness in order to think more clearly about the connections between violence and faith.[54] On the one hand, we want to understand why violence emerges and especially to understand the way that violence itself may symbolize the cry for the end of oppression, whether in Ferguson, Missouri or Cairo, Egypt, especially as the powerful suppress what they label as rebellion among the oppressed. James Cone, for example, demanded that theologians, pastors, and churches see the assertions of Black Power in the 1960s as an act of God, which accords in some important ways with the prophets' interpretations of violence and war as acts of God against injustice. On the other hand, the biblical text witnesses to God's confession of letting anger go beyond its bounds so that it produces violence. Even the prophets themselves – Jeremiah above all others – protest the way that God's actions put their bodies in jeopardy. The prophets' protests ground our own concerns, including what might be called our Jeremianic defiance.[55] We know all too well that anger can easily lead to violence that goes too far, as evidenced by the modern term "collateral damage." If communities of faith believe that God creates and sustains the universe, then it seems we must continue to ask how our God, and we ourselves, are implicated in violence

---

[54] Following Yvonne Sherwood, "'Tongue-Lashing' or a Prophetic Aesthetics of Violation: An Analysis of Prophetic Structures that Reverberate Beyond the Biblical World," in *The Aesthetics of Violence in the Prophets* (ed. Julia O'Brien and Chris Franke; LHBOTS 517; New York: T&T Clark, 2010), 88–111.

[55] Robert L. Davidson, *The Courage to Doubt* (London/Philadelphia: SCM Press/Trinity Press International, 1983), 128–129, notes in Jeremiah's cursing of the day of his birth (Jer 20:14–18) a sense of defiance, shaking his fist at God, as it were.

and war and called to confession and repentance, as well as defiance and repudiation of the ongoing violence in our world.

Encased within this concern for violence generally is a concern about violence against women, especially. So, perhaps we might consider God technically innocent of the rape of women referred to in Zech 14:2 because the verbs are passive. But in the text God claims, "*I* will bring the nations to Jerusalem for war," knowing that rape will result. Furthermore, though the "Woman Wickedness" image in Zech 5:5–11 does not introduce violence, there is certainly evidence that using dehumanizing language makes it easier to enact violence, as demonstrated in the recent history of Rwanda.[56] The overall trajectory of images like these and the dismembered body of the Levite's concubine in Judges 19 and the "Strange Woman" of Proverbs 1–9, along with images of God acting out spousal violence in Hosea 2, Ezekiel 16, 23, and 24 present real problems. Language matters, including metaphorical language, because, as Renita Weems has observed, these words may give a young person in a church their first lesson in stereotyping, bigotry, and marginalizing others.[57] Given that we know the biblical writers used this language to shock rather than edify,[58] it seems that, if we call these texts Christian Scripture, we need to comprehend why the prophets found such language necessary and consider what language is appropriate to our place and time to shock the church out of its slumber. Simultaneously, we need to go further to also revolutionize structural oppression in local and

---

[56] See, e.g., Roger Bromiley, "Beat, Vermin, and Insect – Hate Media and the Construction of the Enemy: The Case of Rwanda, 1990–1994," *At the Interface / Probing the Boundaries* 75 (2011): 39–59.

[57] Renita Weems, *Battered Love: Marriage, Sex, and Violence in the Hebrew Bible* (OBT; Minneapolis, MN: Fortress Press, 1995), 107.

[58] Ibid., 115.

global spaces.⁵⁹ The context in which the Bible is now read is even more important, in the contemporary moment, than the context in which it was first written. Only by constructing communities and spaces of liberation, justice, inclusion, and participation will we really have the freedom to leave behind oppressive readings of the text that marginalize women (and others) in clear and subtle ways.

Divine Command

Although the word for "return" (*šûb*) with the idea of "repent" occurs only three times in the Book of Zechariah (all in Zech 1:1–6), it nevertheless sets the agenda for the book and is the book's key imperative. Preexilic prophets mainly announced God's judgment on the people,⁶⁰ but prophetic exhortations generally aim at repentance.⁶¹ Not surprisingly, therefore, the prophetic texts frequently urge their audience to turn away from injustice.⁶² When we see that the word exhorts people "to return," the implication is that people who repent do not return only to practices of justice, but also to relationship⁶³ with God and neighbor. Repentance calls people to return to God and to do things God requires ethically. Repentance also calls people to return to their neighbor, to treat them well and help them flourish.

---

⁵⁹ Musa W. Dube, *Postcolonial Feminist Interpretation of the Bible* (St. Louis, MO: Chalice Press, 2000), 123.
⁶⁰ Donald E. Gowan, "Repentance in the Old Testament," in *NIDB* 4:764.
⁶¹ Marvin A. Sweeney, *The Prophetic Literature* (IBT; Nashville, TN: Abingdon Press, 2005), 163.
⁶² Gowan, "Repentance in the Old Testament," 764.
⁶³ On *šûb* meaning a "return to relationship" in various contexts in the Old Testament see William L. Holladay, *The Root šûbh with Particular Reference to Its Usages in Covenantal Contexts* (Leiden: E. J. Brill, 1958), 72–74.

Following on the heels of repentance, it makes sense that the next key imperative calls people to do justice in the court and in the community, as this pair of commands pervades Scripture and contributed to the wholeness of a community. Israel was to appoint just judges throughout the cities and towns as the foundation of the community in the Promised Land. Their failure to appoint judges put their life in the land at risk.[64] Likewise, caring for the poor constitutes justice in God's sight while exploiting the poor is sin before God and threatens the peoples' security.[65] The prophetic books, including Zechariah, confirm that injustice leads to exile and that justice can either prevent exile or lead to a full renewal in the land after exile.

In Gary Anderson's study of one of the key words for joy (śimḥâ) in the Old Testament, he observes that the Book of Deuteronomy commands Israel to "rejoice before the LORD" nine times, almost always in a ritual context.[66] If we place Zech 9:9 in a festal celebration for victory, then this conjures images of people making offerings to God, as in Hos 10:5.[67] In Zech 9:9 the prophet summons the people to celebrate what God is doing: giving them victory (9:1–8) and bringing them a king to rule and lead them in times of war (9:9). Ethically, joyous festivals recognize the dependence of the community on God, that God supplies grain for bread or grapes for wine or deliverance from

---

[64] See the discussion in Robert L. Foster, *Wrestling with God and World: The Struggle for Justice in Christian Scripture* (Dallas, TX: A Journey Publication, 2013), 8–29.

[65] Ibid., 50–4.

[66] Gary A. Anderson, *A Time to Mourn, a Time to Dance: The Expression of Grief and Joy in Israelite Religion* (University Park, PA: The Pennsylvania State University Press, 1991), 20.

[67] The term in both texts is *gyl*.

Egypt or, in Zech 9:9, salvation from surrounding enemies with a king to guide and protect them. Obeying the command to rejoice challenges pride that makes a person think they possess the power to grasp what they desire while promoting a sense of dependency because it is God, not someone's own assertion of power, that provides victory or bread or wine or whatever.

According to John Barton, "[o]bedience to the declared will of God is probably the strongest model for ethical obligation in most of the books of the Hebrew Scriptures."[68] This is not blind obedience to the divine whim but, instead, must align with the good behavior the people see in God.[69] Haggai and Zechariah, like many other books in the Old Testament, demand obedience, particularly by honoring God in worship and by working for justice for one's neighbor. As a person moves to the modern context in this regard, there are plenty of commands in Scripture that do not require debate about *whether* to do them (do justice and steadfast love, speak truth to one another, and so on) but invite continued investigation on *how* best to do so.

Another ideal that emerges in the Books of Haggai and Zechariah that carries across much of the Old Testament is the search for just leadership. The shepherd-sheep metaphor concept is one obvious strand of this emphasis. J. David Pleins, writing about the collection of Nehemiah, Ezra, Esther, Ruth, and Daniel, observes a shared theme of the need for active agents in order to build up a just commonwealth. Such persons exemplify personal integrity, assist the poor, and enact social reform.[70] The hope in both Haggai and Zechariah was that Zerubbabel would embody this

---

[68] John Barton, *Understanding Old Testament Ethics: Approaches and Explorations* (Louisville, KY: Westminster John Knox Press, 2003), 47.
[69] Ibid., 48.   [70] Pleins, *Social Vision of the Hebrew Bible*, 204.

kind of leadership, with the Book of Zechariah placing nearly equal weight on Joshua the high priest. The unfolding argument of Zechariah, however, conveys to the audience that neither Zerubbabel nor Joshua achieved the lofty visions set for them. Even so, these books and many others in the Old Testament still uphold the ideal of just leadership, despite the frequent failure of human leaders.

In close connection with the call to just leadership and the effort to hold leadership accountable stands the institution of the prophet. From the days of Moses the role of the prophet entailed, to a significant degree, challenging empires. Sometimes this challenge is direct, as in Samuel's confrontation of Saul, Nathan's challenge of David, or the oracles in Isaiah against Assyria and in Jeremiah's against Babylon. A short book like the Book of Habakkuk might be fairly summarized as "Israel's God shakes the pillars of empire."[71] The Books of Haggai and Zechariah do this same kind of work.

Prophetic Witness

I hesitate to reduce the rich interaction of the Book of Haggai and Zechariah with the rest of the Old Testament to a few ethical essentials. Even so, as the last words in this theology of the Books of Haggai and Zechariah, I offer three foundations for the prophetic witness of contemporary communities of faith in light of these texts.

First, motherly compassion must be cultivated. If justice is to emerge in our world, there needs to be the kind of devoted commitment to those on the margins that is implied by "motherly compassion." In fact, it seems important to recognize that a

---

[71] Ibid., 394.

certain fierceness attends to this virtue because the deep connection one feels toward another on the margins naturally gives rise to anger because they are being exploited or harmed by the system. One must exercise caution in cultivating motherly compassion so as to avoid feeling superior to others. This virtue seems especially important for white, middle- to upper-class people. Physical spaces remind us that as we gain wealth we too readily build gated communities or border walls that keep us distant from those who might need our compassionate action. An essential element of prophetic witness in our times is to nurture a deeper motherly compassion for the marginal in our neighborhoods and for those living in the so-called Third World countries.

Second, prophetic witness that follows the imperatives in the Book of Zechariah and elsewhere in the Old Testament will focus on practicing holistic justice in courts and communities. This calls for *advocacy*, in partnership with the groups actually effected by policies and practices of injustice, and *generosity* that goes beyond charity to helping others flourish. It is troubling to know that communities where people are most economically at-risk are often the same communities that experience the greatest number of arrests and interaction with the criminal justice system. Local churches responsive to the commands of the prophets will work for changes in the criminal justice system that promote fairness and a true concern for the marginalized, while also working for economic development for individuals and families in these communities. Larger-scale efforts at reparations for African American and Native Americans in the United States, or sustainable economic development (as opposed to development run predominantly by "First World" businesses) in "Third World" countries seem like good places to start in the work of social justice.

Finally, doubt also plays an important function in prophetic witness in the world. I advocate for avoiding all violence, a countercultural move at any point in history, including and perhaps especially now. To me, the pursuit of nonviolence and peacemaking means emphasizing the places in the prophets and across the Old Testament containing visions of nations as participating in the life of God and as cared for by God, even and especially when the group in question acts as an enemy toward us and those with whom we work for justice. Each person has a spirit that the Great Artisan formed in them and we must look to treat those individuals, cities, and nations as people with whom we want to commune rather than those we want to physically harm. If communities of faith worldwide committed to these basic components of prophetic witness, I believe that the world would not only find that witness to be authentic but would also see, perhaps for the first time, what it means to be a community of faith.

In the end, then, and as a result, the community of faith that models these virtues and these practices would honor the God whom both Jews and Christians believe has spoken a word through the Books of Haggai and Zechariah.

Further Reading

COMMENTARIES ON HAGGAI AND ZECHARIAH

A number of good commentaries exist on the Books of Haggai and Zechariah. The field of modern research on these books changed significantly with the production of the volumes by Carol and Eric Meyers and David L. Petersen. Authors working in the field of the studies of the Book of the Twelve as a unit have produced several commentaries and bring a welcome perspective, including Michael Floyd, James Nogalski, and Marvin Sweeney. Hans Walter Wolf's commentary on Haggai remains a classic. Edgar Conrad's work intends to read the Book of Zechariah as a whole, a perspective which I appreciate.

Boda, Mark J. *The Book of Zechariah*. NICOT. Grand Rapids, MI: Eerdmans, 2016.
Conrad, Edgar W. *Zechariah*. Readings. Sheffield: Sheffield Academic Press, 1999.
Floyd, Michael H. *Minor Prophets, Part 2*. Forms of Old Testament Literature XXII. Grand Rapids, MI: Eerdmans, 2000.
Meadowcroft, Tim. *Haggai*. Readings. Sheffield: Sheffield Phoenix Press, 2006.
Meyers, Carol L., and Eric M. Meyers. *Haggai, Zechariah 1–8*. AB 25B. Garden City, NY: Doubleday, 1987.

Zechariah 9–14. AB 25C. New York: Doubleday, 1993.
Nogalski, James D. *The Book of the Twelve: Micah–Malachi.* Smyth & Helwys 18a. Macon, GA: Smyth & Helwys, 2011.
Petersen, David L. *Haggai and Zechariah 1–8: A Commentary.* OTL. Philadelphia: The Westminster Press, 1984.
Zechariah 9–14 and Malachi: A Commentary. OTL. Louisville, KY: Westminster John Knox Press, 1995.
Sweeney, Marvin A. *The Twelve Prophets.* Vol. 2. Berit Olam. Collegeville, MN: The Liturgical Press, 2000.
Wolff, Hans Walter. *Haggai: A Commentary.* Translated by Margaret Kohl. Minneapolis, MN: Augsburg Publishing House, 1988.
Wolters, Al. *Zechariah.* HCOT. Leuven: Peeters, 2014.

STUDIES

Recent years have produced a number of excellent articles and monographs on Haggai and Zechariah, though, as with the recent commentaries, the field still lacks much in-depth work in the area of the theology of the two books.

Assis, Elie. "Composition, Rhetoric, and Theology in Haggai 1:1–11." *Journal of Hebrew Studies* 7 (2007): online.
"A Disputed Temple (Haggai 2,1–9)." *ZAW* **120** (2008): 582–596.
Bedford, Peter Ross. "Discerning the Time: Haggai, Zechariah, and the 'Delay' in Rebuilding the Temple." Pages 71–94 in *The Pitcher Is Broken: Memorial Essays for Gösta W. Ahlström.* Journal for the Study of the Old Testament Supplement 159. Sheffield: Sheffield Academic Press, 1995.

Boda, Mark J. "Terrifying the Horns: Persia and Babylonia in Zechariah 1:7–6:15." *Catholic Biblical Quarterly* **67** (2005): 22–41.

Boda, Mark J., and Michael Floyd, eds. *Bringing Out the Treasure: Inner Biblical Allusion in Zechariah 9–14*. Journal for the Study of the Old Testament Supplement 370. Sheffield: Sheffield Academic Press, 2003.

——— *Tradition in Transition: Haggai and Zechariah 1–8 in the Trajectory of Hebrew Theology*. LHBOTS 475. New York: T&T Clark, 2008.

Butterworth, Mike. *Structure of the Book of Zechariah*. Journal for the Study of the Old Testament Supplement 130. Sheffield: JSOT Press, 1992.

Curtis, Byron G. *Up the Stony Road: The Book of Zechariah in Social Location Trajectory Analysis*. SBL Academia Biblica 25. Atlanta, GA: Society of Biblical Literature, 2006.

Finistis, Antonios. *Vision and Eschatology: A Socio-Historical Analysis of Zechariah 1–6*. Library of Second Testament Studies 79. New York: Bloomsbury, 2011.

Floyd, Michael H. "Cosmos and History in Zechariah's View of Restoration (Zech. 1:7–6:15)." Pages 125–144 in *Problems in Biblical Theology*. Edited by Henri T. C. Sun et al. Grand Rapids, MI: Eerdmans, 1997.

Foster, Robert L. "Shepherds, Sticks, and Social Destabilization: A Fresh Look at Zechariah 11:4–17." *JBL* **126** (2007): 735–753.

——— "Undoing the Future: The Theology of the Book of Zechariah." *HBT* **34** (2012): 59–72.

Kessler, John. *The Book of Haggai: Prophecy and Society in Early Persian Yehud*. VTSup 91. Leiden: Brill, 2002.

Petersen, David L. "Zechariah's Visions: A Theological Perspective." *VT* **34** (1984): 195–206.

Petterson, Anthony R. *Behold Your King: The Hope for the House of David in the Book of Zechariah*. LHBOTS 513. New York: T&T Clark, 2009.

Tiemeyer, Lena-Sofia. *Zechariah and His Visions: An Exegetical Study of Zechariah's Vision Report*. LHBOTS 605. London/New York: Bloomsbury: T&T Clark, 2015.

Tollington, James E. *Tradition and Innovation in Haggai and Zechariah 1–8*. Journal for the Study of the Old Testament Supplement 150. Sheffield: Sheffield Academic Press, 1993.

Tuckett, Christopher, ed. *The Book of Zechariah and Its Influence*. Burlington, VT: Ashgate Publishing Company, 2003.

Wenzel, Heiko. *Reading Zechariah with Zechariah 1:1–6 as the Introduction to the Entire Book*. Contributions to Biblical Exegesis and Theology 59. Leuven: Peeters, 2011.

THE BOOK OF THE TWELVE

One of the important turns in the study of the Minor Prophets has been a study of the formation of the Book of the Twelve as a coherent literary unit, which includes following theological themes that develop throughout the corpus.

Ben Zvi, Ehud, and James Nogalski. *Two Sides of a Coin: Juxtaposing Views on Interpreting the Book of the Twelve/The Twelve Prophetic Books*. Analecta Gorgian 201. Piscataway, NJ: Gorgias Press, 2009.

House, Paul R. *The Unity of the Twelve*. Journal for the Study of the Old Testament Supplement 97. Sheffield: Almond Press, 1990.

Nogalski, James D., and Marvin A. Sweeney, editors. *Reading and Hearing the Book of the Twelve*. SBLSymS 15. Atlanta, GA: Society of Biblical Literature, 2000.

Redditt, Paul L., and Aaron Schart, eds. *Thematic Threads in the Book of the Twelve.* BZAW 325. Berlin: Walter de Gruyter, 2003.

SURVEY OF LITERATURE ON HAGGAI AND ZECHARIAH

Boda, Mark J. *Haggai & Zechariah Research: A Bibliographical Survey.* Leiden: Deo Publishing, 2003.

Author Index

Adams, Samuel L. 11, 157, 165
Anderson, Gary, 46
Arnold, Bill T. 77, 109, 135, 188, 190

Balentine, Samuel E., 220–221
Barr, James, 58
Barton, John 207, 224, 231
Becking, Bob, 4
Ben Zvi, Ehud, 8,
Benjamin, Don C. 167
Betlyon, John W., 5, 10
Boda, Mark J. 67, 75, 82, 88, 130, 134, 190
Bonfiglio, Ryan P., 133
Bonhoeffer, Dietrich 150
Boring, M. Eugene 79
Briant, Pierre, 3, 8, 36, 43–44, 61–62, 64, 76, 86, 88, 103, 126–127, 135, 147, 189–190, 193
Bromiley, Roger 228
Brueggemann, Walter, 210–211, 221, 223, 225–226
Bryce, Trevor, 126

Carter, Charles E., 5
Chan, Michael J., 35
Choi, John H. 77, 109, 135, 188, 190
Clark, Herbert H. 155
Clements, Ronald E. 49–50
Coggins, Richard James 102
Craigie, Peter C. 226

Davidson, Robert, 17, 227
De Geus, C. H. J. 107
De La Torre, Miguel A. 171
Deist, Ferdinand E., 27, 57, 181, 185
Dever, William G., 165

Dietrich, Walter 224
Dube, Musa W., 229

Ellis, Richard S. 130

Feldmeier, Reinhard 224–225
Finkelstein, Israel, 22
Foster, Robert L., xviii, 12, 14, 40, 54, 57, 138, 156, 160–161, 163–164, 168, 175, 217, 230
Fretheim, Terence E., 168
Fritz, Volkmar 182

Gelston, Anthony 88
Gilbert, Allen S., 66
Gowan, Donald E., 32, 205–206, 211–212, 220, 229
Graf, David F. 89

Halpern, Baruch, 10
Hauerwas, Stanley 119
Hengel, Martin, 15
Heschel, Abraham 205, 208, 212
Hildebrand, David R., 38
Holladay, William L., 229
Hundley, Michael B., 24, 26, 32, 93, 182

Janzen, Waldemar 69, 168
Jigoulov, Vadin S., 6

Kaptan, Deniz 133
Keel, Othmar, 34, 42, 164, 175, 189–190, 192
Kelley, Tyler, 25, 74
King, Philip J., 26, 42, 56, 68, 84, 131, 136–137, 156, 176, 186
Knoppers, Gary N. 191
Kuhrt, Amélie, 4, 21, 45, 76, 113, 128, 135

AUTHOR INDEX

Levenson, Jon, 209–210, 213
Lincoln, Bruce 72, 113
Link, Christian 224
Lipschits, Oded, 5, 22
Llewellyn-Jones, Lloyd, 61–62, 93, 135

Marlow, Hilary, 223
Matthews, Victor H., 167
Meadowcroft, Tim, 38
Meier, Samuel A. 173
Menken, M. J. J., 16
Merrill-Willis, Amy C. 214–215
Meyers, Carol L., 31, 38, 45, 66, 88, 90–92, 103, 105, 134, 137, 189–190
Meyers, Eric M., 31, 38, 45, 66, 88, 90–92, 103, 105, 134, 137, 189–190
Moberly, R. W. L., 50, 110, 219
Möller, Karl, 13
Mulder, Martin J., 23

Nissinen, Martti, 27, 53–54, 61, 100, 123, 138, 174, 182–183
Nogalski, James D., 41
Novotny, Jamie R., 130

Ortlund, Eric Nels 189

Peckham, J. Brian, 6
Petersen, David L., 41, 75, 88, 190, 203
Pleins, David J. 223, 231–232
Pritchard, James B., 126
Propp, William H. C., 226

Rendtorff, Rolf 207
Rudolph, Wilhelm 134
Ruzicka, Steven, 3, 9

Sakenfeld, Katherine Doob, 222
Schroer, Silvia, 42, 164, 175
Seow, C. L. 218
Seurfert, Michael J., 145
Shepherd, David J. 216–217
Sherwood, Yvonne, 227
Spieckermann, Hermann 224–225
Stacey, David, 14, 93, 155, 161–162
Stager, Lawrence E., 26, 42, 56, 65, 68, 84, 131, 136–137, 146, 156, 166, 176, 186
Stanley, Andy 198
Stanley, Christopher D., 16
Steele, Gail Corrington 97
Stern, Ephraim 21, 68, 107
Strawn, Brent A. 71, 81, 147, 193
Sweeney, Marvin A., 33, 41, 89, 134, 147, 190, 203, 206–207, 211, 229

Tanner, Beth LaNeel, 63
Tiemeyer, Lena-Sofia, 75, 79, 84, 88
Trible, Phyllis 223
Trimm, Charlie 125

Ussishkin, David, 5, 146

Vancil, Jack W. 134

Waters, Matt 71, 133
Weems, Renita 228
Whybray, R. Norman 212
Wilber, Donald M. 35, 71, 193
Wright, Christopher J. H., 215–216

Zagzebski, Linda Trinkaus, 17

Scripture Index

OLD TESTAMENT

Genesis
  2:7–8, 164
  9:15, 224
  12:1–3, 64
  12:2, 110
  12:3b, 219
  12:8, 175
  15:18–20, 33
  21:8–20, 165
  26:25, 175
  27, 165
  33:19, 175
  35:10, 179
  35:21, 175
  37:10, 75
  37:34–35, 179
  37:35, 64
  43:6, 41

Exodus
  2:24–25, 129
  5:6, 140
  5:10, 140
  5:13, 140
  5:14, 140
  6, 32
  6:26, 2
  6:2–8, 32
  7:4, 2
  11:1–3, 34
  12:17, 2
  12:33–36, 34
  12:37–42, 22
  12:41, 2
  12:51, 2
  13:11–15, 141
  14:30–31, 28
  15:1, 45
  19:5–6, 226
  19:23, 77
  20–23, 220
  20:15–22, 28
  21:32, 164
  24, 132
  24:4, 132
  24:8, 132
  24:16–17, 220
  24:17, 68
  25–31, 221
  28, 29
  28:36, 194
  28:36–38, 46–7
  29:42b–46, 220
  30:10, 194
  32:11, 101
  34:6–7, 117
  35, 29
  35–40, 221
  35:4, 29
  35:21, 29
  35:29, 29
  35:39, 29
  39:30, 194
  39:30–31, 46
  40, 30
  40:34–35, 35, 220
  40:34–38, 29

Leviticus
  7.:4–18, 38
  7:19–21, 39
  7:26–27, 127
  10:9, 74

SCRIPTURE INDEX

10:9–11, 38
16:29, 102
17:10–11, 127
17:19, 38
22:15, 194
23:20, 194
23:26–29, 102
27:9, 194
27:30, 194
27:32, 194
Numbers
  5:11–14, 105
  6:5, 194
  11:1, 68
  16:35, 68
  18:2, 71
  18:4, 71
  18:5, 56
  19:3, 40
  19:11–22, 39
  21:17, 138
  24:4, 79
  24:16, 79
  33:54, 117
  34:17–18, 117
Deuteronomy
  1:9–18, 221
  3:18, 84
  4:1–8, 115
  4:24, 68
  10:19, 221
  15:1, 221
  15:1–6, 221
  15:7–11, 221
  15:9, 221
  15:12, 221
  15:15, 222
  18:15–22, 55
  18;20–22, 122
  24:10–18, 109
  24:19–22, 221
  28:44–68, 222
  29:10, 87
  33:17, 66
Joshua
  7:21, 146
  7:24, 146
  9:20, 56
  22:8, 188
Judges
  11:19–20, 125

15:6, 40
19, 228
20:2, 141
Ruth
  2:2, 179
  2:10, 179
  2:16, 75
1 Samuel
  2:6, 224
  8–9, 77
  13:10, 181
  14:7, 141
  15:3, 156
  15:11, 64
  15:15, 156
  15:29, 64
  15:35, 64
  30:26–31, 188
  36:10, 34
2 Samuel
  3:34, 84
  7:7, 138
  7:10, 84
  10:2, 64
  12:15–23, 180
  17:2, 40
  23:21, 156
1 Kings
  8:10–11, 35
  8:44, 65
  8:48, 65
  10:24, 114
  13:6, 101
  15:12, 182
  22, 78
2 Kings
  1:10–14, 68
  2:16, 84
  8:11, 69
  10:15–28, 105
  22:17, 138
1 Chronicles
  6:21, 179
  23:3, 185
  24:4, 185
  26:12, 185
2 Chronicles
  7:1–2, 69
  11:14, 143
  16:9, 83
  17:11, 122

2 Chronicles (cont.)
  19:10, 56
  21:11–20, 192
  26:7, 84
  26:9, 84
  29:19, 143
Ezra
  1:1, 29
  1:1–4, 55, 215
  1:2–11, 23
  1:5, 30
  3:10, 82
  4, 94
  4:4, 83
  4:10, 82
  4:14, 83
  7:6, 216
  7:8–9, 216
  7:27–28, 216
  8:18–20, 216
  8:22, 216
  8:31–32, 216
Nehemiah
  1:1–3, 72
  1:6–9, 216
  1:11, 216
  2:1–3, 72
  2:4, 216
  5, 146, 157–8, 217
  5:1–13, 157
  5:2, 157
  5:3, 157
  5:4, 157
  5:5, 157
  5:7, 157
  5:10–12, 157
  5:14–19, 157
  5:15, 217
  5:18, 157
  7:2, 217
  7:4, 5
  7–8, 139
  9:36–37, 72
  13:21–31, 72
Esther
  4:13–14, 213
  5:2, 179
  6:13, 213
  8:3, 93
  8:17, 213
Job
  10:8–12, 164
  31:29, 180
Psalm
  7:2, 147
  10:9, 147
  17:12, 147
  22:13, 147
  22:21, 147
  23:1, 160
  29:1, 138, 160
  33:11, 92
  33:13–19, 226
  60:2, 34
  72, 223
  73–89, 217
  74:1, 217
  76:4, 217
  76:11, 217
  77:10, 217
  78.62–63, 217
  79:5, 217
  79:11–13, 217
  84:1–5, 218
  89:6, 190
  89:8, 190
  95:3, 224
  122, 218
  122:3, 219
  136, 117
Proverbs
  1–9, 228
  2:18–19, 97
Isaiah
  1:23, 86
  1:26, 106
  2.6–21, 147
  5:29, 147
  6, 78
  10, 106
  10:1–2, 106
  10:5–7, 107
  10:5–34, 147
  10:12, 107
  10:15–19, 107
  10:20–21, 107
  14:2–23, 147
  19:13, 141
  19:17, 92
  19:19–21, 226
  19:19–22, 126
  20:2, 20

28:1–22, 74
28:10, 74
40:3–11, 211
40–55, 161–2, 183, 225
41:8–10, 211
42, 161–2
42:7, 161
42:16, 161
43:25, 211
44:21, 164
44:21–28, 161–2, 166
44:22, 166, 211
44:23, 164
44:24, 164
44:26, 164
44:28, 134, 164, 166
45:18, 164
49, 161–2
49:5, 141
49:6, 141, 161
49:8, 161
49:9–11, 161
54:7–8, 211

Jeremiah
2:11–13, 181
5:11, 158
7, 210
7:1–5, 210
7:4, 158
7:8, 158
8:18, 158
9:10, 158
13:14, 158
20:14–18, 227
21:11–14, 147
22.1–22, 147
22:24, 45
23, 78, 134
23:1, 138
23:1–2, 142, 211
23:1–4, 167
23:5, 78
24:9, 110
25:11–12, 94
25:18, 110
26:6, 110
29:1–9, 159
29:10, 94
29–33, 183
32:1–15, 108
32:17, 108

32:19, 92
32.23–25, 108
32:27, 108
32:28–35, 108
32:36–37, 108
32:38, 109
33:2, 164
33:14–15, 78
33:14–26, 92
36:9–32, 20
37:2, 20
39:10, 159
43:1–7, 13–14
50:1, 20

Ezekiel
5:2, 185
5:12, 185
5:13, 90
7:3, 158
7:8, 158
7:19, 158
8:10, 158
8:17, 158
9, 158
9:8, 158
9:9, 158
16, 228
16:42, 90
17, 147
21:22, 90
23, 228
24, 228
24:13, 90
31, 147
34, 134
34:1–5, 157
34:1–6, 211
34:1–10, 167
34:11–16, 160
37, 81
37:1–8, 81
37:9–10, 81
37:11, 81
37:12–14, 81
40–48, 157

Daniel
1:2, 87
7–12, 214–15
8:13, 190
9:3, 179
9:17, 179

Daniel (cont.)
  9:18, 179
Hosea
  1:1, 205
  2., 228
  2:8, 42
  2:23, 42
  10:5, 230
Joel
  1–2, 207
  3 (Heb. chap.4), 207
Amos
  1:3–2.5, 146
  3:12, 147
  4:3, 164
  4:9, 41
  8:11–12, 205
Haggai
  1, 213
  1:1, 19–20, 24, 29, 205
  1:1–1.15a, 19, 20
  1:2a, 21
  1:2b, 22
  1:4, 23
  1:5, 19, 25
  1:5–11, 109
  1:6, 25, 49, 137
  1:7, 19, 25
  1:8, 19, 27–9
  1:9, 25, 46
  1:9–11, 137
  1:9a, 26
  1:10–11, 34
  1:11, 25, 49
  1:12, 28
  1:13, 28
  1:14, 29
  1:15b, 19
  1:15b–2.9, 19
  2:1–2, 31
  2:3, 31, 82
  2:4, 19, 32–3
  2:4–9, 2
  2:5, 32, 220
  2:5c, 33
  2:6–7, 34
  2:6–9, 7, 11
  2:7, 34–5, 220
  2:8, 34
  2:9, 36
  2:10, 19
  2:10–19, 19, 36, 38
  2:12–13, 41
  2:14, 46
  2:15, 19, 38–9, 42
  2:15a, 41
  2:16, 39
  2:17, 41–2
  2:17b, 41
  2:18, 19, 38, 39, 42
  2:18–19, 109
  2:19, 41–2
  2:19–23, 11
  2:19b, 42
  2:20, 19
  2:20–23, 2, 19, 44
  2:21, 45
  2:22, 44
  2:22b, 45
  2:23, 45–6
Zechariah
  1–6, 10
  1–8, 122, 124
  1–10, 174
  1–11, 172
  1:1–11.3, 172
  1:1–6, 11, 77, 104, 148, 159, 162, 166, 175, 183, 186, 225, 229
  1:1, 55, 61, 205
  1:1–12, 63
  1:2, 56, 64
  1:3, 55
  1:4, 12, 56, 89
  1:4–6, 77
  1:6, 58, 77
  1:7–2.17, 211
  1:7–6.15, 11–12, 61, 98, 122, 183, 185–6
  1:7–6.8, 101, 211, 213
  1:7–11.3, 121
  1:7a, 62
  1:7b, 61
  1:8–11, 63, 89
  1:8–12, 224
  1:10–11, 129
  1:12, 69, 95
  1:12–13, 103
  1:12–17, 90
  1:13, 64, 69, 196
  1:14–15, 105
  1:15–16a, 64
  1:16, 62–3, 65, 117
  1:17, 62–3

SCRIPTURE INDEX

1:17a, 65
1:17b, 65
1:18–21, 177
1:21–23, 106
2:1–2, 66
2:1–4, 66, 196
2:1–17, 66
2:3, 67
2:3–4, 66
2:4, 67
2:5, 67, 128
2:5–17, 66
2:6, 67
2:6–12, 2
2:7–8, 68
2:9, 68
2:10, 69
2:11, 69
2:12, 70
2:13, 70
2:14, 62
2:14–17, 211
2:15, 71, 94, 98, 180, 208
2:15–17, 72
2:15c, 72
3, 91
3:1, 73, 75
3:1–5, 76
3:1–8, 92
3:2, 75
3:3–4, 74
3:4–5, 76
3:6, 77
3:7, 77
3:7d, 78
3:8, 78
3:9, 78
3:10, 79
4:1, 80
4:2–3, 80
4:4–5, 80
4:7, 13–14, 80
4:8–9, 209
4:9, 83
4:9a, 81
4:10, 13–14
4:10a, 82
4:10c, 83
4:12, 84
4:14, 84
5:1–4, 111, 221

5:2, 85
5:3, 86
5:3–4, 85
5:3a, 86
5:4, 87
5:4b, 86
5:5–11, 88, 96, 228
5:6, 87
5:6–10, 87
5:7–8, 87
5:9–10, 129
5:9–11, 87
5:11, 90
6:1–5, 89
6:1–8, 89, 129
6:5, 89
6:6–7, 90
6:8, 90
6:8c, 90
6:9–11a, 91
6:9–15, 91
6:11b, 91
6:12–13, 13–14
6:12–15, 7
6:13b-c, 92
6:15, 94
6:15c, 94
7–8, 10, 13–14, 98, 115, 118–19, 122, 148, 203
7:1, 54
7:1–3, 100
7:2, 100, 114
7:3, 100–1
7:5–6, 101
7:7, 116
7:7–14, 59, 111, 183
7:8–10, 204
7.:8–14, 11
7:9, 105, 117
7:9–10, 12, 102, 109, 117, 221
7:12, 103
7:13, 103
7:15, 103
8:2–3, 13–14
8:3, 105–6, 115, 118
8:4–5, 107, 112, 116
8:4–15, 105
8:6, 108, 127
8:7, 108
8:8, 105, 108, 115
8:9, 109
8:10, 109

Zechariah (cont.)
  8:10–11, 109
  8:11, 127
  8:11–12, 109
  8:12, 116, 127
  8:13, 219
  8:13a, 110
  8:13b, 110
  8:13c, 110
  8:14, 110
  8:15, 110
  8:15b, 110
  8:16, 105
  8:16–17, 11–12, 105, 111, 204, 221
  8:17, 116–17
  8:17a, 112
  8:18–23, 105
  8:19, 105, 117
  8:19a, 112
  8:19b, 112
  8:20–23, 2, 106, 114, 118, 128, 208
  8:21–22, 114
  8:23, 114, 124
  9–10, 9, 160, 162, 172
  9–14, 9–10, 122–3, 201, 204, 214
  9:1–10:12, 131
  9:1–11.3, 121, 123–4, 146, 148, 151–2, 154, 162, 186
  9:1, 121–2, 126–7, 131, 148
  9:1–8, 128, 131, 191, 230
  9:2–3, 213
  9:3, 125
  9:4, 125, 146
  9:5, 125, 130
  9:5–8, 7
  9:6, 146
  9:7, 126–7, 180, 208
  9:8, 125, 140, 148
  9:8c, 129
  9:9, 123, 129, 132, 230
  9:9–10, 9, 131
  9:10, 125, 130–1
  9:11, 132, 141
  9:11–13, 140
  9:13, 77, 131, 133, 140, 146
  9:16, 133, 138
  9:16a, 134
  9:17, 137
  10:1, 123, 136–7, 139, 145
  10:1–2, 161, 186
  10:1–3, 159, 168

10:1–5, 214, 216
10:1–12, 136
10:2, 137
10:2c, 138
10:2–3, 138
10:3, 137–8, 177
10:3c, 140
10:4, 140
10:5a, 141
10:5b, 141
10:6, 131, 140–1, 145
10:6b, 143
10:7, 131
10:8, 141, 145
10:10, 142, 145
10:11, 146
10:11b, 144
10:12b, 144
11, 13–14, 187
11:1, 147
11:1–2, 123
11:1–3, 147, 154
11:2, 147
11:3, 146
11:4–17, 13–14, 121, 123, 144, 154, 156, 163–4, 166, 170, 172, 174–5, 177, 210, 212, 214, 221
11:4–5, 156–7, 168
11:4–6, 160, 186, 221
11:4–7, 11, 159, 186
11:6, 158
11:7, 160
11:7–11, 159, 161
11:7–8.23, 162
11:8, 160, 186
11:8b–9, 160
11:9, 160
11:10, 160
11:10a, 161
11:10b, 161
11:11, 14, 160
11:12–14, 159, 163–4
11:12a, 163
11:12b–13a, 163
11:14, 14, 163, 165
11:15, 167
11:15–17, 184
11:16, 167
11:17, 168, 218
12–14, 121, 123, 172, 194–5, 197, 225
12:1–13.9, 191

12:1, 122, 172–3, 175–6, 179–80, 183, 186–7, 195
12:1–9, 176–7, 184
12:1b, 174
12:2, 174, 176
12:3, 176
12:4, 176
12:5, 177
12:6, 176, 178
12:6–9, 172
12:7, 176, 178
12:7–8, 176
12:7–9, 178
12:9, 176
12:10, 179, 183
12:10–14, 176, 180, 184
12:12–14, 180
13:1, 174, 180–1
13:1–6, 70, 176, 180, 184, 212
13:1–9, 186
13:2, 174, 177, 180, 182–3, 191
13:2b, 182
13:3, 182–3
13:6, 173
13:7, 185, 218
13:7–8, 185, 222
13:7–9, 13–14, 176, 184, 188–9, 214
13:8, 174, 176–7, 185
13:9, 174, 181, 186, 193
13:9a, 185
13:9b, 186
14, 180, 210
14:1, 176, 187, 190, 192
14:1–2, 207
14:2, 174, 188, 228
14:2a-b, 188, 222
14:2c, 188
14:3, 188
14:4, 190, 192

14:5, 190
14:6, 190
14:6–7, 190
14:8, 190
14:9a, 190
14:9b, 191
14:10a, 190
14:11, 173, 191, 204
14:12, 189, 191
14:12–19, 2
14:13, 192
14:14, 192
14:16, 193, 208
14:16–17, 191
14:20, 194
14:20–21, 174
14:21, 194
Malachi
1:1–5, 202
1:4–14, 203
3:1–5, 203
3:5b-c, 204
3:5d-g, 203
3:6, 203
3:13–24, 204
3:14, 204
3:24, 204

NEW TESTAMENT

Romans
    13:1–7, 151
Galatians
    3.6–9, 219

Subject Index

Aaron, 46–47
Aaronite priests, 71
Abednego, 214
Abram/Abraham, 33, 48, 110, 165, 219
Achaemenes, 9
Achan, 146
Ahaz, 143
Ahithophel, 40
Ahura Mazda, 206
   blessing Persian kings, 128
   "blissful happiness for humankind," 72, 113
   favoring Persian rulers, 114
   granting victory in battle, 144
   worship of, 128
Alexander the Great, 6
Antiochus Epiphanes IV, 214
Ark of the Covenant, 126
Artaxerxes I, 9–10, 121, 124, 128, 134, 189, 214
Asa, 182
Ashkelon, 124
Ashtaroth, 181
Assyria, 65–66, 70, 106, 142, 144–146, 148, 191, 205, 232

Baal, 105
Babylon, 65–66, 70, 90, 108, 173, 205, 222, 232
Babylonian Exile, 34, 104, 185, 191
   end of, 94
   reasons for, 102
   return from, 23, 37, 48, 141–142
Balaam, 79
Bashan, 145–147
Battle of Cunaxa, 189
Battle of Mycale, 133
Battle of Papremis, 9

Behistun inscription, 36, 72
Bethel, 100, 104
Biblical Theology, 15–16
"blood of the covenant," 132
Boaz, 75, 179
Branch, the, 78, 91–92, 178, 200

Chronicler, the, 192
Civil Rights Movement, 18
clean/unclean, 38–39
court justice, 111
covenant
   Abrahamic, 32
   "covenant with the peoples," 161
Cyropaedia, 88
Cyrus Cylinder, 4
Cyrus II, 4, 6, 23, 29, 55, 134, 142, 164, 166, 175, 177, 187, 201, 215

Damascus, 126
Daniel, 179, 214
Darius I, 2, 9, 12, 19–20, 32, 36, 43, 53–54, 64, 71, 75, 89, 127, 130–131, 144, 193, 199, 215
Darius II, 83
David, 40, 126–127, 180, 188, 232
   house of, 174, 178–180, 182
   line of, 92
Day of YHWH, the, 207–208
debt-slavery, 156–157, 171, 221
divine command theory, 17
divine motivation theory, 17

Edom, 202
Egypt, 65, 142, 144–146, 148, 193, 222
   days of Joseph, 143
   rebellion of, 121, 124, 131

SUBJECT INDEX

Ekron, 127
Elijah, 192
Ephraim, 132, 139
Esau, 165, 179, 202
Esther, 179, 213–214
ethical doubts
  abusive power, 50
  divine violence, 149
  marginalization of/violence against women, 229
  religous violence, 226–228
  violence, 234
  war/war crimes, 195
  "woman Wickedness" 96–97
ethics
  accountability, 224, 232
  anger, 59, 152
  to bless, 49, 51
  community building, 171
  courage, 194, 197
  court justice, 98, 117, 169, 221, 230
  covenant commitment, 48
  faithfulness, 222
  generosity, 59
  God's repentance, 96
  gratitude, 152
  grief, 169, 171
  impartial judgment, 223
  joy, 230–231
  justice, 115, 118, 151, 233
  lament, 197
  and leadership, 231
  liberation, 48, 51
  loyalty, 222
  moetherly compassion, 95, 98, 117, 148–149, 223, 232
  obedience, 231
  peace, 117–118
  peacemaking, 98, 151, 234
  pity, 170
  poor, widow, alien, and orphan, 115, 151, 221
  redemption, 149
  repentance, 58, 98, 229
  repentance, divine, 225
  salvation, 149, 151, 195, 222, 224
  social justice, 98, 230
  steadfast love, 117
  truth, 115
  zeal, 119
  zeal/jelousy, 115

Exodus, the, 21
Ezekiel the prophet, 70
Ezra, 216

false divination, 137
fasting, 102
Festival of Booths, 193
Former Prophets, the, 212

Gaza, 124, 130
Gilead, 145–147
Golden Calf, 101
governors of Yehud
  exploitation of the people, 160
  failures of, 138–139, 157, 167
  greed of, 154
  as shepherds, 138, 167, 184, 186, 214

Hadrach, 126
Hagar, 166
Haggai the prophet, 20, 38, 44
Haman, 213
Hanani, 217
Hebrew terminology
  'attâ, 129
  'ašrê, 218
  'adderet, 146
  'al, 174
  'am hā'āreṣ, 80
  'p, 158
  'attem, 23
  'el, 174
  'ĕlōhîm, 184
  'ĕmet, 105–106
  'ênāyim, 79
  'hb, 112
  bayyôm hahû', 172
  bêt 'āb, 165
  bny ḥyl, 84
  bny 'wlh, 84
  bqš, 114
  bryt, 32
  geber, 185
  glh, 79
  g'r, 75
  dqr, 183
  derek, 26, 56, 57
  ha'ôd, 41
  habbayit, 26
  haśśāṭān, 73

SUBJECT INDEX

Hebrew terminology (cont.)
 haṣṣō 'ārîm, 185
 hinnēh, 176
 waw, 57
 znḥ, 143
 ḥērem, 204
 ḥesed, 112, 117, 222
 ḥlh, 101
 ḥmh, 158
 ḥôtām, 45–46
 ḥārāšîm, 67
 yd', 190
 yṣ', 32
 yôṣēr, 164
 kî, 134
 kol nôgēś, 140
 lə-, 188, 190
 lə-yhwh, 207
 lwh, 71
 mahləkîm, 78
 malqôš, 136
 maśśā', 122, 173
 mənûḥâ, 126
 mšpṭ, 89
 ne 'ĕmānâ, 106
 nə 'um yhwh, 173
 nḥm, 64
 nṣl, 158
 nss, 134
 nṭḥ, 175
 nwḥ, 90
 nws, 134
 'ăṣabbîm, 181
 'wd, 77
 'immāk, 190
 'nh, 102
 'qb, 203
 'ṣh, 92
 pdh, 141
 ṣdq, 109
 ṣdqh, 89
 ṣ'h, 74
 ṣwm, 102
 qb', 203
 qədēšîm, 182
 qn', 105
 qrn, 66
 qṣp, 56, 64
 ro'šê haggəbārîm, 185
 rēa', 78
 rəḥôb, 107
 rḥm, 63, 141
 rûaḥ, 29, 80, 179, 183
 shalom, 36
 śym, 46
 śimḥâ, 230
 śîmû-nā ' ləbabkem, 39
 spn, 23
 šwb, 141, 203
 teḥĕzaqnâ, 109
 tərāpîm, 137
 torah, 38, 43
Heldai, 91
henotheism, 224
Herod I, 7
Herodotus, 158

idolatry, 180
Inaros of Egypt, 9
intercession, 65
Isaac, 166
Isaiah the prophet, 232
Ishmael, 166
Israel, 142, 145, 174, 181, 188
 house of, 110, 219
 remnant of, 19, 107, 113

Jacob, son of Isaac, 71, 75, 166, 179, 202
 descendants of, 203
Javan (Greece), 133
Jebusites, 127, 148
Jedaiah, 91
Jehoram, 192
Jehu, 105
Jeremiah the prophet, 232
Jeroboam I, 101
Jeroboam II, 205
Jerusalem
 center of God's rule, 14, 90
 center of the world, 194, 207–208
 chosen city of YHWH, 65
 city of David, 206
 fate of, 206
 future glory of, 68
 future greatness, 65
 as a paradise, 191
Jonathan, son of Saul, 141
Jordan River, 145
Joseph, 75
 metonymy for Israel, 143
Joseph, house of, 140
Joshua, 20, 138, 188

SUBJECT INDEX

Joshua the High Priest, 24, 26, 29, 48, 73–79, 84, 91, 93, 216
Josiah son of Zephaniah, 91, 100
Judah, 20, 26, 90, 121, 137, 139, 142, 164, 166, 172, 177, 181, 209, 212
   house of, 110, 140, 219
   remnant of, 132–133
justice, 102, 104, 106, 109, 131, 203, 217–218

King Ammi-Saduqa, 125
"King's Eye, the," 87–88

Lachish, 107
Leah, 71
Lebanon, 145, 163
   cedars of, 146
Levant, the, 65, 121, 125, 128–129, 185, 191
   southern, 191
Levi
   house of, 180
   tribe of, 92
Levites, 71, 143, 216, 221

Manasseh, half-tribe of, 188
Marduk-mushallim, 125
Memphis (Egypt), 9
Meshach, 214
Miriam, 45
monotheism, 224
Mordecai, 214
Moses, 28, 35, 45, 77
   messenger of YHWH, 28, 32, 46
motherly compassion, 102
Mount of Olives, 189, 191
Mount Sinai, 77, 132, 220

Nathan, 232
   house of, 180
Nebuchadnezzar, 6, 23, 34, 87, 191
Necho II, 191
Nehemiah
   governor of Yehud, 4, 216–217
   mission of, 10
Neo-Assyria, 34
New Exodus, 30, 35–37, 47–48, 51, 200, 211, 220
Northern Israel, 20, 26, 90, 105, 121, 124, 131, 137, 142, 144, 148, 164, 172, 206, 212
   exile to Assyria, 142
   remnant of, 133

Pax persica, 36, 63, 85, 131, 200
peace, 112, 130, 133, 200
Pentateuch, 220
Persepolis, 200
   Apadana Hall, 71
   Apadana reliefs, 193
   reliefs, 35
Persian Empire
   kings, wealth of, 135
   subjection of Assyria and Babylon, 66
   wars of, 54, 70, 94, 121, 130, 142, 189, 194
Pharaoh
   days of the Exodus, 28, 34, 194
Philistia, 126, 146, 148, 163, 181
   pride of, 130
   as remnant to YHWH, 127
Philistines, 141, 188
Phoenicia, 146
Phoenicians, 145
pre-exilic prophets, 7, 11–13, 20–22, 25, 27, 42, 57, 74, 85, 102, 116, 147, 205
Promised Land, the, 33, 37, 48, 143, 193
prophecy
   divination, 182
   dramatic action, 91, 93, 155, 159, 161, 163, 165
   ecstatic, 61
   failure of, 55
   false, 180
   "intuitive divination," 53
   oracles of salvation, 33
   "spirit journeys," 61
   woe-cry, 69, 168
prophet
   as divine courtier, 61
   ecstatic, 183, 212
   as intermediaries, 187
   as messenger of Great King, 173
   true or false, 70, 122, 212
Puah, 28

Ramat Rahel, 5–6
redemption
   of firstborn, 141
Regem-melek, 100–101, 104, 112
Ruth, 75, 179

salvation, 131
Samaria, 181
Samson, 40

Samuel, 77, 232
Sarah, 165
Sargon II, 191
Satan, the, 73–76
Saul, 232
scribes
   of Book of Zechariah, 54, 61, 70, 72, 91, 108, 122, 164, 173, 175, 184, 186–187, 201
   as interpreters of prophets, 54, 183–184, 201
Sea of Reeds, 28
Second Temple, 48, 100
   building of, 19, 23, 29, 31
   centrality of, 4, 37
   future glory of, 34–35, 37, 82, 194
   house of YHWH, 212, 218
   incomplete, 24, 32, 40, 81–82, 94
Sennacherib, 191
Shadrach, 214
Shalmaneser V, 191
Sharezer, 100–101, 104, 112
Shem, hosue of, 180
Sheshbazzar, 23
Shinar, 87
Shiphrah, 28
Sidon, 6, 124
Sihon, 125
Solomon, 114, 179
Solomon's Temple, 23, 31, 37, 48
   destruction of, 70
   filled with God's glory, 69
   glory of, 35, 82
   splendor of, 32
   vessels of, 143
steadfast love, 102
Syria, 148, 163

Tabernacle, the, 29–30, 35, 37, 40, 46, 220
Tel Dor, 68
temples
   ancient Near East
      divine benevolence, 24
      eliciting reverence for gods, 24
      heaven-on-earth, 24, 31
Tiglath-pileser III, 191
Tobiah, 91
Torah, 102, 105, 139, 143, 164, 200–201, 205, 212, 218
   personified as petitioner, 103

Trans-Euphrates, 126
Transjordan, 163
truth, 105–106, 109, 111–112
Tyre, 6, 124, 146
   wealth of, 130

Ur of the Chaldees, 110
Uzziah, 205

Xerxes I, 2, 9, 21, 128, 133, 144, 188, 193
   assassination of, 121

Yehud
   exploitation of, 2–3
   external threats to, 2–3, 128
   part of "middle territory," 3, 49, 194
   province of Persian Empire, 3
   refortification of, 2–3
   as remnant, 29–30
   social divisions of, 2–3, 11, 15, 88, 146, 221
   struggles of, 69, 109, 172, 202, 215
   subject status, 72
YHWH
   anger of, 7–8, 56, 58, 63, 66, 69, 90, 140, 158, 217
   as artisan/creator, 164, 186
   benevolence of, 7–8, 26–28, 30, 36, 47, 49, 114, 206
   cheif of gods, 113
   controlling history, 162, 208
   as creator, 174–175, 180
   deliverer of Israel form Egypt, 45
   devotion to, 145
   divine court of, 61–62
   divine presence, 34
   as divine warrior, 189, 192
   as enemy, 26, 29
   eyes of, 83
   faithfulness of, 204
   as father, 166, 172
   favor of, 103
   as fountain, 181
   fear of, 7–8, 20, 30
   glory of, 220
      departure from Temple, 70
   goodness of, 190
   Great King, 36–37, 43, 45, 47–48, 62, 90, 135
      ensures court justice, 86
      Good Gardener, 190
      Great Judge, 73, 76

in Jerusalem, 193
judgment of, 85, 158, 208, 211
leading Judah into battle, 188
provisions of, 127
sorrow of, 64
victorious in battle, 133
will of, 103, 112
heavenly court of, 78
Holy One, the, 106
honor of, 200–201, 203, 210
household of, 165
jealousy of, 104, 107
"lord of all the earth," 90
love of, 202
mercy of, 206
might of, 146
motherly compassion of, 63, 66–67, 69, 76, 85, 141, 206, 217
punishment from, 7–8, 40
residence of, 126
as savior, 109, 178, 188
as shepherd, 7–8
sorrow of, 69

source of happiness for humankind, 128
sovereignty of, 214–215
as warrior, 137
word of, 20
zeal of, 107
YHWH Sabaoth, 44, 183, 186–187, 191, 193–194, 204, 206–207
chief of the gods, 71
in court of justice, 73
deliverer of Israel from Egypt, 2, 21, 32, 63, 182, 184
the Great King, 14, 34
of the hosts of Israel, 194
the one name of God, 191
rule of, 215
ruler of nations, 7–8, 11, 94

Zechariah the prophet, 53
Zephaniah, 91
Zerubbabel, governor of Yehud, 20, 24, 26, 29, 44–49, 51, 73, 84, 93, 130, 178, 200, 216